Mysterious Places
Mysterious Dreams

Steven Rivellino

Xlibris Corporation
436 Walnut St.
Philadelphia, PA 19106
2004

1. Travel—Adventure—Non Fiction. 2. Cruise ships—World Travel
3. Ocean Liners—Non Fiction. 4. Gay men—Non Fiction.
5. Homosexuality—Non Fiction.
6. Young Adult—Coming of age—Non-fiction

First Edition
2004

To order additional copies of this book, contact:
Xlibris Corporation
1-888-795-4274
www.Xlibris.com
Orders@Xlibris.com
18007

For Rod McCann..

Just because the beautiful bird has flown out of sight
does not mean he's not still soaring off in some other glorious place.

"Sailing is a great metaphor for coping with the future. In sailing, you always come up with unknowns– the weather changes; the currents change; and you hit things in the water."

Bill Koch
Skipper, *AMERICA³*

Author's Note

The story you are about to read is true—a candid depiction of life onboard a luxury ocean liner of great stature and tradition at the end of an era.

We must step back then to "that time, that place"; to days long gone—to a time when circumnavigating the globe by sea was still an envied adventure. And to a time when such voyages were enjoyed by only a familial few. To a changing world just emerging from the societal renaissance of the 1960s.

Our adventure centers around a unique group of travelers quite unable to change, unwilling to evolve. Travelers both privileged and not so privileged; those who held firm—desperately grasping on to the roles and traditions of days long past.

Naturally, I have gone to great depths in order to protect the privacy of those who appear in this book.

Therefore, certain names have been changed; some of those you will read about are presented as composite characters, and the sequence of some events is adapted accordingly.

Steven Rivellino
January 2004

Chapter One

"Impressions"

There was a time in my life when nothing else mattered but being somewhere else. Where exactly, was unimportant. Just somewhere else—any place other than where I was at the time. And when I arrived—wherever *there* happened to be—I soon got restless, and again had the urge to move on. I always wanted something new—something different. I always wanted what I did not have. And so this story goes . . .

New York City. A cold day in January 1973. It was a morning sailing—Norwegian America Line always seemed to favor morning sailings back then—and although I could never imagine, in my limited experience, a passenger vessel being ready and able to sail so early in the day, we pulled away from the pier at 11:30 A.M.—very much on schedule.

For me it was a time to escape, although I was not yet aware of my great need to do so. It just seemed exciting—different, if you will—and perhaps a bit daring too—to renounce academics completely, and to sail away on a great ocean liner. And I always wanted to do what others considered to be different.

It seemed a unique idea—at least at the time. And most seemed to agree. My parents, my friends, even my college professors too—they all said how fortunate I was. "What a wonderful experience it will be."

And so off I went. At nineteen years of age, a novice in the true sense of the word; a somewhat provincial young man with only three semesters of college under his belt; there I was, about to set off on an ocean voyage to circumnavigate the planet—a journey the likes of which I had always thought would be, for me at least, unattainable.

They called it *The Great World Cruise.* How obvious to call it great, I thought. Was there ever a world cruise that could not be considered great? Were there others that were considered mediocre, or just plain awful? Nonetheless, I seemed to luck out, for I was on the great one. And it would take ninety-eight days.

My interest in ships, a fascination mainly in classic ocean liners, began when I was really quite young—seven years old to be exact. I remember watching *The Gale Storm Show—Oh Susannah!* on our old black and white television set in the late fifties. She—Susannah, that is—along with her early sitcom-ed side-kick Nugent and the unrealistically slapstick Captain Huxley too, gave me my very first insight into the great physical and emotional rewards of life at sea; the adventure and the excitement of sailing the world's oceans to exotic ports of call—to the tropically beautiful South Pacific, and to the mysterious Orient too.

That initial spark of interest in ships and the sea was fully and finally ignited when, on an otherwise seemingly unimportant day in February 1962, I had an experience which literally transformed my life.

My parents and I had set off for New York City from the family home in Northern Westchester County—a rare shopping excursion it was, or some other such day trip.

We drove south on the Saw Mill River Parkway through Riverdale and on to the Henry Hudson Parkway, first crossing the massive steel-bridged highway which connects the Borough of the Bronx to the great Island of Manhattan. And as always, I looked ahead from the right rear seat where I sat, just behind my mother. I never sat on the left, you should know. I always became sick and threw up whenever I sat in the left rear seat. So the right it was, that day, and always, to this very day.

I remember the sound that morning. Unforgettable. The frigid friction of rubber tires pressed forcefully against the steel-grid roadway created a high-pitched scream to drown out the world. And even with our windows rolled up tight, and our Oldsmobile's heater blowing full blast, that sound was indelible. Impressive and powerful.

Far off, further down the icy Hudson River that morning, I just barely noticed the two uniquely shaped objects. There they stood, proud and powerful, gleaming in the sun's brilliant face. Was it a new skyscraper, I wondered. But why horizontal? Why was it jutting out into the river? It was far too unusually shaped for that.

Already, in those days, the West Side Highway was quite run-down. The cavernous potholes made for a very uncomfortable ride. Heaps of urban trash, plentiful and quite ageless, was messily strewn about as we made our way further and deeper south to the city ahead—the rubbish placed perfectly along the roadside as if a mad artist's eye may have ultimately been responsible. Its apparent arbitrary placement could not have been accidental—for here, in this landscape, it seemed right. Indeed, I could not have conceived of it any other way.

Whatever that structure was up ahead, it quickly caught my eye. How could it not?—so extraordinary standing there, blatantly majestic. It seemed so out of place. The rubbish—no. The rubbish was expected. But those two structures! Yes, indeed. I knew they didn't belong, at least not there.

I yelled excitedly as the realization quickly crystallized. I leaned further forward in my seat. A ship. It had to be. It was in the river after all.

"Look, a ship is in port" I shouted. And then my parents too began to take notice of the quite unusually shaped object just ahead.

The traffic became heavier as we penetrated the city. Soon it engulfed us. We surrendered to it; we had no choice. We were already at the 57th Street exit ramp. My father—then, and now, the only driver in our family—had to quickly swerve into the left lane of traffic. We headed downward and directly onto the highway's lower level—West Street as it was called. Quite skillfully, he dodged the maniacal taxi cabs and graffiti-ed delivery trucks, all of which appeared to be headed in every possible way. I leaned forward then even further, and crouched down even lower, to look and to see, and to get a better view. A view, I wished, could remain forever.

You must understand that for me, at that time in my life, the anticipation of seeing a ship—a real ocean liner—for the very first time was overwhelming—almost orgasmic, if, at that age, I knew what that word meant. It was a dream becoming real. It was the focus of my entire—be it young—life. And through all the nerve-racking bumper-to-bumper traffic that day, with horns blowing frantically and drivers of all kinds and all colors making forceful hand and finger gestures to each other—most of which I did not quite understand—I got to see a ship—a real ship—for the very first time.

There were endless strings of multi-colored flags flapping violently crisp in the cold sea breeze; but they disappeared just as quickly as they came into view—a highway stanchion from the overhead roadway soon blocked my sight. Then again they appeared —crisply pressed from the heavy hand of the wind.

And then, just below, several large images came into view. Letters they were—giant letters—standing tall and proud between two huge blood red and coal black winged smokestacks. Quite futuristic they were. And mesmerizing in their stature. But they too fell out of view even before I was able to read their message. Was it all an illusive dream? I wondered—at one point seeming to be reality, yet disappearing before it could even be savored or touched?

The aging pier jutted straight out into the river. And as we approached 54th Street, I was finally able to see her clearly for the very first time. She loomed up from the ice-strewn Hudson like an alien giant, her colors as vivid as only the eye and the mind could imagine. She frightened me, and yet I couldn't take my eyes off her. Her strength, her grace, her beauty, existed only for me. And there, emblazoned upon her piercing black bow was her name—*France*—in letters as high as I was tall.

I was mesmerized by the force she proudly—perhaps

arrogantly—displayed; her cold silent spirit. And as the old cliché might say, time stood still for the moment—at least it did for me.

We had stopped at a traffic signal; and all of us . . . mom, dad, and I . . . just couldn't help but stare at her in silence—lying there peacefully, at rest—an unforgettable symbol of a maritime world of mystery and adventure we did not understand. Her massive size, and her incredible strength. The power; the beauty.

The very tip of her piercing black bow seemed to extend well over our heads as our car pulled up along side. At her waterline, chunks of brackish ice gently kissed her hull—softly, caressingly; her fresh paint appeared barely blemished by the Atlantic's cruel touch. *France* glistened like new that day in the fickle warmth of a mid-winter's sun. And all I knew was that I simply had to go onboard.

My parents were already well aware of my great interest in ships and ocean liners, and fantastic adventures on the world's great seas. Interest? Hell. It was an obsession. And perhaps that morning, it was just to appease their nagging pre-adolescent son that they decided to stop—if only briefly—by the liner's berth so that I might have a better look.

To my surprise, however, they too seemed interested in the ship. It may have been the very first time I remember my parents showing an interest in my life—in the things which truly intrigued and fascinated me. My father, in particular, stood in awe of the ship's great size and stature, her design and engineering operation; and my mother too had to admit to some curiosity of just what the great ship was like on the inside. You see, my mom also had a bit of the wanderlust in her, and would, from time to time, dream of great travel adventures and ever new places to visit. The great liner *France*, then lying just before us, would no doubt make for endless fantasy.

A scruffy longshoreman—cold and wrinkled, and quite ruggedly dressed—said the ship had arrived only days before, after completing her maiden voyage from Le Havre.

"They claim she broke the record" he shouted as his breath

seemed to crystallize just inches from his face. "Fastest crossing ever, them frogs keep saying." He paused a moment, and turned toward the ship.

"But the guys don't believe 'em. You can't trust them French" he said. "The Big 'U' still has it, as far as I'm concerned."

His colloquial reference to America's greatest flagship *United States* was understood I'm sure, only by me. Surprising too, as I would have thought it common knowledge that the *United States* had captured the cherished Blue Ribband as the fastest passenger liner in the world on her maiden voyage in July 1952—ironically, the year of my birth. And to this day, after more than three decades out of service, she still proudly holds that record.

As he spoke, the longshoreman appeared a bit agitated— impatient, perhaps, by our tedious conversation—and told us he needed to get some coffee. Before moving on, however, he mentioned that visitors were allowed onboard. "For a buck" he said. "They say it goes to the Seaman's Fund, but you never really know where it's going with those French."

We parked our car, and together walked under the huge, rusted, already aging neon sign whose vivid red tubular veins formed the famous French Line logo. We continued through the security gates at the pier's West Street entrance and up the steep stairway to the second level of the nearly frozen passenger terminal.

We could see little of the ship from where we stood. In fact, the only access to her seemed to be by way of a narrow and some-what even darker companionway, just to our right, which was set, rather casually, at a sharply inclined angle—most likely the result of the sea's rising tide.

Hesitantly, my parents and I inched up the gangway, quite care-ful not to trip on the skid dividers placed at every step; nervously grasping on to the worn wooden banisters—eroded smoothly, no doubt, by the endless hands of unknown travelers. Faceless they were. Indeed, the sea had its stories; if only those railings could talk.

When we reached the top, I stopped—only briefly—and stood for a moment before finally stepping onboard. I looked to my right and then to my left—from bow to stern; indeed, I was mesmerized by her vastness. The sensuality of her lines, the curves, the swells, the piercing contrasts of her colors. The vivid smell of the ship's fresh paint—intoxicating as it was—seduced my senses and swelled my heart; the crisp slap of a frozen wind mixing together with the unmistakable scent of the salty sea air all contributed to a moment in my life I could never forget.

Now let me be clear that that very first step I took onboard *France* that morning into her brilliantly lit purser's lobby was, for me, a transformational seduction—a rebirth into an entirely new world, into an entirely new life. From that moment on, I became even more obsessed with the grand ships this remarkable vessel represented. Ships of the past and present—their ageless histories and unique construction and design specifications, and the very personal diaries of life onboard too—all began to dominate my teenage interests far more than sports or music or classroom studies or even adolescent sexual experimentation which so seemed to transfix my fellow schoolmates. I read everything I could find written about steamships in books and magazines and newspapers and various travel pamphlets too. I fantasized often about exploring the world in these floating cities, and lived, at least in my own mind, the imagined life of a handsome young sailor continually setting foot on great foreign lands, on distant continents—sailing off to far-away places which had remained embedded deep within my imagination from elementary school geography books and from faded black and white films shown incessantly on lazy afternoon *Million Dollar Movies*.

And so it was that my professional career path was determined. The strategy was clear. I wrote to all the New York-based steamship companies listed in the Manhattan telephone directory requesting their latest brochures and information and schedules. And I built miniature models and cardboard constructions too to recreate existing ships of great history and stature, and to create my own nautical designs as well.

It was three years later, and no doubt the result of my continued insistence and insufferable pleading, that my parents finally agreed to a twelve-day Christmas/New Year's cruise to the Caribbean's West Indies. It was to be our—my—very first ocean voyage.

Our travel agent had arranged for us to sail for what we had hoped to be fourteen glorious days onboard the newly refurbished *Caribia*—which I, of course, knew was actually Cunard Line's former "Green Goddess" *Caronia*, the pride of the renowned Cunard cruise fleet at the time. But due to the cancellation of *Caribia*'s maiden voyage—for technical reasons, it was said—we were, just one week before our scheduled departure, re-booked onboard Holland America Line's already classic *Nieuw Amsterdam*.

The *Nieuw Amsterdam* is, to this day, my favorite ship—perhaps because she was my first, or perhaps because she was simply one of the great ones. She had all the old-world charm that one would imagine and indeed anticipate—the thick rich carpets; the dark walnut and mahogany walls; the black linoleum lobby flooring which was polished, nightly as we slept, to shine like mirrors; the double-decked and balconied Grand Ballroom; and the beautifully appointed brass and etched-glass elevator cabs in which young blond Dutch boys in white gloves and pill-box hats waited to assist you to your desired deck destination. The sumptuous dinners onboard were served magnificently in the spaciously vaulted Dining Salon where an aging string orchestra played soothing classical music from the luxurious overhanging balcony alcove.

It was while onboard that twelve day Caribbean sailing that I formally decided, at the impressionable age of thirteen, that I wanted to become a part of that world, that life. I wanted to live with those blond-haired/blue-eyed alien people—with their winning smiles and engaging cultures; to become one of them. I wanted to leave my home and my home town, my schooling and my tediously mundane life in Westchester County, and actually live—actually experience—those mysterious places; my mysterious dreams.

In early 1968, while still only a high school junior, my persistence succeeded when I was engaged onboard Home Line's flagship

Oceanic as a children's counselor and "after hours" musician in an ad hoc rock band—a group whose members I was asked to assemble from among other high school friends whose interest in ships I quickly created and eagerly nurtured. Indeed, I could hardly be considered a rock musician of any stature, even though I had studied music theory and classical piano, and performed one or two seasons with my high school marching band's drum corps. But when a Home Lines representative whom I had met as a result of my assertive letter-writing campaign called my home and asked if I was interested in assembling a musical group—one which I believed the teenaged-passengers onboard *Oceanic* would enjoy, and which would, at the same time, keep them out of the other—more adult—public rooms, there was no further decision to be made. No discussion. At that time in my life, I believe I would have said and agreed to almost anything in order to work onboard a passenger ship. So naturally—immediately—I accepted the employment offer and the musical task ahead, and quickly assembled a trio of seemingly like-minded high school musicians who would agree to be silent accomplices in carrying out my charade. Terrible as we were, we set out on a glorious nine day Easter cruise to St. Thomas and Nassau on the beautifully sleek white Italian liner, with subsequent holiday cruises to follow in the coming seasons. Musicians changed with each voyage, as did my experience and my perspective on my life, and my future. Yet I remained focused on only the next possible voyage. When the Easter cruise ended, I eagerly awaited summer. And then Christmas. I was living the dream I had always dreamed, and all I wanted in life was for it to continue, and never ever end.

So for me, at least, it was all perfectly clear. My goals were always consistent—to work on a ship. Not just once or twice, but to permanently work on a ship. To make it my job; my career. My life. And so as I continued to live my dream, seasonally, at least—the more reluctant I became to return home and to the academic arena—first high school, and then college—to courses and to subjects with which I was by then totally disinterested.

Clearly, I wanted only to travel. It was all that mattered. I became impassioned with the idea of going to sea in those remarkable giants. For me, they were symbols of unusual adventure and great exploration. I felt special when I was onboard ship. Indeed, I felt like I was someone. I felt important. I was a part of "the ship's staff." And I loved being a part of something—anything. More and more I became strengthened by how that made me feel. I continually dreamed of belonging to that stalwart team of young foreign sailors with the world's sunlight in their hair, their faces gloriously tanned by beguiling days at sea. I dreamed of joining the family of those special crewmembers so fortunate to experience that wonderfully intoxicating feeling at the end of each and every voyage of already being home—of knowing that as passengers were disembarking, *they* would be staying onboard ship, ready to welcome new passengers into their world, and together set off again for great new adventure. Yes, the ship was their home. And I wanted it to become my home as well. I knew then, instinctively or otherwise, that my true education was not to be in the classroom at all, but in traveling the world by sea.

And so my search for permanent employment continued—successfully securing interviews with *Nieuw Amsterdam*'s Holland America Line, as well as with the North German Lloyd, a steamship company which then successfully operated the historic *Bremen* and the perhaps more popular yet physically smaller *Europa*. Both companies were pleasant enough in their form-letter responses, and consistent in their rejections as well. "Too young" each would say. "Perhaps in a few more years."

And then, as if by destiny or fate, I was interviewed by Cruise Director Bill Branton to be his personal assistant onboard Flagship Cruises' new *Island Venture*—her maiden voyage scheduled for February 5, 1972.

Needless to say, I was thrilled—excited about actually achieving my goal. But, I was also a bit perplexed. Clearly, this opportunity was just what I had wanted and waited and prayed for. But after the pragmatic rejections from both Holland America and North German Lloyd—two steamship companies of great stature and repute—I did wonder why Flagship Cruises would actually want to hire me. It was true after all—I was young. And with all my passion aside, I had little actual experience in the industry. Flagship Cruises was a very new company, with little history or experience of their own. Indeed, no matter what their popular reputation in the industry may have been at the time, how good a company could they truly be if they were actually interested in hiring someone as young and as inexperienced as I?

Nonetheless, for whatever their reasons, I was hired. I didn't really want to question it too much. So as the year turned and the winter snows came, I eagerly packed my bags, and headed south once again to a cold New York City.

Island Venture was the 20,000-ton sister to the already popular *Sea Venture* which began her service just twelve months before. With Norwegian registry and Italian service crew, both ships quickly and easily established themselves quite successfully in an industry already crowded with newer, more modern vessels no longer built for the transatlantic trade but specifically designed for the newer, more lucrative cruise market.

I sailed onboard *Island Venture* for eleven months— an itinerary of ten and eleven day cruises to the West Indies and Bermuda; happily experiencing and eagerly learning all I could about my new life at sea.

But what I enjoyed most of all was the dramatic feeling of achievement and satisfaction. Finally, I had become a full-time staff member onboard a luxury passenger ship. And with that knowledge and that security then behind me—feeling that I did actually belong somewhere, someplace—a newfound confidence was built. I found myself easily getting to know the other staff and crew members onboard, the ship's wonderfully friendly Norwegian Captain Johann Dahl, and some of his younger officers too.

But in November of that same year, the glorious fantasy ended. For some odd business or economic reason—we never really knew which—the new and increasingly successful *Island Venture* was suddenly withdrawn from active and regular cruise service, and prematurely sold to the then fledgling Princess Cruises of Los Angeles. I was out of a job and land-based once again. And so, like a shameless barker blatantly hawking his wares, I once again offered out my services to the first taker in the shipping industry.

It was but two weeks later when I received an employment offer with Norwegian America Line—the appointment of which I now write. It was certainly a coup. Few people would argue that Norwegian America Line was considered the finest—most elegant—cruise operation in the industry. And my first cruise with NAL was the World.

Sagafjord's 1973 Great World Cruise then was to become my inauguration into the longer, more affluent, cruise market; and with whom my circumnavigational virginity would be lost.

New York's Pier 40 on the Hudson's North River—a passenger terminal then shared by both Holland America Line and Norwegian America Line—was quite busy with pre-sailing activity by the time we arrived. And just as we had done nearly twelve years before, my mom and dad and I turned off Manhattan's West Side Highway, parked our car, and together walked up a shaky wooden gangway—this time though, with baggage well in hand.

Stepping onboard, we stood in the beautifully elegant Purser's Lobby midship on *Sagafjord*'s Upper Deck. Passengers were boarding as well, and as they did, they were warmly greeted by members of the ship's social staff. And reminiscent of an earlier time onboard *Nieuw Amsterdam*, blond stewards—this time Norwegian—in crisp white jackets and equally white gloves were hurrying about carrying baggage and checking tickets, and escorting *Sagafjord*'s guests to their previously assigned cabins.

I felt great excitement that day. Yet, I had to admit I shielded great fear and anxiety as well. For my appointment onboard *Sagafjord* was that of Shore Excursion Assistant. And with no real experience in this field whatsoever, I feared I had to bluff my way through as best I could; as I had so successfully done onboard

Oceanic and *Island Venture*, and perhaps—all too often—in other areas of my life as well.

For a moment or two, I had no idea how I had gotten where I was. The cockiness of the professional pride I often felt amongst non-sailors ashore was quickly doused. The small-fish-in-a-big-pond syndrome then literally took on new meaning.

Nonetheless—with neurotic fear hidden deep—I marveled at the thought. Of where I was, about what I had already accomplished, and about what I was about to do. I was to become a member of the *Sagafjord*'s Tour Office staff—a Tour Office staff about to set off on a ninety-eight day cruise around the world. No matter how I chose to interpret it, I was clearly proud of that achievement, and exhilarated too. And I'm certain that glow of pride was noticeable by all. I was eager to have it begin; and I looked forward to what I knew would be an incredible voyage.

So my excitement was energy that morning, and it intoxicated us all. Quite distractedly, I adjusted my luggage in my hands and walked through the dimly lit lobby—across deep-blue carpeting, past cream-colored leather sofas and high-backed armchairs, and pots of lush palms and tropical greenery—and descended the two decks below to my single berth cabin—Number 54 on A-Deck aft.

Almost immediately—even before I had had the chance to put the heavier bags I was carrying down onto the cabin floor and some smaller ones onto the bed, my mother began a brief inspection of my cabin and its adjacent private bath. Was it large enough for her son? Was there enough light with only one porthole? What would the view be like?—as if the view, like anything on this particular voyage, would be constant. Was the cabin located too far aft?—the vibration would certainly keep me awake at night. Perhaps a cabin so far aft would not take the sea well. And on and on it went—her motherly concerns were many. I knew it would not simply end. So quickly, before any of her queries could actually be addressed, I suggested we leave the cabin just as it was, and set out to explore the ship.

Walking forward on A-Deck portside and finally up to Main

Deck, we first discovered the Saga Dining Room; continuing then up to Veranda Deck aft to the swimming pool area and the Veranda Cafe; then forward through the spacious Grand Ballroom, and even further forward to the Dance Studio, Theatre, The Ibsen Library, the North Cape Bar, and the beautiful Garden Lounge with its impressive panoramic views overlooking the ship's bow. There we sat for a moment—stewards were serving morning coffees and teas and small bite-size pastries and scones to the passengers and their guests. We sipped our tea, and chatted awkwardly about the countries I would visit and how wonderful it would be. And when our cups were empty—when we could shift no more in our seats; when we could avoid no longer the real issues at hand—we knew instinctively it was time.

And so we moved on—back to the Purser's Lobby, that is—Purser's Square, as it was sometimes called. It was there that we awkwardly exchanged farewells, hugged our final hugs, kissed our final kisses, and wiped my mom's tears away. I watched them both walk down the gangway and wave one last time.

It was then—when they finally moved out of sight—that I first felt the terrible loss. A pain I had never before known. Suddenly, I realized, I was completely on my own. And what exactly did that mean? Where did it leave me? Alone, abandoned onboard a Norwegian luxury liner with nowhere else to go—nothing else to do but embrace the world. I could no longer be the innocently naive nineteen year old from Westchester County New York. I could no longer be that neurotic teenager so able to manipulate others quickly and easily with his broad smile and his all-too-pleasant disposition. I had to be a man—whatever that meant. Perhaps I was one already—in taking on such a challenge, welcoming the unknown. I found myself unsure. And suddenly, and quite uncontrollably, my mom's tears became mine.

Yes, I was indeed on my own—just as I had dreamed I would someday be. And for the very first time in my life, I began to wonder if this was truly what I wanted. It seemed a great idea in theory, I thought. But reality, well that was certainly something else. What was I doing, after all? What was I searching for? Traveling to the

Caribbean for ten days at a time was one thing; sailing around the world, quite another. That was commitment. And commitment—of any sort—frightened me greatly.

Two Norwegian sailors with dark woolen coats and gleaming white caps began to untie the gangway's support ropes. It was clear there was no turning back. Was it anxiety, or panic? I didn't know. I didn't have time.

Robert Brooks was Norwegian America Line's Sales Promotion Manager at the time, and the gentleman actually responsible for my contract onboard ship. It was Mr. Brooks who interviewed me for this very appointment several weeks earlier, and it was his decision after all which placed me onboard.

Brooks stood with an elderly couple—they all seemed elderly to me back then—just to the left of the Purser's Office. He appeared bored yet polite to the couple—seemingly preoccupied as he spoke. His focus moved about; his attention drifted. His nodding seemed mechanical, his movements quite rehearsed. But when he turned just a bit and noticed me watching him, he abruptly put an end to his conversation and joined me at the open port, just aft of where the staff still stood in militaristic formation waiting to greet any last minute stragglers who were now quite late for sailing.

Brooks was unequivocally British and quite popular with the passengers and the ship's staff alike. He wore a charcoal-gray suit that day, a three-piece, naturally—wearing it so well, I might add, that it looked as if it would be inconceivable to picture him wearing anything else. His short dark hair was just a bit splattered by gray; his pencil-thin moustache simply made him a caricature of good ole British charm.

"Good morning" Brooks said as he nodded just a bit. His highly polished "upper class" accent was loud and strong as he firmly extended his hand in greeting; a heavily loaded briefcase occupied the other. "Are you all set to sail?"

"I think so" I answered with a smile no doubt, and perhaps some trepidation. "My parents just went ashore. They came to see me off."

"Oh dear" he said. "I'm sorry I missed them."

Brooks sounded sincere about missing my parents, then abruptly changed the subject.

"Have you been to your cabin? I do hope it's satisfactory. A-Deck, isn't it?" He smiled again with a certain gleam in his eyes which made me understand, quite clearly, that my answer had better be "more than satisfactory, Mr. Brooks, thank you."

And just then I realized that someone else had joined us. He appeared to be in his early '40s, conservatively well dressed, with dark brown—almost black—hair and a fairly dark complexion. His smile seemed plastered on his face as he first looked my way, and then back at Brooks.

"Oh Lar" Robert greeted him.

"Hello Mister Brooks" the man said quite formally, yet with just a bit of sarcasm too. His eyes sparkled, as he glanced quickly in my direction. His demeanor appeared warm, almost sincere, and he seemed as if he could be a good deal of fun.

"Have you met Lar—Laurence Vandelis? Tour Office Manager" Brooks emphasized. "He's your new boss."

"Welcome aboard" Vandelis said as he hardily shook my hand. "I've heard a good deal about you. We're all quite pleased you'll be with us."

What could he have heard, I wondered? And from whom?

We talked a bit more, the three of us, about the cruise ahead, about some passengers who both Brooks and Lar seemed to know well from past cruises and social events ashore; and about nothing very special at all. We knew our time together—with Robert Brooks, at least—was limited. And so were our words.

The Purser's Square began to fill with embarking passengers and their families and friends. The haunting sound of simultaneous goodbyes quickly overpowered our conversation. We all were shaken by the ship's massive whistle as it abruptly blasted out its final call—the universal signal that visitors must leave the ship.

"Don't worry about coming to the office just yet" Lar said as the whistle's blast faded off slightly in the distance. "There's plenty of time for that. Maybe you'd like to go up on deck and watch the sailing. There will be a cruise staff meeting at twelve noon in the

Dance Studio" he continued. "You'll meet everyone there."

Sagafjord was quite a stately vessel. She was one of the few cruise liners still in service at the time of this writing (although no longer under the Norwegian America flag) which exhibited classic lines in design and architecture, old-world service, and a highly sophisticated style of cruising. Her reputation is still quite unique in an industry which most often caters to the mass and middle-market traveler.

I stood alone on a nearly frozen Sun Deck waiting—just waiting—to experience first-hand the lavish festivities and lively celebrations I had visualized through the years from reading epic travel books and viewing classic films, all of which showed glamorous ocean liners sailing off to great adventure.

But this was different. There was only stillness in the cold that day—silence. There were no crowds. There was no celebration. Where were the bands playing lively festive music? Where were the streamers of every color of the spectrum? Where were the vibrant passengers lined up shoulder to shoulder along the rail, waving excitedly to friends and loved ones who eagerly gestured back from ashore? Where were Nugent and Captain Huxley—now, when I needed them most?

Nervously, I walked further forward and stared ahead over the rail. The Hudson below was dark and filthy and scattered with stained chunks of ice.

Perhaps they were too old, I thought. That's why no one else was on deck. That's why I stood alone, when what I wanted and needed most of all was to share this incredible moment in my life with someone.

They're veterans, I told myself. World Cruise veterans. They had no interest in the usual, perhaps nonsensical, sailing rituals I so looked forward to that day. They had no reason to stand shivering on a frigid deck as a fitting farewell to a New York devoid of any warmth whatsoever.

The ship's whistle blew then a second time. It was my last chance to run ashore.

Down below in Purser's Square, I was certain the passengers too—knowing they had only moments left before departure—were perhaps just as anxious in anticipating the crushing uncertainty of what was to follow during the next three months at sea. Their guests must have been anxious as well—anxious about abandoning their elderly loved ones, alone and onboard—and, I'm sure, anxious about something as simple as reaching the gangway in time, before it was finally lifted and pulled away.

I looked ahead, over the rail, below to the ship's bow where Norwegian sailors were untying the massive ropes, ready to toss them ashore. A frigid New York City stood blatantly as a backdrop; the sun just barely peeking out through a shroud of overhead clouds. The sailors sang as they worked—Norwegian folk songs or legendary Nordic Sea chanteys—I could not tell which. But the sound of their voices rose strong and clear that morning; the enthusiasm with which they worked boasted an intense feeling of pride in their jobs and in their choosing the sea as their life's commitment. I envied them. I wanted to be one of them.

Who were they, I wondered? That blond sailor with his cap slightly askew, his jacket bellowing in the wind. Would I get to know him during this trip, I wondered? Will I become his friend? Or maybe it will be that sailor over there, with his somewhat darker hair blowing straight back past his face. And maybe it will be all of them. Perhaps none.

Their voices continued in song as three diminutive tugs approached from our portside. Gently, they kissed our gray hull with the very tips of their padded bows, and slowly and carefully inched us away from the pier—our sole escort into the Hudson's great North River.

We stood there for a moment, drifting quietly mid-stream. And with a startling burst of strength and blinding anticipation, the powerful voices of my potential new friends were drowned out by what seemed the loudest and longest blast of *Sagafjord*'s massive whistle, sounding off for the third and final time—signaling to the world that we were well under our own power, and heading proudly out to sea.

The gentle movement of the ship, silently turning and drifting in the Hudson's strong current, was cinematically visual—as if a camera slowly panned New York's famous skyline of excessive concrete and jagged angles to offer the viewer a keen understanding and deep insight into the strange new world they were about to describe.

I remained alone on deck—my jacket collar pulled tightly around my neck, my hair blowing back powerfully against my face.

We sailed south, passing each city street and each massive building and each landmark too; they slowly—and quite unceremoniously—drifted behind, and soon far from sight. I had stood there before, but there was something different about that sailing that morning. It was unlike any onboard *Oceanic* or *Island Venture* when weekly voyages to the Caribbean meant the safety of home every seven days. This was *the world*, and thus a departure symbolic of a whole new experience, with powerful new meaning.

Yet in a strange way, it was calming and peaceful—as if pieces of my life, of my very own soul, were fading away as well—as if the essence of the person I thought I was and the identity of the person I always knew, was slowly being lost or stripped away or abandoned. I knew—just instinctively knew—I would and could never be the same again.

Indeed there seemed no escape. Clearly, I was the explorer I had always dreamed of being, destined by my own discovery to become someone new—to search and to find and to become the man who would be more comfortable in, and far more appropriate to, these new and frighteningly unfamiliar surroundings onboard *Sagafjord*. Someone who could better relate to a host of new people—to passengers and to crewmembers alike—to those who had become, perhaps through destiny or fate, my accidental traveling companions.

I shivered as I realized I could no longer rely upon the childlike persona I had created and accepted during my lifetime, a persona which I had so cleverly developed and so brilliantly used to manipulate and even exploit those around me. Those qualities—that naive and youthful image—would certainly not do in these new and quite sophisticated surroundings.

I felt naked and exposed, and very much alone out there on deck as the Statue of Liberty, as cold and as green as ever, came into view. In years past, she had held out her welcoming light to hundreds of thousands of adventurers seeking new lives in a new land. She didn't appear welcoming that day—at least not to me. She was, in fact, setting me free. Wasn't it freedom, after all, that she stood for? Freedom to explore, and freedom to be.

And suddenly, like out of a dream long past, she was there. *France*—proudly steaming towards us with bellowing black clouds bursting from her twin winged smokestacks—having completed another brisk North Atlantic winter crossing, and heading to her Hudson River berth, not far I'm sure, from where we had just come. Her decks were alive with hundreds of excited passengers no doubt eager to catch their very first glimpse of a winterized New York. They became witness to our sailing—some waving, others with cameras well in hand. Their presence made it real. It wasn't my imagination, after all.

Up ahead, the Verrazano Narrows Bridge stood vast as the city's metropolitan gateway, with the Ambrose Light Ship just off in the distance. As we approached, I felt *Sagafjord* roll slightly; the seas were beginning to pick up just a bit. Over the side, I watched as our navigational pilot hurriedly climbed down the rope ladder. He seemed to hesitate a moment before leaping onto his bobbing motor launch which then sped away—he turned with a final quick wave of his hand up towards the bridge. *Sagafjord's* starboard side port was closed and sealed shut. Our engines increased in power and vibration. The rhythm of our voyage had begun.

The last of a family of wandering albatross circled the ship as we steamed full ahead. They glided with the wind, silently away, back toward the land they knew and relied upon, and well, well out of sight—toward home.

Sagafjord's Dance Studio was a small uninspiring room just forward of mid-ship on Veranda Deck portside. The outside wall framed a series of floor-to-ceiling window units; opposite, full-length mirrors reflected the vastness of the open sea beyond. It had a rather common, and quite uninteresting, black-and-white linoleum flooring with a slightly domed ceiling alcove overhead into which was set several indirect fluorescent lighting fixtures which cast a hew of harsh cold light over the entire area. An aged spinet piano was bolted to the forward wall; a curved banquette with red leather cushions just opposite.

I opened the door at twelve noon sharp, not wanting to appear too anxious; certainly not wanting to be late. The room was already humming with audible activity; the sound not wavering in pitch or volume or tone. Everyone seemed quite animated—talking openly, laughing loudly; each person continually calling attention to himself as exaggerated gestures became more and more pronounced.

Many heads turned as I stepped purposefully into the room. "Who's the new guy?" had to be the question in everyone's mind. "How will he fit in?"

The door slammed loudly behind me—less, I'm sure, from my pulling it shut; most likely due to the increasing roll of the ship. I must have appeared nervous and perhaps even a bit self-conscious that morning, although I tried to look confident and ignore them all—I dared not glance into anyone's eyes and chance openly revealing my fear and anxiety. Rather I looked passed those threatening faces to the ocean view beyond. The massive sea was quite beautiful well into the distance; deep blue, surging still, and cold—uncertain and uneasy. My feelings exactly.

I felt awkward and out of place—not really knowing how to act, or with whom I should first speak. The confidence I once held proud and strong from my months onboard *Island Venture* was now gone, lost perhaps in those choppy waves I admired so. What was it that was different onboard *Sagafjord*, I asked myself. Why was it that I felt so uneasy?

I noticed Lar Vandelis at the far corner of the room. He held a mixed drink in one hand, a cigarette in the other, and was surrounded by five other gentlemen who huddled together in their own very private conversation—all were dressed impeccably well in what appeared to be dark navy jackets and charcoal-gray trousers. His smile, which seemed so warm and friendly when we stood together in Purser's Square just moments before, now seemed calculated—permanently and insincerely painted on his face. He seemed somehow bigger and perhaps even stronger than he did when Robert Brooks was with him—far more confident—definitely more secure.

Lar waved me over to join him and his colleagues. As I crossed the dance floor, a waiter approached and asked for my drink order. "A ginger ale, thank you." No alcohol for me. I could take no chances that day.

Lar was openly enthusiastic as he shook my hand; although his movements and his vocal tone made it quite clear, at least to me, as to where I should stand, and with whom I should speak. He began introducing me to the group, and I quickly realized that these were the men with whom I would closely and intimately spend the next ninety-eight days; the other members of the Tour Office staff.

Not unlike Robert Brooks, Percy Hayes was unequivocally British. He looked to be about thirty five years old, and was perhaps the most animated of them all. His already thinning hair was blond—its color, no doubt, aided a bit by the sun and perhaps even by his hairdresser. Percy was slightly overweight—rotund, if you will—and as the well-known Clement Moore holiday verse goes—when he laughed, his stomach shook "like a bowlful of jelly"—that was Percy perfectly. And as he stood there that day, he too was impeccably dressed in his elegant tweed slacks, and his well-tailored navy blazer, with a multi-colored silk handkerchief in his left breast pocket. Yet somehow, the uniform fell differently on Percy—more perfect, more right. He held his "tall" gin and tonic with the same hand on which he wore a gold pinky ring, dominated by what must have been, no doubt, the Hayes' family crest.

Percy was in heated conversation with Archibald Hannon—a somewhat older gentleman, who appeared to be in his late '50s or early '60s. Archibald had faded gray, almost white hair—a swatch of which seemed to fall continually into his eyes; his rather annoying affectation of constantly pushing it to one side and out of the way seemed more a calculated gesture than a mechanically natural response. He wore exceptionally thick, dark-rimmed glasses which regularly slid down his nose—elongating his face like a worn rubber mask. Although he too wore a jacket and tie, Archibald seemed far more disheveled than any of the others—looking more like an absent-minded professor than I had ever dreamed possible. Clearly, he appeared quite out of place. Perhaps even more so than I myself felt. Nonetheless, he was certainly well cast. Archibald, I soon learned, was the ship's intellectual, and it quickly became quite clear that he never let anyone forget it. He was formally introduced to me that morning as the ship's official historian and lecturer.

"My only problem now is raising the money" Archibald told Percy as he leaned haphazardly against the ship's bulkhead. "You see, my producer thinks it may be a bit of a problem because of the esoteric subject matter—you know, the mystical setting and the themes of confused identity and unspeakable love."

Archibald slid his glasses further up his nose, and took a long, somewhat exaggerated, sip of his drink. It was clear from the conversation that he had written some sort of theatrical work, and was trying to obtain the needed financing.

"What about your friend from Madeira?" Percy asked. "What was his name?" Percy was obviously hoping to be helpful.

"Martin? He wouldn't invest a penny, that cheap son-of-a-bitch" Archibald snapped back quickly.

"Why not? He tried to kill you once, didn't he? I would think he owes you." Percy sipped his drink.

"Yes, but that was on a cliff near Hong Kong—in another place and another time. I'm sure he's forgotten all about that. Besides, he's much too conservative to invest on Broadway. He's far more interested in his daily trysts with the locals of Funchall—but we shan't discuss that right now."

They both casually glanced in my direction, and then continued.

"Besides, there are other sources for money. You, of all people, know that Percy. Don't you? These passengers, for example. There's certainly lots of money here."

"Old money too" Percy added, and smiled. "That's the best kind."

"Old or new, I'm not fussy. Who the hell cares?" Archibald shook his head and smiled somewhat satanically. "You're just a snob Percy. You know that, don't you? A pompous British snob." They both laughed.

"Snob? I think not!" he said as he waved his hand away. "But thank you anyway."

"Yes, a snob. And you know it too! And don't dismiss me like that."

Archibald suddenly seemed to get a bit agitated, for a reason clearly unapparent to me.

"Now now dear Archibald. Don't you get your knickers in a twist."

"Be nice to me Percy, or I won't mention your name when I win the Tony Award."

"Ah, be still me heart." Percy rolled his eyes and grabbed at his breast in a comedic mock swoon, directing his attention then fully towards me. It appeared more an escape than desire.

"If I raise the money and the play's a hit" Archibald continued, "I'll take my profits and buy a new wardrobe. I have that right, you know. It's a part of the American dream. Besides, I have an awful feeling it's going to be a winner Percy. A big hit. I have a sinking feeling of success."

"Dreadful, isn't it?" Percy said as he sipped his gin and tonic one more time.

"Dreadful indeed."

They both stopped their conversation long enough to personally welcome me onboard. Percy, first, chuckled in true British fashion as he shook my hand, and quickly asked where I was from. While the others around us eavesdropped quite openly, I told him of my home in Westchester County, and how I left college in mid-stream, so to speak, in order to accept this opportunity—to sail around the world. As I spoke, I noticed Archibald staring—watching me intensely, quite strangely—a peculiar grin on his face; a haunting, piercing glare in his eyes. He seemed different from the others. I'm not sure what it was, or why, but he made me even more uncomfortable than I already was.

I sensed that something was not right. I felt odd with him looking at me like that; almost dirty. Somehow I just sensed that Archibald Hannon might be a queer—a homosexual—or at least he seemed to act as I would have thought one would act—like a vulture eyeing his prey. And I was not, in the least, interested in becoming one of his conquests. I wanted no part of this individual whatsoever, and I guess I tried to make it clear to him too by turning my back, and moving just a bit closer to Lar, somewhat out of Archibald's reach—at least out of his gaze.

Just then, the door to the Dance Studio burst open and Cruise Director Ted Jones came sweeping into the room. His partner Anne Dickson was at his side. A stunning couple they were—both exquisitely dressed, glamorously social. The room was stilled at their entrance; they sailed across the floor with an impressive, almost regal, presence. It was as if they owned it. In a sense, they did. And even to my young novice's eye, it was quite apparent that they were much loved and respected by those in that room.

I watched closely as they warmly greeted their friends and long-time colleagues. Appearing unusually sincere for the group thus far, Ted and Anne moved from person to person—kissing some (on both cheeks, mind you), and simply hand-shaking others. From where I stood, they seemed the perfect couple; with a look and style others would eagerly seek. It was Percy who confirmed my thoughts.

"They're a couple you know. Been together for years. Ted's married—to someone else—naturally. But that's unimportant."

With their grace and enviable elegance quite evident, Ted Jones and Anne Dickson seemed to illustrate the grand style and sophistication clearly synonymous with Norwegian America Line—a style and sophistication the likes of which I was not yet accustomed.

Ted Jones, I soon learned, was not only *Sagafjord*'s Cruise Director; he and Anne Dickson were the ship's dance team as well. Together, they would perform in specially themed shows throughout the voyage. In addition, they would offer private dance instruction to any interested passengers during the many days at sea.

"They're considered the finest dance team afloat" Percy told me. He clearly wanted me to understand just how lucky we were to have them onboard. I tried to look impressed. Although I wasn't quite sure just what sort of an achievement that was.

Ted raised his hand, the room fell silent, and the more formal introductions began. The customary procedure, I soon learned, was for each of us to say a few words about ourselves as the focus and the attention moved about the room.

Margaret Sinclair, the Senior Social Directress, was an extremely elegant woman, in her late sixties or early seventies, dressed quite conservatively in a classic white and navy-blue suit with matching purse and shoes. Margaret appeared to be quite open and personable, yet boasted a grotesquely animated, forceful style. Her movements were abrupt and erratic as she spoke, and she made it quite clear, at least to me, that this was *her* ship, and it God-damned will be run as she saw fit. It was said that Margaret Sinclair began her sailing career onboard Cunard's *Mauretania*, after a short and perhaps somewhat unsuccessful career as a grand music hall songstress. Although her given and formal name was Margaret, everyone called her Maggie.

Hal Carter was Ted Jones' Assistant Cruise Director, and he too looked very much the part. With his white cotton pants, white shoes and socks, and double-breasted navy blazer, he seemed quite characteristic of the classic—perhaps a bit tacky—cruise director. He whined a bit when he spoke, or at least appeared to have a rather distinct and unusual way of speaking—a manner I had not heard before. He shuffled neurotically from one leg to the other as he spoke.

"What kind of accent is that?" I whispered to Percy as Hal told us that his office was located just behind the Purser's Office. "Where's he from?"

"He doesn't have an accent, you twit. He's a queen! A poof. He's a pansy."

Lar overheard Percy's comments, and giggled mischievously. Archibald widened his already sardonic grin and closely watched my reaction to Percy's harsh words. I was embarrassed and disgusted, and tried my best not to let my feelings show. Yet I'm sure my face had by then turned the color of Lar's Bloody Mary.

The introductions proceeded, and quickly moved about the room—everyone trying to be even more jovial and even more clever than the speaker immediately preceding him. It appeared as if they were all trying just a bit too hard to be liked, or perhaps to attract as much attention to themselves as possible. To me, it was obvious that each of them clearly savored the spotlight—albeit for just a moment or two.

As they each spoke, I felt a great unhappiness among these people, a phoniness I simply could not understand—and it troubled and saddened me greatly. Their lives seemed uncomfortably dishonest. Forced. Why did they act so insincere and insecure, I wondered? With such wonderful jobs and such exciting careers, why weren't they happier? Why weren't they satisfied with their lives?

I was angered by the truth my thoughts queried, and by these people too. It was not at all what I expected onboard *Sagafjord*. And most definitely not what I expected onboard the Great World Cruise. I hated them all for manipulating my feelings so, and for making this—perhaps the most important time in my life—seem so unimportant, so unhappy—and so, so negative.

I glanced out the windows for a moment as the introductions continued. The voices bounced about the room with great speed and accuracy—I dodged their direction so as not to be struck.

The ship had clearly picked up speed; the sea—each wave— moved along swiftly past us, and quickly out of sight. I tried to focus on one particular spot in the vast ocean surrounding us—just a patch of white foam in a palette of deep blue. It was impossible. Confusing; lost in the ever-changing movement. But it didn't matter. It was just a diversion. Anything, I thought, to escape the dreaded atmosphere in that room.

No matter how much I tried to camouflage it, change for me had always been a trauma; it created great uncertainty in my life. I was trying so very hard to like these strange new people. But somehow, I knew instinctively—in my gut—that no matter what I did, or what I told myself, I really did not like any of them. And more importantly, I did not want to be like any of them. I wanted none of them as my friend. I did not want to admit it to myself, but all I wanted was to go home. Or at least to go out that Dance Studio door and come back in again, and have it all be different and wonderful—just as I had imagined it would be; just as I had dreamed. But I couldn't, and it wouldn't be. I was there, and I knew I had to deal with it just as it was. Make the best of it, as my mother would say.

I pulled my focus back into the room just as Marshall Smith began to speak. Now let there be no doubt that Marshall Smith was a very unattractive man, with a densely thick bushy mustache and even thicker, rounded glasses. He had severe, shortly cropped black hair, just a bit speckled with gray; with a good amount of dandruff which fell from his scalp in flurries as he spoke.

Marshall had a heavy lisp or sibilant "s" as it is called—I could not tell which because he mumbled so. Lar nudged me with his elbow.

"That's no accent either" he said as he giggled uncontrollably.

Percy and the others laughed as I tried to ignore Lar's comment. Marshall explained that he was onboard to conduct bridge lessons. And he made it quite clear that his was the finest bridge instruction on the high seas.

The tour office staff was next to speak, and Philip Pound commandeered the floor. Pound was from Australia, with deep blue eyes and two huge feet which somehow supported his towering height of well over six and a half feet—although he did slouch a bit when he stood, and swayed from side to side as he walked. His arms moved frantically about his body as he described his hometown of Ferntree Gully, Tasmania; then led the staff in a brief and quite uninspiring rendition of *Waltzing Matilda*. An abundance of overly accented "mates" were thrown in for effect and good measure, I'm sure. Philip seemed to have many in-jokes among the permanent staff members onboard. I disliked him immediately.

Lar then took control and introduced the rest of our group— first Archibald and Percy, and then Ornulf Johnsonn, and Per Sanden; finally introducing me as the newest and the youngest addition to the tour office staff.

Ornulf—whose name I soon learned meant "wolf" in Norwegian—and Per had heavy Scandinavian accents. They joked among themselves—in Norwegian, no less—while the others spoke. They seemed distantly pleasant—not open or warm, or at all eager to meet new people or invite them into their very cloistered group.

Focus then moved to Jan Walesky, the Polish orchestra leader, and his pixielike wife. Carmen, it turned out, was the Walesky Orchestra's lead singer and chief tambourine player, and she certainly acted the star.

Seated together with her on the banquette was Gennifer Gray, an aging folksinger from Fort Lauderdale with shoulder-length strawberry hair. Why she brought her nylon-stringed acoustic guitar with her that morning, I never really found out. But it was there, clearly as an appendage to her pale personality. Gennifer was a bit too earthy for me—a Floridian flower child if you will, already quite matronly yet only in her mid to late 30s. It was evident that she and Marshall Smith were great good friends. Whatever they had in common though, I was unable to imagine.

To Gennifer's left were Roger Rolande, a middle-aged Frenchman and his much younger part-time assistant and full-time girlfriend Elizabeth, whose job it was to create various scenic effects for the entertainment shows onboard. They were typically French—Roger, believe it or not, was even wearing a somewhat lopsided black beret on his head, with a half-smoked Gauloise hanging from his lips. Casting here simply could not have been better.

And finally, we met John Marratisch, the all-too-slick and quite nondescript golf pro, and the four gentlemen surrounding him—*Sagafjord*'s "dancing boys"—hired solely to socialize with the single women onboard. All of the "boys" were well past middle age and quite severely dressed; some with shoe-polished-black hair and bad toupees, shiny leather shoes and bulky pinky rings. Their personalities had an austere slickness to them, and I imagined just what their jobs really did entail. I was disgusted at the thought.

The meeting continued on a bit longer. The drinks flowed freely, as did the incredibly nonsensical self-congratulation. Ted discussed that evening's schedule of *Fun and Games* in the Ballroom—whatever that was—and our mandatory attendance for cruise staff introductions—the "dog and pony show" as Percy called it. He then went on to address proper procedures and shipboard protocol—as snickers and groans and some jeers too were heard. Numerous pairs of eyes rolled.

At last, it was over—the formal part of the meeting at least. Yet the alcohol still flowed; the mingling and shallow talk lingered. It was chaotic, the audio level back to deafening. So I was relieved—saved by the bell if you will—when that same young waiter interrupted us all with the chime of his hand-held gong announcing that luncheon was being served in the Saga Dining Room. His real message? Get the hell out, no doubt. I've got to clean up.

Percy Hayes was raised in rural Wales, the product of a broken home. Although he often spoke of a personal assignment as a member of the famed Queen's Guard, no one has yet been able to confirm or document that appointment. After first moving to London as a young adult, Percy finally left Europe in the mid-1950s on a Cunard liner not unlike *Sagafjord*, hoping to establish a new life of prosperity, personal freedom and privacy "off in the colonies."

Percy's homosexuality was, at that time, somewhat of a social embarrassment, and that, in part, led to his rather youthful and quite premature departure from Britain. And although he claimed somewhat of a solid family heritage, he had little actual money to his name—Percy was barely able to scrounge and borrow for the shipboard passage alone.

Yet it was while onboard that ship, traveling cabin class westbound across the Atlantic, that Percy met a younger, first-class passenger—an American called Billy—and they soon became close and intimate friends. Percy spent the remainder of that voyage sharing Billy's first-class accommodations, as well as his affections, and by the time their ship docked at New York, their relationship had been sealed.

Unable to abandon his new British lover in what, for Percy, was a strange new country; in what was perceived to be such a dangerous city as New York—Billy invited Percy to share his family's Connecticut home . . . to live there with him, and with his parents Elizabeth and William Sr., at least until Percy was well settled-in to his new life in the Americas.

But once ashore, however, with the glamour and the romance of their grand ocean voyage behind them, Percy and Billy's relationship quickly soured—the passion once nurtured by crisp Atlantic nights soon waned. And it was quite soon thereafter that their inseparableness was indeed separated—disrupted by each pursuing his own very personal interests, and perhaps even more exciting and intriguing lovers.

Nonetheless, they continued to share their Connecticut living arrangements for just a while longer—a situation which eventually paid off quite well for Percy. For it was during that time that Billy's mother Elizabeth—the dominate matriarch of the family—became quite fond of the young Mr. Hayes, regardless of her own son's faded affections or disruptive concerns.

Percy, it turned out, was no fool. He knew a good thing when he saw it. And so as his own personal affections for the young Billy lessened, Percy's respect, camaraderie, and admiration for Billy's mother grew. And so it was *their* bond—not Percy's and Billy's, but rather Percy's and Elizabeth's—which prospered. It was she who then encouraged Percy. It was Elizabeth who supported him both psychologically and financially—much to the dismay, and intense jealousy of her dearly embittered, soon to be estranged, son. However long and often Elizabeth and the young Billy argued over Percy and his continued interference in their family life, it was Elizabeth's strong will and even stronger purse-strings which won out, as her actions and her own personal desires were quite determined. And Percy and Elizabeth have been great good friends ever since. Percy and Billy, though—well, that was clearly another matter. As Percy eventually moved on to his own apartment somewhere deep in the cavernous streets of lower Manhattan, it became clear that he and Billy would never speak again.

I trust by now it is quite obvious that my very first impressions of Percy Hayes were not exactly complimentary. He appeared shallow and quite a bit flamboyant; far too homosexual for my tastes. Clearly, he was a man of many sexual experiences—that was obvious to anyone—and for some unknown reason, I feared people of many sexual experiences. Perhaps I feared their perceived power over me for having such knowledge and experience. Or perhaps I felt that they would, in some way, encourage me to act in a similar manner; make me do as they have done. I wasn't interested in any of that. I had never been what one might call a sexual person. I had never had a girlfriend during my teenage years when others were clearly running to parties and to high school dances; when others just couldn't seem to get enough of that all too provocative female companionship. Sex was neither an interest nor an issue during my adolescence. There was something about it—about the concept of it I guess—that I didn't really think about and, yes, perhaps even feared. I don't think it was the actual act itself—in fact I was clearly fascinated by its physicality. But more likely and more realistically, it was the intimacy which the act represented that I was quite unprepared to accept. That was indeed more threatening to me than anything else. I wasn't sure why, but it was.

So I didn't think about it very much. I successfully avoided getting myself into sexual situations of any sort. I would breathe a sigh of relief when I knew I had escaped once again—without having to kiss a girl at school, or make out in the backseat of my father's beige Oldsmobile on the night of my junior prom. It was not that I had never felt sexually aroused. Indeed, I did. And quite often too. But I soon learned that that was easily remedied—quietly, quickly —and I was then able to move on to what really mattered in my life; to what really occupied my interests.

When I was twelve years old or so, I did masturbate with a school friend, as most pre-teen and teenage boys might do once or twice in their adolescent years. Yet other than that one rather uneventful and somewhat embarrassing experience, I never consciously, and wholeheartedly, sought out another person for sexual reasons.

Percy, however, was quite the contrary. He was different. And although I often pursued what others considered to be different, I clearly did not want to be like Percy. I was uncomfortable with his presence and his obvious homosexual ways. I felt threatened by him. And that troubled me greatly.

No doubt I wanted, and usually welcomed, new experiences in my life—after all, one just had to look at what I had already accomplished. But at the same time, I kept those experiences—especially those experiences of a sexual nature—at a good safe distance. In my personal life, I took little steps—just one at a time. This voyage, however, with all these strange new people with whom I was now thrown together, already made it seem as if I was tumbling down an entire flight of stairs.

Our first days working together were spent organizing the Tour Office—planning how we would operate, and discussing our overall selling strategy. Those early days also offered us the much needed time to get to know one another a bit better—personality traits, neurotic defenses, and all. Ironically, it was through our own particular working styles and our individual daily tasks that this exercise was achieved. But with all our daily pleasantries, it could not be ignored or forgotten that since that very first day onboard—stemming back to our initial meeting in the Dance Studio—first impressions do take hold. What seemed to be unscalable walls and unpierceable barriers were solidly established; and penetration, of any kind, appeared—at least at that point—to be impossible.

My personal uneasiness with Percy continued to grow as the

days went on. In the office, he continued to be gratuitously open about his sexuality and his numerous anonymous sexual exploits. His crude and distasteful comments on just about every sexual topic one could imagine were indefatigable, and extremely off-putting. He blatantly and continuously made sexual innuendoes whenever and wherever he could—not only in the office, but out on deck and sometimes even in the presence of passengers. I tried to avoid being alone with Percy as much as I could and wherever I could. And I quickly found myself becoming angered by the stressful atmosphere I felt he created.

Lar announced the various tour office assignments and responsibilities at our first official staff meeting that next afternoon. He described in detail how each of our particular roles fit in to the entire tour operation, and how important we all were, as individuals and as a team, to the overall success of the cruise itself and to the full enjoyment of the passengers.

Per would be the tour office cashier, handling all financial transactions and settlements; Ornulf and Philip Pound, with some assistance from me, would be in charge of the over-the-counter sales and ticketing; while Percy alone was to be in charge of any and all private arrangements. Being the most junior member of the staff, I was assigned some additional duties as well—to type, distribute, and file all office memos and other lists and correspondence, which, on a world cruise, I soon learned, was considerable. From extensive rooming lists to passenger manifests, to specific tour itineraries, and the mandatory "shore tips," I quickly became proficient at what was expected of me. I also learned an invaluable lifetime lesson—how important it was to know how to type well and efficiently, but never, under any circumstances, reveal that secret talent to anyone.

I like to pride myself on being exceptionally well organized, and I quickly took delight in the seemingly endless praise from the others about my administrative abilities and exceptional typing and organizational skills—praise, I'm sure stemming from the fact that none of them could type a single letter. And so I ended up doing all their personal work as well. A back-handed compliment, no doubt. Nonetheless, it was praise—and for whatever reason, I was willing and quite eager to accept it. Clearly, I liked the attention and the compliments, and openly welcomed more—all I could get. It energized and encouraged me to take on even more duties than what was actually expected. And it was because of that great support and encouragement from my tour office colleagues that I began a project of my own—setting up an entirely new filing system onboard, and constructing charts of all kinds to make our tour operation run even more efficiently. One chart in particular illustrated each tour, its appropriate booking number, and the escort assigned to be in charge. At a glance, it clearly detailed any tour scheduling conflicts, and this effort alone dubbed me the wunderkind of *Sagafjord*'s shore excursion office.

Yet with all the satisfaction of knowing that I was so appreciated and so well liked by my co-workers onboard, I continued to distrust them. I continued to wonder just what their real motives might be—why did they so easily accept me as they did? Was I really as special and as talented as they claimed? And if not, then why did they want me around? Perhaps I flattered myself, but I couldn't help but feel that it was sexually motivated—at least with Percy and Archibald. It had to be. Who really knew about the others and their own motives or agenda? Whatever the reasons, my curious fear and uneasiness remained; the uncertainty it created, profound.

Of everyone, Percy was truly the enigmatic dichotomy. It was Percy who both disgusted and fascinated me at the same time, and it seemed the more I despised his overt mannerisms and his flamboyant ways, the more I found myself mysteriously drawn to him, or more importantly, to his all-too-winning image and enviable style. Indeed, I envied his sweeping popularity with both passengers and crewmembers alike. I envied his custom-made suits which Percy proudly boasted were designed by his very private tailor in Tangier. His shoes were designed by Gucci, he told me, and were always polished to shine like mirrors. And he prided himself on showing off his $1,800 Cartier Tank Watch which he defiantly wore with just everyday blue-jeans and a pullover shirt. "It's the height of chic" Percy would boast.

Clearly, my experiences were quite different. I had never yet dreamed of having a suit tailor-made, let alone a private tailor, or even visiting Tangier; a Timex watch was the only timepiece I owned; and my shoes came directly from the not-so-private collection of Thom McAnn.

Admirably winning, yet curiously repulsive in his pretentious manner, Percy indeed appeared to be the perfect image of chic sophistication. His popularity onboard seemed to grow each day. Yet I could not understand why he was so liked. Most everyone knew full well that Percy was a homosexual. It was so obvious after all, and yet they seemed quite indifferent to the fact—quite disinterested actually. It bothered them little that he was so open about that very personal part of his life.

I too wanted to experience a similar kind of popularity. Yet I feared altering my personality in order to achieve such acceptance. My personality, indeed. It's all I had.

What frightened me most was the fear of the unknown; that I would perhaps have to change . . . become someone else, or even become more like Percy in order to win that same acceptance and that enviable popularity from those around me—to become more outrageous in my appearance; more flamboyant in my mannerisms. No, that just could not be. Certainly one didn't need to be or act like a flamboyant homosexual in order to gain the acceptance of the world—at least our world onboard *Sagafjord*.

And that's the world that mattered. And what a world it was—a world unlike any other. Who really knew what was normal here— what was accepted behavior, after all? Indeed, what was expected? Was life onboard *Sagafjord* truly that unique—albeit tantalizingly dysfunctional?

Yes, to me, Percy was clearly a dichotomy; his social success certainly an enigma. But until then, he appeared my only role model of success and popularity. And ironically then, he unwillingly became the center of my attentions. My resistance to certain aspects of his life and his personality remained instinctive however; I just couldn't allow it any other way. I could not, and would not, under any circumstances, model myself after Percy Hayes.

So from that day forward, I made it a point to become more observant of the others on board—other staff members and passengers too—people who were clearly held in high regard, and who commanded great respect. It was research, after all. I needed to actively study their personal mannerisms and their individual styles in order to more successfully develop my own social image and personality. It was becoming quite obvious to me that I wasn't yet secure at all with who I was, and with what type of person I was becoming. I only hoped it wasn't that obvious to the others—the insecurity, that is. Out of fear of discovery, I quickly had to decide what I needed to do, and who I needed to be like, in order to become popular onboard ship, in order to be fully accepted. And if it did indeed turn out to be anyone like the infamous Percy Hayes, I just didn't know what I would do.

There existed many rules of conduct for cruise staff members onboard Norwegian American Line vessels—most of them quite simple, yet all hard and fast. One in particular—and perhaps the most important—was that all staff members, men and women alike, must socialize with the passengers as much as possible. Socializing, according to NAL standards at the time, entailed not only talking with passengers while in the lounges or on deck, but joining them for drinks perhaps at the North Cape Bar or in the Club Polaris, or even in the Verandah Cafe or out on deck by the pool. But most of all—for the male staff members at least—socializing meant dancing, as much and as often as possible, with the many single women onboard—all of whom were quite elderly, and very very rich.

There was no doubt that single women—whether or not permanently unattached, or divorced or widowed—all seemed to flock to *Sagafjord's* annual winter escape for many reasons. Some, perhaps, for a change of routine; others, to simply follow the sun westward. But it became more and more apparent that many traveled onboard solely for the camaraderie. Naturally, they all preferred male companionship to that of other females. Maggie Sinclair —or any of the other female passengers, for that matter—would clearly be considered competition for the attentions of the far fewer men onboard. So the more gentlemen Norwegian America Line could engage then—in whatever capacity—the better.

For whatever their own particular quirks or eccentricities might be, most of the female passengers seemed to have one true commonality—they all loved to dance. Perhaps it made them feel attractive once again, or it brought back memories of their more youthful days when dancing in the great ballrooms of mid-century America was their main social intercourse. Or perhaps it was simply a passive sexual thrill to fox-trot with a handsome younger man. Whatever the reason, dancing became the main focus of the male staff's attention. In particular, golf pro John Marratisch and his troupe of dancing boys were indeed kept busy in the lounges after dark. And as Cruise Director Ted Jones continually reminded us in staff meetings and in shipboard memos as well, they—the dancing boys—needed all the help they could get.

One night at sea, quite early on in the voyage, I arrived in the Ballroom just after dinner, perhaps a bit too anxious to fulfill my dancing responsibilities—"pushing the old bags around the floor" as Percy would say. I wanted to finish early enough to take in that evening's movie *Public Eye*—a then recent comedy starring Topol and Mia Farrow. Perhaps not *Gone with the Wind*, but it was all that was offered. And even at such an early stage in the voyage, I clearly needed some diversion.

The Jan Walesky Orchestra was already playing as I entered the Ballroom. The music was quite loud and full. A number of female passengers sat quietly alone, at individual tables, near the edge of the dance floor. The remainder of the room was open and vacant—most of the passengers were still enjoying their dinner service two decks below.

I noticed a well-dressed, rather sensitive-looking older woman with shoulder-length gray hair pulled stylishly back behind her neck. She wore an elegant deep blue evening dress. I watched her for a moment as she sat pensively on portside—at a table for two, just off the dance floor. And like all the others, she sat alone—staring blindly at nothing in particular . . . her toe slightly tapping to the steady rhythm . . . hoping, perhaps, to be noticed. Jan and Carmen were performing their own bouncy arrangement of *You Made Me Love You.* Hesitantly, I approached her table.

"Good evening" I awkwardly stumbled out. "Would you like to dance?" I am certain I asked the question hoping her answer would be in the negative. She paused for a moment; her slight hesitation caused embarrassment for us both, although I'm sure she meant no harm. She must have been just as uncomfortable as I. No doubt she was taken aback by the scenario—a nineteen year old asking a quite elderly woman to dance. But that was my job; that, she must have known.

"Yes" she finally said as she stood. "I'd love to." And together we walked to the center of the dance floor.

The woman must have sensed my intense self-consciousness and unease—anyone would. But as I took her in my arms, she beamed—just a bit—with the smile of a young girl who had just been asked to her first high school social.

We began to foxtrot; I of course led with my ever-versatile box step.

After a moment of awkward silence, I introduced myself as Carmen sang "I didn't want to do it, I didn't want to do it." The woman knew who I was, however. She remembered me from the first night's cruise staff introductions.

"You're easy to remember" she told me. "You've got to be the youngest person onboard."

"Then of course you know I work in the Tour Office" I said to her. I was indeed proud of that fact, and I almost expected her to visibly react in utter amazement at just how special a person I must be.

"So very nice to meet you" she said. "I'm Harriet . . . Harriet Woodward."

We continued around the dance floor in frozen silence, my

box step becoming just a bit more daring and confident with each new twist and turn. It was obvious Mrs. Woodward was a very good dancer.

"Where are you from?" I finally asked—I just couldn't think of anything else to say. Mrs. Woodward then spoke of a small town just outside St. Louis where her family had been in residence since 1805. Old money, I thought. I knew Percy would be pleased. I couldn't wait to tell him.

She talked a bit about her grandchildren and the impressive schools they attended. I tried to act interested in what Mrs. Woodward had to say, and I hoped to God I was convincing.

"Have you ever taken a world cruise before?" I asked.

"No, no." she replied hesitantly. "This is my first." She paused, and looked away. Our dancing continued. I began to realize just how long Jan and Carmen's musical arrangement really was.

" . . . so what made you decide to take this particular cruise? Why *Sagafjord?*"

Suddenly, and quite unexpectedly, Mrs. Woodward began to tremble; her eyes welled up with tears.

"I'm here to bury my husband" she said.

She began to weep quite openly then, nearly collapsing in my arms.

For several years, Mrs. Woodward and her husband Charles had planned to take the *Sagafjord* Great World Cruise together, in celebration of their 60th wedding anniversary. Just one month before sailing, however, Charles Woodward suffered massive heart failure and died suddenly, quite unexpectedly. His last wish was to be buried at sea.

I escorted Mrs. Woodward back to her table, and sat with her for most of that evening. Mia Farrow and Topol would have to wait. I didn't want Mrs. Woodward to feel any more alone than she already did.

Ironic, I thought—that Mrs. Woodward and her husband would be traveling together after all.

Gretal heckettson was infamous onboard. And very much like Percy Hayes, she too was an enigma. Her name was tossed about constantly in the Tour Office, and among the other staff members too, with an almost sacred reverence. Everyone onboard seemed to know the woman, or know *of* her at least, although I had yet had the opportunity to meet or even see her walking about the ship. Maggie told me that Mrs. Heckettson was perhaps Norwegian America Line's most valued customer. The previous year alone, Maggie said, Mrs. Heckettson had "lived" onboard ship for ten months, spending the remaining two in Buck's County Pennsylvania—most of which, Percy boasted, she owned. "Old cattle money" he told me "...from way back."

Percy explained that it was probably less expensive for Mrs. Heckettson to live onboard ship full time—even in accommodations as grand and as extravagant as NAL's Trigvassen Suite—than to maintain her huge estate back home, with servants and utilities and the like.

And she must have loved that suite very much . . . it was said that Mrs. Heckettson hadn't left it since sailing from New York. She traveled with NAL so often, I was told, that the cruise reservationists in the New York office automatically held the Trigvassen Suite in Gretal Heckettson's name. It was the unwritten rule. They just blocked it off in all the berthing books—completely. Not available to anyone else. Norwegian America Line had to be able to accommodate her whenever she decided to sail. Mrs. Heckettson's revenue was far too valuable for Norwegian America to lose.

While Percy shared with me the particulars of the Gretal Heckettson story, he unknowingly revealed more about himself than about this infamous passenger. His own truths began to emerge shamelessly through his words. Willingly or not, Percy's powerfully camouflaged personality was striped bare. And it was then that he came alive—for me, at least—for the very first time.

His words made me wonder if perhaps Percy was, in reality, not as wealthy as he would have liked us all to believe—with all his flashiness and his Cartier watches, and hand-made suits. Perhaps he only lived his rich-man's fantasies by proxy so to speak, vicariously through these very wealthy passengers he so admired and respected, and with whom he socialized with at every conceivable opportunity. By talking about their wealth as often as possible—thereby making it real... in his mind at least—perhaps Percy actually believed he was one of them; one of the fabulously wealthy social set. Mrs. Heckettson's Buck's County Estate, for example, became his then, if only by inference, and if only for a moment. He made their lives all too familiar, but only to himself. It was others then, who thereby created Percy's own reality.

Although rarely witnessed, it became clear that Percy had a close, personal relationship with this mysterious lady, dating back, I was told, at least several world cruises and one or two South Pacific sailings as well. She trusted him; and he obviously amused her in some odd way. That was their unconscious social agreement. And so she gave Percy all of her travel business. If Mrs. Heckettson ever decided to step ashore while in port—which, I was told, was an extremely rare occurrence—her private car specifications or hotel accommodations, or even specific restaurant reservations were pre-arranged personally and only by Percy Hayes. Mrs. Heckettson's personal escort ashore though was not Percy at all, but Chief Steward Bjorn Anderson—a charming, somewhat older, Norwegian America veteran whom she grew to love and to trust over the many years traveling the world.

I'm sure you realize by this time that Mrs. Heckettson was not only rarely seen about the ship, but she rarely socialized with other passengers at all. In fact, it would have been suprising if she did. She seemed to dismiss them as uninteresting or unworthy, and she seldom, if ever, acknowledged their presence onboard. Continually, she stayed within the luxurious confines of her suite, and Percy would spend hour after hour in her company each and every morning over coffee and burnt dry toast, discussing her future travel plans—however real or imagined they were. In a way, by so doing, he was fulfilling his own very special social responsibility. No Ballroom dancing for Percy Hayes.

I was fascinated by this Mrs. Heckettson, and couldn't help

but create in my mind my own personal image of her—not only of what she might be like, but of what she represented. And still often—far too often—I would wonder why such a sophisticated woman like Gretal Heckettson—no doubt the richest and most powerful woman onboard—would ever want to be associated with an openly flamboyant homosexual like Percy Hayes. What, if anything, could they ever have in common?

Early one morning, just after opening, an old woman shuffled in to the Tour Office. Unsteadily feeble, she wore only a wrinkled pink bathrobe; her thinning, snow-white hair seemed completely untouched after a restless night's sleep. She walked barefoot, stepping up to the selling counter quite hesitantly, almost fearful.

"P-e-r-c-y" she whispered slowly. "I must see Percy." Her eyes rolled back into her slightly tilted head as she spoke in breathy delirium. Her hands moved wildly and erratically about her face as she repeated—faintly whispered—his name over and over, as if in a dream. "Percy" she whispered again. "Where is Percy?" A Norma Desmond of the seas, I thought. Who was this woman?

Percy came running in from the Purser's Office as soon as he heard her whispers. He greeted the woman warmly—quickly turning her around, escorting her back into the hallway and out of sight, as if he were protecting her from being seen by any of the others onboard; from shattering her alluring image in everyone's eyes.

This, I was told, was the glamorous and distinguished Gretal Heckettson.

The Saga Dining Room was beautiful—warmly reminiscent of the classic dining salons of the great transatlantic liners, not unlike Holland America's vintage *Nieuw Amsterdam*. One entered the great hall from Upper Deck aft by first descending an elegant two-deck-high grand stairway, expertly fit with plush-red carpeting protected on each side by shiny brass banisters and elegantly spoked railings. An equally magnificent double-deck high, ceiling-to-floor, etched glass door stood grandly at the entranceway.

The dining room itself was decorated in shades of royal reds and regal golds. Above was a beautifully vaulted ceiling which housed a galaxy of indirect lighting fixtures specifically designed to create various moods of light.

At the time of *Sagafjord*'s design and construction in the mid-1960s, the most unique feature of the Saga Dining Room—a true marvel at the time—was its dual escalator system which lead to the kitchen facilities one deck below. These escalators greatly facilitated service maneuvers for the waiters and other dining room staff who otherwise would have had to balance trays while attempting to navigate up and down stairways during extremely rough seas. Additionally, the Saga Dining Room was one of the few floating restaurants at the time able to comfortably accommodate all passengers at one sitting only—dinner was served comfortably from 7:30 P.M. to 9:00 P.M. nightly.

Percy said the mark of a true well-seasoned world cruise traveler is that he will inevitably request, if not demand, a dining room table for two. No one, at least no *experienced* traveler, would want to risk a ninety-eight-day three-meal-a-day commitment with others who might be unpleasant, or rude, or constantly complaining or otherwise negative. Those *real* travel professionals—world cruise veterans—know well just how difficult other passengers could be.

In 1973, even onboard a sophisticated world cruise liner like *Sagafjord*, social class attitudes were still a consideration. It was unheard of for Sun Deck passengers to dine—or even be seen seated—with those occupying space on A-Deck; rarely would those passengers fortunate enough to be chosen to dine at the captain's table be seen at horse-racing or enjoying bingo, or even in the audience of one of Ted Jones' variety shows. Social snobs they were, and outwardly proud of it too.

So, then, the endless demand for private tables-for-two became a constant issue for *Sagafjord*'s maitre d'hotel. There just wasn't enough of such tables onboard, or room for any additional tables to be set. For us then—the cruise and tour staffs—there was little else to do but dine at temporary tables set up specifically for that purpose—not in the Dining Room itself, but rather in the Main Deck entrance foyer—just slightly aft, and at the foot of the grand stairway. Personally, I thought this arrangement was a bit second-rate, although I seemed to be alone in my thinking. In fact, Percy and Archibald were both thrilled that they did not have to dine near passengers at all. Most of the others agreed. They welcomed our dining arrangements with open arms. And so if the others didn't complain—those who I felt were far more experienced and far more sophisticated—then why should I?

The staff tables were set, and seating specifically assigned, according to job or department or onboard responsibility. There were the two entertainer's tables on starboard side, just adjacent to the social staff's table; Ted and Anne's essential table-for-two was tucked away in a quiet corner just under the stairwell and nearly out of sight, with Roger and Elizabeth's table—also for two—just nearby. Our table, seating the five members of the tour office staff and Archibald Hannon too, was located on the portside of the ship, just to the left of, and slightly under, the grand stairway.

Our waiter was called Hans, a young Norwegian boy who could not have been very far from my own age. He was in training to become a full-service passenger waiter and, as is usually the case, was first assigned to serve the cruise staff as an intern. Once proficient at handling the oftentimes obnoxious and perhaps even more demanding cruise staff, these waiters then were more than likely to be congenial and therefore far more successful with even the most arrogant passenger onboard.

As one would expect from his limited experience, Hans was somewhat lacking in the culinary arts, specifically in attending tables. Clearly, his desire was there. But skillful expertise was not. Yet I liked Hans. He was uniquely personable and always shared with us a wonderfully refreshing sense of humor and a warm radiant smile. It did not matter to me, for example, that we would receive green beans for asparagus, or roasted potatoes in place of mashed. Once the error was brought to his attention, Hans would blush and nervously shift from one leg to the other; he'd grin sheepishly with embarrassment. Sweat beaded up on his forehead and sometimes even rolled down his cheeks. He realized his mistakes—always did—and tried his hardest to make things right. To be better the next time. And to most of us, it really didn't matter at all. Except for Philip Pound.

Philip was quite authoritative with Hans, and freely and quite openly scolded him for his lack of restaurant finesse.

"One should treat servants as servants" Philip said one afternoon in his guttural Australian drawl, just loudly enough for the young man to hear. "Hans needs to learn, and that's all there is to it."

And so it was with Hans and Philip—a match soon doomed to ignite.

Now let there be no doubt that Philip's outbreaks were quite an embarrassment to us all. For me, I was intensely angered by his insensitivity. So much so that I became quite uncomfortable with Philip's presence at meals; we never really knew when he would erupt and again lash-out at poor Hans.

One afternoon, Philip's luncheon Chateaubriand was served medium-rare instead of medium, as he requested. Immediately, Philip flew into a rage—his fork, still well in hand, moved wildly about the airspace in front of him as he arrogantly and unnecessarily chastised Hans for his unprofessional inefficiency and great inexperience.

"My luncheon is ruined" he shouted, slamming his fork down with such rage, passengers no doubt heard the outburst well into the Dining Room.

All of us at the table fell silent. Hans, too—his head bowed downward in shame. Philip then stood, angrily tossing his linen napkin onto his plate.

"I'm lunching on deck" he said as he dramatically left the table.

We were stilled; few of us even shifted in our seats. My biting anger was replaced by deep concern that Hans would think Philip spoke for us all, and that we too were unhappy with him and with his work. I spoke first, and tried—however awkwardly—to make it clear to Hans that we all, in fact, thought he was doing a fine job, and not to let Philip intimidate him in any way.

"Philip was upset about something else" I said to him. "A problem we had in the office." Hans smiled and said "Mange Takk—thank you." He may have been inexperienced, but Hans was not a fool.

However brief it was, my conversation with Hans that day was clearly a risk. It was a practice openly frowned upon by NAL executives. And so it was a behavior heavily policed by shipboard officers and some crew members too.

When first hired onboard, I was given a pamphlet called *Instructions for Cruise Staff* which listed specific rules of conduct, and discussed the personal behavior expected onboard ship. "The staff onboard should be 'friendly but not familiar' with the ship's crew" it said. Any socializing between staff and crew was strictly forbidden. Guideline No. 1 it was—clearly important if they ranked it so. It was also the one regulation which I instinctively feared would be impossible for me to uphold. Archibald told me that previous staff members had severely abused the privilege of socializing with crew members, sexually and otherwise. Some staff members, he said, were discovered buying liquor from the onboard store under the guise of their personal staff discount, and in turn, selling it to crewmembers in order to turn a fast profit. The result? Certain crew inebriation. And a quick change of rules.

It was clear NAL management believed that socializing with crew members would make it routinely difficult for the social staff to then delegate work to their "friends", or to reprimand them if need be, if strong bonds of friendship were clearly intact. Personally, I believed that Philip's own philosophy of treating "servants as servants" had a good deal more to do with overall company policy than first thought. It was clear, at least to me, that the unwritten class distinction onboard *Sagafjord* must be maintained at all costs.

That one particular ruling was the only directive of onboard social behavior which disturbed me. The ship's crew—dining room waiters, cabin stewardesses, and the sailing and navigational crews too—were the only people onboard ship who were anywhere near my own age. They were the only people onboard who, I felt, I could be close to and with whom I could be myself; perhaps visit each other's cabins in the evenings when off duty, listen to music, or even go ashore together—to the beach or shopping, or just to see the local sights. Yet out of fear of losing my job and being scandalously sent home from the next port of call—indeed, what could be worse?—I complied with the ruling as best I could. My appointment with Norwegian America Line was an important one to me; one which I wished to maintain. I was not at all interested in, or eager to, jeopardize that contract.

We sailed for two days from New York to Port Everglades—the port of access for South Florida and the greater Fort Lauderdale area. During this time, onboard activities were uneventful, with just the usual getting-to-know-you games and socials played over and over again. Cruise Director Ted Jones was unable to delve into his usual bag of entertainment tricks and activities programs until the majority of passengers boarded the ship at Port Everglades—the final and remaining group of passengers was scheduled to join ship at Los Angeles.

For us though, it was during those initial few days of the cruise that the entire staff learned to adapt to each other and work well together as a team. And the development of early passenger relationships had begun.

The seas became a bit heavy while passing off of Cape Hatteras; a frigid north wind—blowing strong and full against our stern—was our only escort south. No one was allowed on the open decks for fear of being swept over the side by a massive gust of wind or a powerful rush of the angry sea. The mood onboard was as sullen as the sky and sea around us. And although I was never much of a fan, our first sight of South Florida that January morning was certainly welcome.

Entering Port Everglades harbor around midday was truly a memorable sight, and perhaps even substituted for the lack of festive celebration I so longed for at New York. A flotilla of private crafts sailed out well past the break water to greet our ship. After surrounding us at the pilotage, they all, quite ceremoniously, accompanied *Sagafjord* to her designated berth.

A massive concrete condominium structure stood on our starboard side as sentry to the harbor's gate. From a lone center balcony hung the red, white, and blue NAL house flag—the only color in its huge mass of gray—no doubt a salute from a former Norwegian America Line passenger as a loving tribute to his favorite ship, and the nearly century-old company still operating her.

Port Everglades was not a port-of-call per se, but rather our second port of embarkation. And although we were alongside just long enough to take on the expected passenger complement, I made it a point to step ashore for even a few minutes at least, if only to telephone home, and visit with a longtime childhood friend who had recently relocated to the Fort Lauderdale area.

Passengers waiting to embark that afternoon were already lined up in the terminal building as our gangway was placed into position. All in a row they stood, fidgeting and fanning themselves as a futile protection from the intense southern heat. I knew I had to leave the ship before the massive steel gate on the edge of the pier was lifted and that horde of overly heated passengers began to move onboard. Once that happened, getting ashore, I knew, would be impossible.

Even so, it was difficult maneuvering through the crowd. Each of them seemed unusually anxious to embark; like me, perhaps they too were searching for a far better life than the ones they were so eager to abandon in beautiful South Florida. And *Sagafjord* was that hope. *Sagafjord* was their dream.

Or perhaps it was simply the intense Florida heat that they longed so much to escape.

Carefully, I pushed my way through the crowd, to the nearest public telephone. They were elderly, most of them—gray-haired, some even hostile, with excessive tans and the overly leathered skin which only the baking Florida sun can produce. Some had their children with them; others, their children's children. I thought about the incredible power *Sagafjord* had over these people—and to us staff members too. Perhaps it was what she represented—the hopes, the promises, and the potential romance of an intimate winter at sea. Whatever the reason, it was incredible how one ship—or at the least what she symbolized—was able to influence all those people's lives, as she was then so influencing mine.

The actual selling of land tours began in earnest that next morning. Some passengers, after diligent research and what some might envy as a lifetime of dreams, pre-booked their shore excursions prior to sailing. Most of that day then was spent simply delivering to passengers their pre-paid pre-packaged tickets.

Cruise Director Ted Jones strongly encouraged all passengers to attend Archibald Hannon's two-part travel lecture scheduled to begin that same morning in the Grand Ballroom. Hannon's talks, I was told, would describe the Shore Excursion Program in brilliant detail—offering passengers the opportunity to be well informed about our entire tour program and its operation before purchasing additional tours or making changes within their already pre-arranged program. It was in light of my great lack of experience, no doubt, that Lar suggested that I too attend Archibald's lectures.

Sagafjord's Grand Ballroom was the largest public room onboard, located directly mid-ship on Veranda Deck. It was a beautiful salon, decorated in antique gold and forest green fabrics, with just a touch of burgundy and light natural woods as accents. The open stage with its retractable dance floor was set into the forward portion of the room; the vaulted ceiling which encircled it was fitted with a concentric series of oblong light rings—the colors of which could be altered, if desired, from various shades of gold and green, to a very patriotic Norwegian red, white, and blue.

Archibald stood at the center of the dance floor with a music stand before him as a makeshift lectern. He seemed to hobble about, nervously checking this and checking that. As his audience filed in and took their seats, Archibald looked just as disheveled as he did when we first met in the Dance Studio just four days before.

His gray hair was plastered down with Brillecreme perhaps, or some other similar outdated hair tonic, and as he began to speak, I couldn't help but think how unsightly and how unattractive this man really was. I felt embarrassed for him, and wondered how soon it would be before everyone onboard—passengers and crew members alike—would be laughing at him, making him the center of ridicule, as school kids made fun of the weirdoes and the nerds and the others they simply disliked in their classrooms and school yards back home. I could just hear them shouting out "four eyes" and "sissy" perhaps even before Archibald had a moment to utter a sound. But no such calls were made that morning; Hannon's audience simply fell silent.

Archibald began his talk with focus and strength—as if, to him at least, nothing else mattered. And as he spoke, indeed, nothing did.

It was as if all of my personal considerations about this man's outward appearance and his rather unkempt style were just that—meaningless considerations. What seemed important to Archibald—and to me and perhaps to all of us present that morning—was his subject matter only, which he attacked with a passion and a confidence unlike anything I had ever before witnessed. His words created pictures as vivid as one could imagine, and his exciting histrionics—both physical and vocal—made me realize just how talented and skillful this man really was.

It was clear that Archibald was indeed an intellectual—a master, if you will—commanding his subject and his language with great ease and superb style. He was passionate too about his presentation. The sharpened modulations of his voice—from great highs to a soft dramatic bass—was as skillful and just as calculated no doubt as his pacing. He seemed to control time—the hour passed as if it were only minutes; as if we were all in a mesmerizing dream.

As Archibald described Tour #1—*A Panamanian Evening*—it was clear that he was much more than just our ship's port lecturer. Indeed, he was an historian, with great psychological and sociological insight into the people and the cultures we were all soon destined to visit. His lectures, I knew then, were to become, for me at least, one of the highlights of the voyage ahead.

The long awaited Captain's Welcome Aboard Cocktail Party for all passengers who boarded ship at New York and Port Everglades took place that evening—January 8, 1972—at 6:30 P.M. in the Grand Ballroom. Those passengers who had not yet embarked—who were scheduled to join ship at Los Angeles—were to receive their own very private affair in the Club Polaris several days later.

The Cruise News—our onboard daily news and activities journal which was slipped under our cabin doors each night, silently as we slept—requested that all passengers first assemble on Veranda Deck forward starboard side, just aft of the Theatre entrance. There, they would wait patiently in line for the large glass doors to open—an action which in itself would announce that Captain Sven Brookstad was in residence, ready to begin the tedious process of shaking each and every passenger's hand, personally welcoming them onboard, greeting each one individually—both repeat passengers and newcomers alike.

Captain Brookstad was a figure one could not easily forget. He stood nearly six feet tall. His was a somewhat stocky build, with long and unusually thin strings of greasy brown hair carefully folded over his rather smallish head—no doubt in an unsuccessful attempt to hide his advancing baldness. His stance was strong and stiff, so much so that it seemed as if he had forgotten to remove the wire coat hanger from his white dress uniform jacket. His cold Nordic eyes pierced through me as he shook my hand for the first time; his pre-set smile seemed as insincere for my greeting as it was for the many passengers who were soon to follow.

He entered the ballroom as a thunderbolt might light up the evening sky. Following him was a trail of officers who seemed to mimic the Captain's very unique image, and actions, and intense personal electricity. When finally in position, just aft of the main doors, Staff Captain Magnar Berntzen stood immediately to Brookstad's left, and to his left stood Chief Officer Kai Julsen, followed by Chief Engineer Olaf Anders, Hotel Manager Thor

Christiansen, Chief Purser Ingvar Torsen, and finally the ship's physician and surgeon Roald Dalle and dental surgeon Hans Mitter. All in a row they were, each one more starched and stiff than the next. Maggie Sinclair brought the only animation to the group. She stood at the Ballroom's entrance, and to the captain's right, in a floor-length evening gown of pink organza and lace, with matching pink pumps. The fractured image of an aging Bette Davis in *Whatever Happened to Baby Jane* came to mind—although I could only assume, and hoped too, that Maggie Sinclair sang a bit better during her earlier musical career, than that disturbed and rather demented fictional child star.

It was Maggie's responsibility to greet each passenger, or each passenger couple as it may be, first at the doorway and then present them, individually and by name, to the captain and his staff of officers. Maggie did her job well, pushing the passengers along at a very steady pace while making sure that none of them was monopolizing the captain's attention. It was clear that she felt she was, in a way, protecting the captain—from what, I wasn't quite sure, and perhaps she wasn't sure either. But her movements and actions made it seem as though he, the captain, was her own personal property, and she, at least in her own mind, was certainly responsible. And trust me when I say that she filled those pumps well; Maggie was very much in charge.

I asked Maggie why she wore her dainty white gloves which buttoned at the wrist.

"How would *you* like to shake the sweaty hands of 450 strangers?" she said. "Think of the grease and the dirt; the diseases I could catch!"

I was amused by Maggie's unexpected, yet rather well thought-out answer. Being a borderline hypochondriac myself, I would never have thought of such a concept, and that disappointed me. But I certainly think of it now. To this day, whenever I shake anyone's hand, I secretly wish I had previously donned a pair of Maggie Sinclair's little white gloves.

Cruise Director Ted Jones finally arrived wearing a midnight blue tuxedo. And as usual, Anne was at his side—stunning as always in a sleek black evening gown. Anne was no doubt the most beautiful woman onboard. And as she graciously greeted the captain and his officers, she moved about with her usual grace and elegant style. One couldn't help but admire Anne Dickson for the lovely woman she was. Indeed, I had already signed on to the list of her long line of admirers

"Let's begin" the captain said firmly as he slightly nodded his head. And the awkward silence and uncomfortable small-talk amongst the staff was sharply broken. The Walesky Orchestra struck up a highly subdued version of *As Time Goes By*. Maggie then opened the Ballroom's glass doors, and those very first passengers, with hands already outstretched—smiles already plastered across their faces—entered the room.

Gesag Dichosian—known to everyone onboard as Dick—was the ship's photographer. He held the photo concession monopoly onboard all Norwegian America Line ships since the days of their once proud flagship *Oslofjord* in the early 1950s. And no doubt because of this onboard longevity, Dick often—quite openly and sometimes arrogantly—boasted to staff and to passengers alike about his keen business acumen and, at least in his mind, his permanent job security.

Dichosian was a short man—rotund if you will—balding too, with his remaining snow-white hair cleanly encircling his head. He had an overly thick white moustache which invariably collected the drippings from the yogurt he consumed daily at every meal—no doubt a nutritional ritual resulting from his youthful Armenian upbringing. Theatrical casting directors would no doubt choose Dick as the quintessential Santa Claus—but in physical appearance only. In actuality, Dick was the antithesis of old St. Nick and everything he stood for. He had quite a volatile personality and a contemptuous attitude towards most other people, and, it appeared, to life in general. He would often, and sometimes quite ferociously, argue with passengers over the smallest of details—over a question innocently posed or a comment constructively made. And ironically, with all of the obnoxiousness and the uncomfortableness he caused most people, I felt that the quality of Dick's work was certainly not synonymous with Norwegian America Line's first-class image and reputation. I often wondered why NAL kept him onboard at all—I would have thought it quite easy to release him from his seemingly open-ended agreement. Certainly no unions or employment contracts to worry about here, way out at sea.

But I soon learned that there was much more to it. You see, Dick and Captain Brookstad were friends—intense golf buddies, to be precise. At most ports-of-call, Dick and Captain Brookstad, and sometimes accompanied by Staff Captain Berntzen too, would be the first to leave the ship, as soon as she was anchored or tied up—sometimes stepping ashore even before the usual announcement could be made that the ship was cleared of customs and immigration formalities, and passengers were free to go ashore. With their golf bags carried by NAL's lowest ranking seamen, they would proceed to the most beautiful golf courses or county clubs in the world, always as the very special guests of the local port authority or the club's proprietors directly. And so it was, with a number two wood, that all too important sportsman's bond was made secure. Dick was in, and that was that. The quality of his photographs was simply irrelevant.

The spirited sounds of music and voices and laughter, and the tinkling glasses increased in intensity as more and more passengers entered the Ballroom and the Welcome Aboard party swelled to its climax. Consciously aware of my social obligations—clearly everyone of importance was there and would most likely be watching our social performances that evening—I busied myself about the room, seeking out the loneliest-looking women with whom to dance. Indeed, I wanted to do my duty, be seen doing it, and get it over with as quickly as possible. Naturally, I was still put off a bit by my traumatic experience with Mrs. Woodward just a few nights before. So reluctantly, and rather cautiously, I approached each potential dance partner with obvious trepidation.

With Hasselbladt well in hand, Dick snapped away as if there were no tomorrow—with each click, I'm sure his mental cash register rang.

"Never get their approval beforehand" he said to me later that evening. "Just shoot. They can't buy a photo I haven't taken."

Designers Roger and Elizabeth had chosen pastel colors as their decorative theme for the evening. And indeed, the room looked beautiful in celebration of the Welcome Aboard Show which was to be performed later that evening. The staging area itself was swagged in a crisscrossed style, with a pink and violet scrimlike material elegantly draped from one end of the room to the other. Huge displays of freshly cut flowers highlighted the platform at each end; the orchestra played, back lit, from within.

It was at that party that I first began to realize just how much I was already fitting in onboard ship. The older female passengers, in particular, were responding to me quite well. Perhaps it was my youth, which must have been such a refreshing change from all the others onboard—perhaps because I helped rekindle for them some very pleasant and endearing deep personal memories—"You look just like my grandson" they would say, and then I would be shown photograph after photograph of the child with whom I was, at least in their minds, identical.

I noticed too that members of the social staff were beginning to respond quite positively to me as well, although I felt their motives still quite mysterious. As I've already mentioned, I liked being liked by my co-workers, yet I felt I had little reason to trust any of them, and I continued to question their outward warmth and open sincerity. For quite sometime, I continued to mistrust their interest in me, believing that the attention I was receiving was purely physical—sexual, if you will. Conceited? Perhaps. But those feelings were real. It concerned me greatly. I really did not want to have to face the fact that any one of these men with whom I now worked might do anything necessary in the hope of sharing my bed.

But the most exciting of all was that some of the ship's crew members appeared to want to get to know me as well. For obvious reasons, however, their interest had to be expressed much more discreetly and far more privately. Waiters, stewardesses and some

of the sailing crew too began to speak to me more and more often—something I enjoyed and, in fact, actually began to seek out
as time went on.

You see, such forbidden friendship created enticing discretion,
and this too, was attractive to me—the antithesis of my tour office friendships. I instinctively responded more positively to the
very private nature of potential friendships with the crew. I was
sure that the similarities in our ages would in itself create a strong
bond between us, and I looked forward to our relationships growing stronger. For whatever it meant, I was lonely in the midst of
nearly five hundred others; and I wanted their companionship
very much.

The rhythmic handshaking on the receiving line seemed
nonstop throughout the hour, as did the patronized dancing by
the social staff and entertainers. Carmen and Jan mechanically
performed their usual Welcome Aboard repertoire of standards
and easy-listening show tunes. The atmosphere appeared festive,
yet formal, and everyone seemed purposefully proper; somewhat
insincere perhaps, yet proper nonetheless.

Between dances, I studied the passengers intently—indeed a
very wealthy and sophisticated group. I wanted to learn as much as
I could about what made them successful, what made them popular,
at least in their own social circles. They had achieved achievements
of which I could only dream. They had reached certain pinnacles in
their lives. This was clearly a segment of society I had never before
experienced; a lifestyle I unknowingly envied; a status to which I
greatly aspired.

"Would you like a drink?" I turned just then and noticed the
same young waiter who served our initial staff meeting that very
first day onboard. He smiled and offered me a ginger ale.

"How did you know I drink ginger ale?" I asked, as I too
smiled.

"I remembered" he said. "Would you prefer something else?"

"No, no" I quickly answered, somewhat embarrassed, clearly

impressed. "This is great. Just perfect, thank you." I accepted the drink and sipped it slowly. Quite unexpectedly though, my companion lingered a moment at my side.

"Isn't it a bore?" he continued in a strong Scandinavian accent. He smiled as he gazed at the overly crowded dance floor, and slowly shook his head. "I don't think I can take another one of these parties." He grinned then, and nervously looked about the room. His mischievous look was inescapable.

"Oh, it's all right" I said. "This is my first world cruise, so I'm kind of in awe of all of this."

"I'm Arne" he said. "Arne Christiansen."

"I'm . . ."

"I know who you are" he whispered, and then he was off, before I could respond further. I noticed the Chief Steward, his supervisor, approaching. Another tray of complimentary champagne needed to be passed.

At last, the trumpet fanfare rang out. The lights in the room dimmed just a bit, while those on the bandstand brightened stronger with intensity. Everyone's attention shifted from each other then, directly to the stage.

Ted Jones stepped to the microphone and formally introduced Captain Sven Brookstad to the world. The applause was deafening. Brookstad was clearly the star of the evening—the favored Norwegian son who had come to escort us all on a spectacular journey around the world. He was adored and respected simply for the position and rank he held, so the audible adulation therefore seemed fitting.

The captain took the stage as an emperor mounts his throne. As the applause lessened, he began an obviously prepared welcoming speech. It was the usual tidbits of shipboard trivia often heard by most well-seasoned travelers—100,000 eggs will be used on this voyage; 35,000 loaves of bread, and on and on.

Although no doubt an intelligent man, and perhaps quite worldly too, if indeed "worldly" means more than circumnavigating the globe several times, Brookstad seemed to enjoy playing the role of the naive Norwegian gentleman, appearing to be somewhat unfamiliar with the English language and all its innuendoes and subtleties. He seemed to enjoy, at least in a public forum like this one, creating the impression that he didn't quite understand what he was saying in this—not his native—language. By so doing, he was able to innocently succeed at making several choreographed mistakes—clearly for laughs; many double entendres for effect—without having to accept or take responsibility for the sometimes harsh and opinionated judgments which would usually accompany such grammatical and basic errors of syntax. The passengers willingly fell for his performance—some giggled, most were amused. The ladies, no doubt, thought him adorable, and more than likely created fantasies of what the next ninety-eight days in his company—perhaps in his suite—might bring.

Percy and I stood alone at the back of the room, as far from the action as we could. As the captain spoke, I watched an already inebriated Percy Hayes grimace and roll his eyes as if to say "I've heard this same old boring speech so many times before."

Brookstad introduced his staff of officers again one by one, and then lifted his glass in salute to the passengers, to the ship herself, and to the long voyage ahead.

"Skoal" he said proudly, and the group echoed his toast as four hundred glasses were simultaneously raised. Ted then took the microphone and announced that dinner was being served in the Saga Dining Room.

The 1973 Great World Cruise had officially begun.

Chapter Two

"Transitions"

It is globally recognized as one of man's greatest achievements. Historian David McCullough referred to it as *The Path Between the Seas*. Its series of locks which raise and lower ships of all kinds and shapes and tonnage to the various levels of the Atlantic and the Pacific—functional through the years from gravity alone—is an ingenious feat of engineering design—a keen workmanship long gone from our present-day world; its eight-hour maritime transit becomes a highlight of any voyage for passenger and crew member alike.

The Panama Canal. We had arrived.

Archibald was the chief source of history here. Days before our arrival, he had shifted into character just as one would expect—a cruise ship chameleon of the colorless sort. He hobbled about the ship with an air of cockiness—an intellectual arrogance, if you will. He was the expert—no doubt about it; the Canal Zone authority, or so he would let us believe. It was written all over his face. Was it the fish-in-the-small-pond syndrome? Or was it, in fact, who he really was? Was Archinald Hannon the true fountain of knowledge he well portrayed and hoped we all would believe? Was he truly a kind of intellectual dandelion—recklessly tossing its seeds to the wind in every which direction, for whatever unknown reasons? Whatever the case, it really didn't matter very much after all—real or perceived. I was a sponge, so eager to learn. From where that knowledge came, I was not in the position to choose, or to judge.

No doubt Hannon loved the attention. You could see it in his face. You could taste it in his eyes. He would do it whenever he could, at any opportunity, and with whomever he could—just open up his mental almanac and throw out tedious yet fascinating facts, and then sit back and wait for the lavish praise and awesome acknowledgment. "Did you know..." I heard him tell the Evans one morning "that the canal's Atlantic entrance at Cristobal is further west than its Pacific entrance at Balboa, and that the levels of the two oceans differ by several feet?"

That particular morning, I raced from my cabin even before the Panamanian dawn illuminated the sky. With Nikon in hand, I took early breakfast out on the open deck. Tea and a blueberry scone it was. The usual. Indeed, I had already become quite a creature of habit, already well settled in to my shipboard routine. Quick, and practical—especially that day. I was determined to experience it all—and not to miss a moment of our fifty-one mile transit.

It was too important. We were finally approaching what I considered to be our first real foreign port of call. And just as I initially felt when leaving New York—the excitement, the anticipation, and yes, perhaps even some of the anxiety too—I experienced it all again that morning with the Isthmus just ahead; a renewed enthusiasm for the voyage, a feeling that I was once again on the verge of a new life; on a journey of vast and enriching adventure. And with it came a passionate exhilaration and a new-found freedom—not really knowing where I was headed, but eager to go nonetheless, longing to absorb all that I could—burning to learn, impatient to grow.

To me, transiting the Panama Canal with the vast Pacific ahead symbolized the beginning of a new life—a spiritual awareness and an emotional passage which I knew would take far longer than the eight hours it took *Sagafjord* to navigate that celebrated waterway. Several months, perhaps even years to fully develop; to appreciate. I was anxious to begin though—frightened no doubt, but anxious nonetheless.

As we edged our way into Gatun Lock, Archibald was already on the Bridge from where he was broadcasting historical and factual commentary through the ship's public address system and out onto the open decks. In illustrative detail, he described the canal's overall design and construction, and emotionally told of the great number of men who had lost their lives from malaria, cholera, or through the usually tragic construction accidents; getting the project up and underway, and finally to completion.

The humidity that morning was oppressive, the heat overwhelming. Dense rain forests surrounded us, and smelled of decaying leaves and fresh palm sprouts. The air was heavy and stilled as if in a vacuum. For someone not as young or as foolish as I, it might have been unbearable. But I would not surrender. I was determined to remain on Signal Deck—*Sagafjord's* upper-most point just above the navigational Bridge itself—with an unobstructed view over the ship's bow and the great tropical landscape beyond; intensely lush, passionately green.

Access to that particular area of Signal Deck was secluded and quite difficult to find. It was therefore rarely frequented by passengers. Consequently it became a safe and popular recreation area for the social staff and entertainers to congregate without being disturbed—a place to escape; a place to relax without having to deal with social responsibilities and the endless and oftentimes inane passenger questions.

Gentle rains seemed to kiss the air; cleansing, renewing. It focused an almost surreal experience into a realistically tropical perspective.

Sagafjord moved about slowly to her proper position within the lock itself—rarely under her own power but rather pulled forward by the canal's uniquely designed motorized mules. The massive aft gates then closed behind us, and the water level rose slowly, as did the ship herself, finally reaching the level of Gatun Lake—expansive, serenely tranquil; whose fresh waters I was sure were as deep as I imagined. Then Gatun's forward gates creaked open, and we slowly steamed forward and onward towards the next lock—and the next—and ultimately to our final Panamanian destination—the vibrant city of Balboa. Indeed, it was an amazing process. Something I had certainly read about in books and often discussed in elementary schoolrooms, but never fully understood or appreciated until actually experiencing it for myself.

As we continued our journey through the Canal Zone that day, I found myself drawn to the exquisite landscape we seemed to dissect. There was a stillness. A Peace. There was mystery; the unknown. I wondered what was out there, in those incredibly dense jungles and tropical forests. It was a landscape quite unfamiliar to me. I didn't want to miss its language. I wanted to stop, and hear its message. I wanted to explore. I wanted to see for myself, not just pass through. I wanted to experience whatever that something was that I was not to see.

I adjusted my position on the rail where I sat, and leaned further forward—truly a photographer's dream. I clicked away as I'm sure Dick Dichosian would, and most probably was, just aft of where we all stood.

Far below, the ship's bow section stood open and naked; fully exposed for all to see. I noticed the crew's swimming pool—small but no doubt functional—awkwardly set atop the storage hatch below. I couldn't imagine that that swimming pool was well within the keen mind's eye of *Sagafjord's* original designers; no doubt an afterthought by the Norwegian shipboard hierarchy; the hatch being the only logical place to set it. A bit unsightly, but logical nonetheless. The pool, I was told, was for male crew members only—the ladies onboard had a more private area on the upper deck aft where sunbathing for them alone was allowed; women were not permitted to swim or visit here. It all made sense after all. I wouldn't think the stewardesses onboard—all young, and most quite attractive—would enjoy sunbathing in bikinis, some topless too—on that very open expanse of bow, with the all-male officer team well positioned high above, well equipped with focused binoculars and other such nautical toys of the highest magnification.

That day, the pool and its surrounding area was packed with veteran sun worshippers and amateur photographers comprised of off-duty sailors, and waiters, and stewards, and the like—most of them no doubt eager to document their Canal Zone experience on film for friends and family back home.

The sea of blond heads and tanned bodies was impressive; indeed beautiful, as I watched them high from my perch—anonymous; powerful and submissive. They lounged and played and sunned and swam; others just sat on the bulkhead extensions and watched the incredible scenery go by. And suddenly—hitting me like a powerful gust of wind, forceful and quite unexpected, seemingly coming from nowhere in particular—the Panama Canal didn't seem to interest me any longer. I had an overwhelming and unexplained desire to be with them all—those young men—down on the bow, sitting by their pool, sunning, and laughing. Being together; sharing that experience.

Arne Christiansen leaned against the ship's starboard rail. He sat alone wearing a pale-blue bathing suit, nothing more. He looked off in the distance—intently pensive, seemingly oblivious to all I observed. He was in fine shape—his chest was strong; his legs powerful. His radiant tan only enhanced his body's clear definition. I watched him intently, and I knew—just knew—that we would be friends.

Yes, a waiter called Arne. Someone my own age with whom I might share this incredible trip. Someone quite unlike the outrageously flamboyant Percy Hayes or the lascivious Archibald Hannon. Someone with whom I could feel more comfortable and less threatened, and with whom I could better relate on a personal and more human level. Someone who could best understand me, and I him.

And so that day I believed that Arne would be that friend. He did, after all, seem quite amiable the few times we'd met, somewhat interested in developing a friendship. After our brief conversation at the captain's Welcome Aboard reception just a few days before, I felt confident that our paths would inevitably cross again sometime during the voyage. I wondered when that would be. I wondered how long I would have to wait.

I found myself often thinking of Arne and about how I could get to see him, to meet him again, to know him better. But that's the sort of thing I was so unaccustomed to doing—get to know someone, that is—without seeming too forward. I didn't want him to think that I was queer or anything—especially since most of my co-workers were clearly so inclined. Identification by association, I feared. Clearly, the dilemma was real. I was intrigued and excited at the prospects of a future friendship with Arne, yet nervous as hell about talking with him again. Simply put, I didn't want to blow it.

Arne turned and noticed me watching him. I couldn't hide. He waived, somewhat discreetly, so as to not draw attention to either himself or to me. Shyly, I waived back and saw Arne smile—his teeth beamed white in the intense Panamanian sun.

Archibald's voice began again over the ship's public address. With Gatun then behind us, our transit, I realized, was only just beginning.

Sagafjord pulled alongside at Balboa later that afternoon—a rather seedy port city located at the Pacific entrance to the Canal Zone. And immediately after ship's clearance, Lar and I began dispatching our first tour—*A Panamanian Evening*.

Cocktails were served onboard in the Garden Lounge for the sixty or so pre-booked tour participants. We then boarded the local excursion buses for a brief panoramic drive around the city, finally arriving at the El Panama Hotel where a typically local dinner of rice and beans and a strangely flavored meat dish of unknown origin was served. The after-dinner entertainment was presented by a popular Panamanian folk dance troupe. The singers and dancers were colorful and lively, reminding many of us of the Caribbean's *Folklorique Martinique*—the energetic song and dance theatre which entertained cruise passengers while their ships lay at anchor off Fort-de-France.

Our passengers laughed and ate and danced to the primitive sounds of the musical trio. The tour was clearly an early cruise success. For me, it was a benchmark. It gave me the confidence I needed as a tour escort, encouraging me to prepare for the operation of the more complex tours still yet to come—many of which included overnight stays and involved baggage arrangements, air ticketing, restaurant reservations and hotel accommodations. Now it was evident—at least to me—that I could actually do the job. Finally, I was beginning to believe it; at least with a bit more confidence.

We sailed from Balboa at midnight. I settled into bed—my cabin lights were put out—just as the last ropes were thrown ashore. As I closed my eyes, I heard a tug boat's shrill whistle from just outside my porthole.

Sometime during the night, I was awakened by a loud banging coming, it seemed, from deep below deck. There was a tremendous shifting movement of the ship upward and then back down again, and sideways too. We were embraced by a storm, and the darkness of the night and the intensity of the waves against the ship made the experience both frightening and depressing. From where it came, and when and how it all started, I did not know. Just hours before, it was calm; it was peaceful. Now, the intense noise and the violent movement—the banging, the crashing— made it seem as if the world was ending. I shut my eyes tight and prayed it would all soon stop.

Suddenly, there was another banging. This time, though, it was more personal. Closer. Someone was knocking on my cabin door. Indeed, I was startled by the nearness of the disturbance, and wondered just who the hell would be calling at such a late hour—in such an incredible storm, in the middle of a seemingly endless and horrendous night. I switched on my bedside reading lamp; it was 4:10 A.M.

Two Norwegian sailors stood in the hallway, one of whom I recognized from gangway duty earlier that evening at Balboa. He was called Jan. He smiled and nodded slightly as he too remembered our brief meeting. The other seaman, whom I did not know, appeared to be of a bit more senior rank in the onboard navigational hierarchy. It was he who spoke, first apologizing for the late-night disturbance, then announcing that the sea was beginning to pick up. I laughed. Quite an understatement, I thought. I could barely keep my balance as he spoke, even though I was bracing myself tightly against the door jam, trying to prevent it from slamming shut, while shifting my body weight in order to hang on for dear life.

They needed to secure my porthole, the senior officer said, with a steel plate cover. It's only a precaution, he explained as they both quickly, and rather assertively moved into my cabin—to protect the glass from shattering in the night should it be struck by heavy seas.

"Like shrapnel" Jan volunteered as he turned and looked my way. At that, we both smiled. I wondered for a moment, even in my sleepy stupor, how a young Norwegian sailor would have known such an obscure English word.

The more senior seaman then explained that the porthole glass, if smashed by the sea, could be shot in thousands of pieces, all over the cabin.

Still half asleep and a bit disoriented by the cabin's blinding darkness and the ship's massive movement, I could do nothing more than stand and watch passively as the two men worked. They, too, had lost their sea legs, having to continually fight to keep from falling off balance as the ship ferociously moved up and down, and violently from side to side. They were silent momentarily as they tightened up the last bolt and finished their work. They then took up their tools in both hands and turned to leave my cabin almost as quickly as they had appeared.

Jan smiled and nodded again as he and his colleague excused themselves. They wished me a good night—the older seaman in English, Jan in Norwegian; they apologized once again for the disturbance, and were gone, closing the cabin door gently behind them. It was then that I realized that I had been standing there all along, watching them both work, wearing nothing but my underpants.

I staggered across the cabin and forcefully fell back into bed—the mattress appearing to rise up to meet my body as I dropped. Within seconds, I heard the sailors begin their now familiar routine at the next cabin door. I thought about my neighbor—whoever he was—and what he would be wearing when he answered his door.

The sailors' nocturnal visit concerned me greatly; I could not easily fall back asleep. "The sea is picking up" they said. They had to seal the porthole shut. I knew the navigational crew would never disturb passengers in the middle of the night unless the storm we were already experiencing was indeed a serious one. Was the ship in jeopardy, I wondered? Were we all in danger of our lives?

Their statement was in fact an understatement. The seas were indeed building to an even more frightening pace. I heard the intense power of the waves pounding against my cabin wall, shattering hard the silence of the night. Bottles fell from my bathroom shelves, glass smashing to the floor in a crash. Books and other personal items slammed to the deck too—the sounds were echoed, over and over, muffled if at all, from adjacent cabins just forward and aft of my own. I knew it would be futile to tidy-up just then. I knew if I stood, I would likely get sick. And whatever I was able to retrieve at that time, and put back in its place, would inevitably be thrown again about the room as the ship continued to move throughout the night.

So I decided to ride out the storm in bed. I thought it best to try to get some sleep, although I somehow knew that that was the remotest of possibilities. The crashing and the pounding and the constant—almost eerie—creaking of the ship as she angrily moved about disrupted any hopes of silence, and brought only frightening images to my mind.

At times, the sea's ferocity thrust the ship up and out of the water, so much so that her rudder and propellers broke through the surface, sending terrific vibration throughout the ship—shaking her violently—before eventually slamming back down again, crashing into the sea, only to be swooped up again with the next massive crest. Fear of the ship foundering, whether real or imagined, now replaced my fear of seasickness, and thus the night was spent. I fell in and out of restlessness, and prayed to God that it would all end by morning.

But it didn't. And eventually, I had to leave my cabin—I just couldn't stand such intense movement in such a small space any longer. I wanted to scream, and get the hell off the ship.

The steel plate which the sailors secured against my porthole had succeeded in concealing any trace of the approaching daylight. Time then was indeterminable in the natural sense. I switched on my bedside lamp once again, and looked about the room.

The cabin was in chaos. Everything I had onboard—everything I owned—was thrown to the floor in a massive heap. I scooted around it all, grabbing the first pair of pants I could find and the shirt I had worn the previous night, and left the cabin as quickly as I could. Death or vomit? I was unsure which would come first. But the queasiness won out and was fast approaching, and I knew I had to get out and on to the open decks. I had to get some fresh sea air into my lungs—before it was too late.

The ship seemed deserted. There was an eeriness about. *Sagafjord* creaked hauntingly as she slowly cut her way through the massive waves. I stumbled forward and down the corridor to the stairwell leading up to Main Deck and further on to Upper Deck, then Veranda Deck—the thought of breathing cooler, crisper air was reassuring. It seemed my only hope. Breakfast would have to wait. Breakfast . . . just the thought of it made me want to throw up.

Walking was difficult. With each step, the ship seemed to respond with an angry, purposeful jolt—pounding and shaking violently around me. I fought simply to maintain my balance and to stay clear of the companionway walls which seemed to assault me from all sides.

The true severity of the storm became evident as I turned the corner on the Main Deck landing, and saw that the double-deck glass wall at the aft end of the Saga Dining Room had shattered during the night, and lay in pieces at the foot of the stairway.

"Shrapnel" I thought.

Stewards and sailors were hustling about, busily clearing the area before passengers could even notice.

Jan, the quartermaster, was there as well—obviously still on duty. He seemed amused by it all—the frantic fuss no doubt. He was more animated then, and far more talkative than I had so far seen him—most likely a reaction to his superior officer not being anywhere in sight. I didn't want to be rude to Jan, yet I didn't have the stomach to stay and listen to him for long. But even in my state of utter disgust, I couldn't help but be won over by his winning Nordic charm. So I did. I stayed just a bit. I listened with open eyes.

Jan was almost childlike that morning, with an all winning and quite refreshing innocence. He spoke with the excitement and the enthusiasm seen only in a young adolescent who tells his dad about a really gross caterpillar he just squished, and how really cool it was.

Jan couldn't wait to tell me about the damage in the Ballroom; the concert grand piano which was bolted to the stage had pulled off its brackets sometime during the night and smashed against the wall. The ballroom furniture too had fallen in the night, and slammed against the picture windows portside, shattering some. He talked about other damage around the ship as well. It was clear Jan and the other sailors enjoyed this sort of weather. It kept the passengers in their cabins, he told me. So they didn't have to deal with them.

"It's fine with me" the chief steward's assistant added. "The less I see the grey hairs, the better."

I couldn't even react to their comments, although I tried to seem amused and in some sort of compliance.

Nonetheless, I could stay no longer. I had to get to the open deck quickly.

With little letup, the gale continued throughout the day. Most passengers, and some crew for that matter, were incapacitated in their cabins for the duration, and it seemed to be the longest day and night I had ever experienced. The headache, the nausea, the depression, the crankiness—I just wanted it all to stop, or I simply wanted to die—I didn't really care; whichever came first.

I wondered why Captain Brookstad just didn't turn the ship toward shore—toward shallower water. No doubt the sea was calmer closer to shore. Surely, that would stop the horrible, sometimes unbearable, movement.

But that, I later learned, was just what Captain Brookstad

would not do. Our ship was much safer well out at sea, in the very deepest water. Nearer the shore, the ship would be uncontrollable and in tremendous danger of slamming against reefs or submerged rock formations, and foundering for sure.

So which was worse? Seasickness, or sinking the ship? At that point, I would be open to any suggestion not to throw up. All I knew was that if we did hit the rocks and sink to the depths of the Pacific, my unbearable headache, and constant nausea would end. I might be dead, but at least it would stop. That's all that mattered.

And so I had no choice but to trust the Norwegian seamen and their sea-wise expertise in knowing what was best. I let them do their jobs. Indeed, I had no choice.

The storm lasted nearly twenty-two hours, at times blasting Force 12 winds and 40-foot seas. And to this day, it remains the worst sea storm I have ever experienced. All of us received a certificate signed by the captain to commemorate our surviving such a gale. A record, the captain told us. A record perhaps, but one I am not too eager to break.

What was most amazing however, was not the storm itself, but what occurred when the ship's violent movement finally stopped. In an instant, it was as if it had never occurred at all. The headaches and the nausea were gone in a flash; quickly forgotten, until of course the next time. The sea was a lake, and the silent calmness of the brilliant sun that next morning overpowering.

At sea, I learned, one forgets easily. Forgiveness, however, well that's another matter altogether.

The stewardess who serviced my cabin was called Bruni, an attractive young German girl whose name was the diminutive of Brunhilde—one I had long associated with excessively overweight opera singers with long blond braids and piercingly sharp horns jutting out from metal helmets.

But my Bruni was different. Rather dark haired and almost petite in stature, Bruni came from a small Bavarian mountain village in southern Germany, just outside of Munich. Together with her Austrian boyfriend, Gerhard, who worked in the main kitchen as a pastry chef, Bruni had signed onboard *Sagafjord* for a one-year stint. She and Gerhard were pooling their savings in order to open an inn somewhere near the Bavarian capital. Working just one year onboard *Sagafjord* would easily amass their start-up funding.

Bruni was a charmer in every way. When she spoke, her very slight German accent was winning and endearing, and the periodic grammatical errors she made made everything she said seem simply adorable. One couldn't help but smile when Bruni was present. And unlike with Captain Brookstad, her errors of syntax were honest and sincere. I admired Bruni's beautiful blue eyes and her beaming smile which appeared whenever she saw me. She called me her *schatz* which, she told me, meant "little treasure." Naturally, I was thrilled. I often thought that if it weren't for Gerhard, perhaps I would ask her out—whatever "out" meant onboard a luxury cruise ship steaming somewhere off in the vast Pacific. But Gerhard was indeed onboard—so naturally, I wouldn't.

Percy and I were alone at breakfast the morning following the storm. He too looked a bit exhausted from the experience. It was unusual to see Percy at breakfast at all—he preferred his morning coffee and croissant in his cabin "as the French do" he would say.

"Guten morgen meine schatz" Bruni said to me as she passed our table; her arms weighted down with a load of clean bed linens. "Did you hear about last night?" Bruni laughed uncontrollable as she paused by our table for just a moment, and leaned a little closer—first checking to be sure no one would see.

Bruni then told us about Gertrude Arkin, a middle-aged passenger traveling alone, who occupied cabin A-42—just several cabins forward of my own, but still in Bruni's allotment of service responsibility. Mrs. Arkin had apparently been to the ship's cinema that night—no doubt to escape the abusive remnants of the storm. She returned to her cabin just past eleven. By then, the ship's movement was certainly calming down, although periodic swells would still throw one off balance, and caution was still advised.

But Mrs. Arkin paid no mind to warnings—she, being the strong-willed New Yorker that she was. Warnings, no doubt, meant little to a woman who had spent the previous two hours well settled in on her favorite stool in the North Cape Bar.

Back in her cabin, Mrs. Arkin began to undress and proceeded to hang up her clothing in one of her three walk-in closets. Mrs. Arkin was a short woman, Bruni told us—just under five feet—and as she stepped inside to reach the clothes bar, the ship lurched to starboard, slamming the closet door shut behind her, locking her within.

Naturally, the woman attempted to escape, fumbling in the dark for quite some time, but to no avail. She tried, unsuccessfully, to pry the closet door open with the only tool available to her—a wooden clothes hanger. Mrs. Arkin was forced then to spend the entire night crouched down on her closet floor, uncomfortably sitting atop her immovable iron shoe rack. Bruni had only just found her moments before. Although Mrs. Arkin appeared physically fine from her overnight ordeal, she was a bit shaken and a touch angry. No doubt a bit embarrassed too, I would think.

"What a great advertisement" Percy laughed as he spoke. "Sail *Sagafjord* on a world cruise—with closets so large one might spend the night in them. Quickly, get Brooks on the ship-to-shore."

Archibald had joined us by then. He order only coffee.

"I like it straight and black" he told Hans. "Just like my men."

I had hoped Hans' student-level English would somehow obscure his understanding of Archibald's unnecessary and quite obnoxious joke. I hated him when he did that sort of thing. Why, I wondered, did Archibald Hannon—and Percy Hayes too—have such a need to overtly push their sexuality on us all so unexpectedly, and most often inappropriately?

As was usually the case when Archibald Hannon was present, the conversation quickly became about him—monopolized by his constantly self-centered focus and opinions. And that morning was no different; he immediately changed our subject—clearly Mrs. Arkin and her closet adventures were of no interest to him. Rather, he began to reminisce about years past when he and Percy shared a cold-water flat together on Manhattan's lower east side; a somewhat surprising fact, the details of which I found quite interesting. And so I was amazed at how eager I was to hear more.

Percy made it clear to me that their living relationship was purely financial—neither one of them, at that time in their lives, having enough money to sustain himself on his own.

"No one else would live with you, you twit" Percy said amusingly to Archibald. "Remember when you first moved to New York, you shared that dreadful little mirrored flat with Frank Sutton from Thomas Cook?" Percy then looked at me, and continued. "Frank moved out within a week. He couldn't take it. He said 'who the hell did you set me up with here Percy? This guy is a nut. He gets up in the middle of the night and recites Greek poetry in the dark. I can't take it anymore Percy. I'm moving out.'"

Percy and Archibald spoke of some amusing incidents while living together, including three major burglaries. Percy was the one who eventually moved out, after the latest thief—apparently Percy's own physical size—conveniently helped himself to Percy's stylish wardrobe of custom-tailored Brioni suits.

Archibald Hannon grew up in Buffalo, New York. And, like Percy, was raised in a broken home—his father abandoning the family when Archibald was but one month old. No doubt this faceless father figure had an indelible effect on the young Archibald, and it was clear to me—even after knowing him for such a short time—that Archibald was obsessively driven in his search for a dominant male figure in his life to replace the father he felt he never had. Indeed, Freud would be proud.

Archibald spoke quite openly about his childhood years—about when, at the age of twelve, he and his friend Walter Levy were playing together atop the Hannon's roof, and Walter coerced the young Archibald into having anal sex with him. "It hurt" Archibald told me, "but I liked it. I wanted him to do it more."

He talked about some of his other school companions too who continually mistreated him because of his intellectual interests and mental prowess. They laughed at him and threw things too. Once after school, they ganged up on the young Archibald, and threw him to the ground, breaking his spectacles; from then on, they called him "four eyes."

He talked about the time, as a teenager, his mother caught him having oral sex with Johnny Benito, another neighborhood boy. She screamed at her son, telling Archibald that if he kept that up, he would be sent to a home for incurables, and would die of cancer of the throat.

And he talked about the time when, at the age of forty-six, Archibald visited his father's grave for the very first time—a nameless plot in a deteriorating Bronx cemetery—a grave with no headstone, only a number. He brought forsythia, and wept uncontrollably asking "Why did you leave me Papa? You never even held me. What did I do to make you leave?"

Although I tried to stay my physical distance from Archibald as best I could—making sure I would never be alone with him—I began to sense, as time went on, that Archibald had ultimately given up on me, finally realizing that I was not to be one of his sexual conquests. With this then well understood between us, I felt a bit more confident, even secure, easing up on my defenses. And from then on, Archibald and I were able to speak more freely; be more open with one another. With the fear of his sexual advances pushed aside, I could then begin to concentrate on Archibald himself—the man, and his indelible influences. I had to admit that unlike his childhood schoolmates, I was deeply enamored by his keen intellectual prowess—his cleverness and witticisms and extensive knowledge of just about every topic coming to mind, and perhaps even some which I never even knew existed had it not been for Archibald's persistent insistence and provocative stimuli.

And what probably fascinated me most of all was that Archibald Hannon had never attended college. He was totally self-taught. He studied the Greek and French languages completely on his own, quickly mastering what for others would have taken a lifetime. He was so successful at such linguistics, in fact, that he was engaged by the French Line to lecture to French passengers onboard the final world cruise of the great liner *France* just one year before. Archibald beamed with pride as he told me that everyone onboard *France*—

passengers and crew alike—simply assumed he was French.

In his early 20s, Archibald Hannon, at the request of his then homosexual lover Michael Rodgers, relocated to London and became emanuences to Cecil Beaton, the world famous photographer, scenic and costume designer, social writer, and—as Percy would say—just plain snob. Although Beaton took full credit for his literary works, Archibald claimed he was in fact ghost writer for most of Cecil's books, and was instrumental too in guiding Cecil's social life during Archibald's years in Europe.

Archibald proudly shared fascinating stories with us of his experiences while in Cecil Beaton's service—of private photo sessions with a topless Marilyn Monroe, and a very moody Greta Garbo; of extravagant social parties with the famous and the infamous of the 1940s and the 1950s.

After several successful years living and working in Europe, Archibald returned to the United States in the early 1960s. It was only days after his landing at New York when a cable arrived. Michael Rodgers, was dead—mysteriously found floating in his bathtub. Although bruises of unknown origin were present, it appeared drowning was to be the official cause of death. Naturally, Archibald was devastated by the news, and went into a self-banished seclusion. He wondered often if it was suicide after all, or murder. Was it rough trade? Someone Michael had picked up that particular night? Someone he might have been seeing? Archibald was haunted by these thoughts, and felt he had no choice but to shut himself inward, away from the world.

It was during those years of intense isolation when Archibald began writing for himself—and a promising career, both in the theatre and in the publishing world, had begun.

First impressions aside, I soon realized that Archibald Hannon was indeed a fascinating person—a remarkable human being. For me he had clearly become an important part of the voyage. For me he had clearly become an important part of my growth—my new life. Time spent with Archibald became an experience more learned and more vibrant than I had ever dreamed possible. There was a uniqueness about Archibald Hannon. I couldn't place it just yet. There was still so much to understand.

I instinctively knew I had to absorb as much as I could from this man about the world, about life, about people—and perhaps even about me. I simply could not let that opportunity escape.

Ever since I was a child, I held a clear fascination with time—or more specifically, with the movement of time. I was enthralled by the philosophical concepts of the past, the present, and the endless time still to come. I thought often about what really is "now"—the moment—and how "now" becomes "then" almost immediately, even before the thought is formalized or completed. I thought often about how much our lives are based upon our own self-created structure of time, and what it all represents.

When digital watches became all the rage in the late 1960s, I continually shied away from owning one. I was never very comfortable with digital watches, mainly because they failed to convey a true sense of the past. No dial, no sweeping hand—I needed a watch which would create the overall illusion of time's passing. The slow, evenly paced, metronome-like ticking of a clock—it made me feel safe and secure; it made me feel satisfied and at peace.

As anyone who has ever been to sea can attest, sailing the great oceans of the world has a unique way of obfuscating that illusive structure which we call time. The ship's whistle blows, the ropes are cast off, and almost immediately, time—as we knew it up to that moment—no longer is measured or defined in the usual manner so customary ashore.

In a strange and unique way, a ship creates her own time—a suspension of time if you will—and it's not uncommon to begin to lose track of one's Wednesdays or confuse one's Saturdays with one's Thursdays. It all blends together to become one time—a shared time—a continuous time which doesn't seem to have a beginning or an end, and there truly isn't any real way to measure it or define it. At sea, time simply exists—alone, isolated, cut off from the world. And perhaps this in itself may just be one of the great lures of ocean voyages for many of us—to be lost in that wonderful and very freeing time suspension, far adrift from the world's structured reality as we know it.

Onboard ship, time pieces—digital or otherwise—are virtually discarded—used only, of course, for the all important fashion statements. Once at sea, we tend to evolve, and shoreside habits quickly fade away. Quietly, without any warning or benchmark, it happens. Passengers begin to discern the passage of time solely by association—by the beginning of certain recreational activities for example, or by the opening of the ship's shops or another shipboard facility. I overheard a couple one day make plans to meet in the Ballroom when the complimentary dance class ended—no time specified, just a reference of focus, of association. After all, everyone onboard knew, in fact, that the end of the mid-day classical concert in the Garden Lounge—whatever actual time it happened to be—signaled that the Saga Dining Room was finally open and ready for full luncheon service. No announcement was needed. No bells had to be rung. When at sea for weeks, or even only days, I challenge any of you to try to decipher what day and time it really is. I'll be sure that you will not reach an answer without at least some difficulty.

Nonetheless, with her own timeless reality well established, a ship is compelled to surrender, at least officially, to popular world practice and maintain respect for the clearly defined time zones dividing our planet.

As you already may have observed, *Sagafjord*'s 1973 Great World Cruise followed a western itinerary—sailing from New York and Port Everglades, beginning her circumnavigation of the globe in a westward direction—through the Panama Canal to Acapulco and Los Angeles, then further west to Honolulu and continuing on across the great Pacific to Yokohama, and beyond. So out of respect perhaps for the well-established longitudinal time zones, our ship's clock was set back nightly, thereby gaining hours as we continued our journey westward.

Sailing in this direction was certainly the preferred route for any seasoned traveler circumnavigating the globe. Clearly, an eastward itinerary would require losing hours nightly, and along with those lost hours go lost sleep, and patience too, and perhaps even some basic human pleasantries.

The morning after our third time change—somewhere between our departure from Balboa and our arrival at Acapulco—I found myself up and in the Tour Office a bit earlier than usual—"steamship lag" some might call it. Within minutes, an elderly woman walked in. She was rather smartly dressed. And yet it was immediately apparent that she was perturbed and had to speak her mind. I was alone that morning, and it was clear that it was to me that she would do so.

"Young man" she stated sharply as she placed her black leather handbag on the counter. "I am furious. It's these time changes—changing the clocks. Why must we do that? It's only us out here after all—I'm fed up with it. I want to speak with the captain."

I explained to the woman about the various time zones around the world—a lesson she obviously missed from early grammar school days—and how the ship must, by maritime law, maintain correct time within them.

"Well, it's driving me mad, you know, and that's all there is to it." She paused a moment, and then continued. "If we absolutely must change our clocks, I don't particularly care for the way Norwegian America Line has decided we do it. My boy—you are the young boy, aren't you?—it certainly wasn't like this on the *Gripsholm*."

I understood her obvious comparison with *Sagafjord*'s only real world cruise competition from the then popular Swedish American Line. I thought perhaps the woman's comment was to make me fear that she might want to disembark immediately—right then and there, mid-ocean in fact—and join our rival somewhere out in the vast Pacific.

"I'm most definitely not a night person" she continued. "I retire precisely at 9:30 P.M." She pulled her crumpled *Cruise News* out of her handbag and unfolded it onto the counter. "You see, it says here—'tonight at 2:00 A.M. the ship's clocks will be set back one hour.' Do you realize, my boy, that last night I had to awaken at 2:00 A.M.—disturb my much-needed rest, mind you—in order to set my clock back one hour. You can be sure I am not the type of woman who likes to have her sleep interrupted, for any reason whatsoever."

Her angry eyes and clear expression of disgust told me that she was not speaking in jest, but was in fact serious. Clearly, she was not only angry, but troubled by her dilemma.

Dumbfounded by her ignorance, I explained that she could certainly change her clock any time before retiring. The result would be the same, I told her; and I, of course, would tell no one. It would just be between us.

After a moment, she thanked me for my help. She then took up her copy of that day's *Cruise News* and hobbled out of the office. So this was the rich. Old or new money, I wondered?

Chapter Three

"Like Ships In The Night"

Later that same morning, there was great commotion in the Purser's Office, just adjacent to our own—a single narrow walkway separated both offices and allowed for easy access. I noticed the purser himself, Per Olesand, and his two assistants in what appeared to be a frantic search—each of them spoke in lively Norwegian; often laughing, sometimes uncontrollably. I poked my head through the doorway.

"What's going on?" I called to Gunnar, the younger of the two assistants. "Can we please have some decorum here?" I asked with obvious sarcasm. "This *is* a business office, you know." Gunnar Olafson, from the Geirangerfjord region of Norway, was smart and handsome and unusually dark haired for his great Nordic heritage. He was amiable with everyone onboard, including the tour office staff.

"Oh, God Dag, my friend. And don't you say anything." He was barely able to speak through his laughter.

"Anything about what? I too, was smiling—for what, I wasn't yet sure. But his mood was clearly infectious. I stepped further into their office.

"Mr. Woodward; he's gone" Gunnar said. "We've lost his ashes—and the ceremony . . ."

"The burial-at-sea?"

"Yes" Gunnar replied. "The burial-at-sea is tomorrow morning."

"How could you lose his ashes?" I asked incredulously. "Where was he last?" The image of Mrs. Woodward and my grave dance floor experience flashed through my mind. And then I too began to laugh at the absurdity of it all.

"We're not sure" Kari answered, as she joined Gunnar by the cashier's desk. Kari Johanson, the other purser's assistant from just outside Bergen, had been onboard for two years and was quite experienced in purser duties and hotel concierge responsibility. The fact that she too was a part of this fiasco—of losing Mr. Woodward—was quite surprising.

"I think I last saw him over here" Kari said as she pointed towards the ship's steel safe. "Near the petty cash box." She walked to the filing cabinet on which the ship's petty cash was kept during daytime hours. "But when I went to look for him this morning, he was gone."

"What will we do if we can't find him?" Gunnar asked, as his laughter continued. He then turned to me. "What are you going to tell Mrs. Woodward?"

"Me? I'm not telling her anything" I said. "Why me?" "You lost him."

"You danced with her" Gunnar answered. "This wouldn't have happened if you hadn't dance with her." Purser Olesand laughed out loud at Gunnar's suggestion.

"What does my dancing with her have to do with anything?"

"We could tell her he just blew away—his ashes, that is." Purser Olesand interjected from behind his desk. And for the first time, I witnessed the officer's sardonic sense of humor, something which so far had not been expressed—at least in my presence—during the voyage. His comments, as dry as they were, were quite surprising, especially coming from such a senior officer of his particular rank and authority. It made me like him all the more.

"Why not just burn something?" I said jokingly. I grabbed a pile of papers from the countertop. "Here, burn these copies of yesterday's Cruise News" I said. "You'll have ashes, and Mrs. Woodward will never know."

Gunnar's eyebrows raised with interest as he listened to my

clearly sarcastic suggestion. For a moment, I feared he might try to do just that if Mr. Woodward's remains were not found.

Eventually, though, there was no need. When the search resumed, Mr. Woodward did indeed turn up. It seemed he had fallen off the petty cash shelf and behind the copy machine sometime during the storm. Mr. Woodward was safe after all. And the pursers, I'm sure, were all quite relieved.

For a tropical sea just off the Mexican coast, there was an uncomfortable chill that next morning. I left my cabin even before daybreak, and stood alone on deck. The sea was still; the pale dawn silent.

The open decks were damp from the previous night's rain. Salt crystals, deposited by the sea and kissed only by the night, made the ship's railings glisten like jewels in the misty early light. I couldn't help but swipe my finger along the wood, and bring to my lips the great taste of the sea, its soul and its life. The sun had risen just moments before, and illuminated the scene—theatrically and dramatically—soft, as if in a dream.

I first heard the scuffled footsteps, and then the voices. Quickly, I moved further aft and slipped behind a bulkhead, just barely able to hide in an alcove overlooking Veranda Deck. I should not have been present; I could not be seen.

Captain Brookstad stood together with Staff Captain Berntzen, Ted Jones, Maggie Sinclair, Chief Purser Olesand, ship's chaplain Father Casey, and, of course, Mrs. Woodward. She held her husband lovingly in both hands, and stared pensively out to sea. The group appeared solemn, the mood intense. Dick Dichosian arrived, late as usual, but with camera loaded and well in hand. He nodded to the captain as he awkwardly repositioned his camera bag over his left shoulder. It was obvious that Dick didn't want to miss out on documenting any shipboard activity for posterity, or profit. Although not listed in the *Cruise News*, this activity—quite private and not open to other passengers—was no different, at least in Dick's business mind. Everything onboard was indeed fair game.

They stood in silence for several moments, the gentle slapping of the sea against *Sagafjord*'s hull seemed soothing and unusually amplified.

Captain Brookstad began with a few words, his heavy Nordic accent, and the good distance from where I stood, made his comments virtually inaudible—clearly indecipherable. His lips moved quickly yet silently. Their message? Irrelevant, no doubt. It was as if the twenty-five years Brookstad spent onboard rusting Norwegian freighters caused him to treat NAL passengers as cargo. They were indistinguishable in his mind. It was only a duty he performed; any personal or human emotion was completely nonexistent.

Maggie warmly touched Mrs. Woodward's arm. She was a strong woman, Maggie was, and she openly offered that strength to Mrs. Woodward, who began to weep softly. As the captain spoke, she wiped her tears away with her gloved hand.

Father Casey gently took the urn from Mrs. Woodward and began his benediction. Dick snapped away, just as he did during bingo or dance contests, or any of the other shipboard activities. His presence alone made this ceremony seem almost routine, perhaps as commonplace as Maggie's ports-of-call shopping talks, or afternoon tea. His diligence was impressive though—he didn't miss a beat. At four bucks a shot, his mental cash register must have been ringing. No doubt Dick wanted to offer Mrs. Woodward a photo album of her husband's memorial service—perhaps with *Sagafjord*'s photo on the cover—to purchase and to cherish for all time to come. I sourly remembered Dick's philosophy—they can't buy a photograph he did not take.

I saw the sign of the Cross being made—first by Father Casey, followed then by the others. I too crossed myself as a lone gull encircled our ship—this far out at sea, it had obviously lost its way. Mrs. Woodward raised her right hand to her lips—kissing the very tips of her gloved fingers—and placed them gently upon the bronze urn; a final farewell to the man she loved.

Father Casey then opened the lid, tilting it gently over the rail. Mr. Woodward's remains were quickly taken up by the breeze, gentle as it was, and graciously scattered upon the sea.

As our ship moved forward, the ashes and bone chips swirled

about in a dramatic vortex, finally settling upon the welcoming waves below. They embraced him quickly, accepting his life and his spirit deep within its own.

The lost gull continued in flight with renewed determination, this time a bit further away, well into the distance. Perhaps it had finally found its way.

The talk onboard ship—the staff gossip, if you will—was centered around a group of people from Norwegian America Line's New York office who inconspicuously boarded ship at Balboa. Rumor had it that they were scheduled to sail with us only to Los Angeles. Why they were on board, no one really knew; and avid speculation was rampant. "Spies" they were called, so all of us were on alert.

During cocktail rounds that evening, I first noticed what I knew had to be the New York contingent seated just off the North Cape Bar. They appeared quite festive—and surprisingly young too—laughing and drinking; obviously enjoying each other's company and their time onboard ship, away from their offices. I was perplexed however. The picture just didn't fit. Even if they were just innocents from the New York office, as we were led to believe—employees of the Line simply out for a sunny holiday onboard ship—they still wouldn't be so obvious. They wouldn't allow themselves to be seen so blatantly in public as they were, seated together, with bottomless drinks well in hand; laughing and having an obvious good time. They were too conspicuous on a vessel which clearly catered to the aged. And even if it were true—that they were all just here on holiday—they would still have some responsibility as NAL employees. At least they should appear to enjoy the charade—invite a seasoned passenger to sit with them—for show, at least. It wouldn't have killed them. No, it could not be as it appeared. Never. Unless, of course, it was indeed a trap. Or perhaps they just didn't care.

Whatever the reason, I had to admit that the group's demeanor was quite attractive to me, their youthful frivolity a cherished joy; something I had not realized I missed until that very moment. I wanted to meet them, yet had to be careful. However conspicuous their sitting together was—during working hours no less and with passengers clearly present about the room—it did concern me. It was clearly against NAL staff policy. Everyone knew that. Guideline No. 23: *Never appear to be having more fun than the passengers* was the rule. It was in the Staff Manual, after all. This then had to be a trap.

Joan Farilucci and Sandy Bradford were secretaries at the NAL executive offices at 29 Broadway. I remembered seeing Joan busily running about when I arrived for my interview with Robert Brooks. Joan was short, and dark haired—her Italian heritage, obvious—and that night, she seemed quite animated in her conversation with Sandy, who was just a bit taller, with long reddish-blond hair and deep-green eyes. They were the first to greet me as I nervously hovered near the bar that evening, awkwardly awaiting for something to happen.

Joan smiled as she glanced in my direction and waved me over. "We've been looking for you—"

"Come and join us" Sandy added. "We can't wait to hear—how do you like the ship?"

"The ship's great" I said as I pulled up a chair, totally oblivious to how it all might look. "I'm really happy to be onboard. I'm having a great time."

Joan took the lead then and introduced the others—there was Leila Jones, an older woman with graying hair and a tired face, whose job was never made very clear to me; and James Arthur who worked in the operations department and dealt with the ship's customs and immigration clearances at the various ports of call; and there was Vincent too, a younger man who was a junior reservations agent at New York. Vincent was traveling onboard for the very first time, I was told—a sort of a familiarization cruise—a "FAM" trip, as it was called in the travel industry.

Vincent sat just to my right so I shook his hand first. And it was then that I realized I had actually seen him earlier that afternoon. He was sitting by the pool wearing a bright red bathing suit and white baseball cap, taking the sun as we sailed north. He was reading a book—and that in itself clearly pulled my focus . . . not his reading the book, but the fact that someone so young would be there at all. Not a typical passenger, to say the least.

When I first saw him lying out on deck, I knew there was something odd about that scene, something unusual. For a moment, I thought he might be a crew member. But a crew member would never be allowed to sit on a passenger deck, especially by the swimming pool—Guideline No. 17. So after meeting Vincent and this group that night, it all made sense.

I stayed with them for the entire cocktail hour; no pre-dinner dancing for me that night. Indeed, it was exhilarating to be in their company. For the first time since leaving New York, I felt I was finally with my peers—with people my own age. I was finally able to relax a bit, and be myself. And although I perhaps shouldn't have done it, I did. And for that one hour at least, I really didn't care at all.

We talked a good deal about the ship that night, about our own personal lives, and of the great adventure ahead—for me, at least. None of them were to remain onboard; they were all to disembark at Los Angeles as the rumor conveyed. Yet they weren't looking forward to that day . . . they all wished they could stay. In a way, they envied my future.

Not unlike naughty children, we laughed as we commented on the passengers around us, and their unique eccentricities. I clearly enjoyed being with this group, and they seemed to enjoy my company as well. Time passed quickly, and before I knew it, the music had ended in the Garden Lounge; dinner was being served. We left for the Dining Room then, and agreed to meet again later that evening.

For me, the dinner hours could not have passed more slowly. I paid little attention to my table companions' conversation that night. Mostly, I fantasized about getting to know my new friends better. I dreamed about what the next few days in each other's company would bring, and how much fun we would all have together. Except for Leila, we were all about the same age, no doubt with similar interests. But even more coincidentally, we worked for the same company. Clearly, it was a natural bond.

It was Vincent who seemed to pay me the most attention that evening—inquiring about my personal life onboard ship, and my particular duties and responsibilities onboard. Who were my friends? What did I do after hours? It was just practical information of life onboard which he needed, he said, to better sell the ship to passengers and travel agents alike.

Vincent was an extremely handsome man, perhaps twenty four years old or so. His jet-black hair and his deep-olive complexion could not disguise his obvious Latin background—perhaps Italian or Spanish, or even Portuguese was a possibility—and I suppose it was my preoccupation with his unusually sharp eyes, piercing dark as the night itself, which caused me to totally miss his last name during our initial introduction. He seemed a little quiet at first, and somewhat reserved. But he smiled warmly when we parted for dinner, and showed a renewed enthusiasm when I joined them later that evening.

The Ballroom was already quite crowded when I arrived. The lights dimmed quickly. The music struck its downbeat, and with a grand flourish, the evening's entertainment began. We sipped our drinks, and commented on the show—how could we not?

That evening, Cruise Director Ted Jones was presenting *Steps in Time*—a simply-produced musical cabaret which we all quickly recognized as nothing more than a star-vehicle for Anne and himself. The show was a romantically contrived recreation of the fancy routines and unique dance styles of the late 1800s to the present. It moved slowly, from decade to decade, in a basic revue format, with sloppy introductions and voice over announcements made in clear view of the audience.

Anne was radiant on stage that night. She was the only performer who created any excitement or interest whatsoever; indeed Anne was the only performer who brought any sense of professionalism to the quite under-rehearsed spectacle.

Other members of the social staff were cast in various roles as well—Norwegian America spared no expense in their entertainment budgets, we could see. Maggie Sinclair appeared in a huge picture hat with multicolored paper flowers and ribbons adorning the brim, a flowing shoulder scarf, and matching parasol. Hal Carter, along with bridge pro Marshall Smith and golf pro John Marratisch were also featured in various song and dance numbers. These unexpected and quite unnecessary chorus additions made the show appear even more amateurish than it actually was. Nonetheless, the "steps" continued and the recreated generations passed. If I had to choose, my favorite would have been the Cake Walk, with Ted and Anne impersonating Vernon and Irene Castle right down to Anne's laced-up high-heeled shoes, and Ted's dark derby hat and gray buttoned-up spats. If that was the high spot, we were all clearly doomed.

The show finally ended; the applause far from deafening. And soon after, our group began to disperse, one by one—first Leila, then Joan and Sandy. Tomorrow would be an early day's start ashore at Acapulco.

Before long, it was only Vincent and me who remained.

It was quite late. I was normally asleep by ten—no question. But I was clearly enjoying myself—perhaps for the first time since coming onboard—and, I guess, I didn't really want it to end. For some reason, I wasn't at all tired. In fact, I was wide awake; the blood racing through my veins with the excitement of the coming dawn. It must be the coffee. Or perhaps the company. There's something about youth with youth, I realized, which enlivens us. It's amazing, I thought, what with all our neurotic considerations cast aside, the energy one gets when one is simply enjoying the moment.

I was feeling a closeness to Vincent then—a camaraderie if you will. I didn't know what it was. I didn't know what to call it. I didn't know where it was coming from. I did know, however, that I wanted it to last. He was young, alive, intelligent and funny. I didn't want to lose that. I couldn't remember when I felt such exhilaration.

Vincent suggested we have a nightcap together in the Club Polaris, *Sagafjord*'s only after-hours bar.

"Just a quick one" Vincent said as he smiled his wonderfully winning smile. I had no choice. I was too intrigued. I was too excited to say no.

The Club Polaris, one deck above on Promenade Deck aft, was where one would find the more "fun-loving" crowd—as the *Cruise News* advertised "dancing till the wee hours" and all that. Yet if such was the anticipation, that evening would most certainly have been a disappointment. Only two or three couples sat at opposite corners of the darkened room which, as I'm sure the ship's original building plans illustrated, was *Sagafjord*'s first class restaurant when on transatlantic crossings earlier in her career. The dancing boys—Alan, Glen and Harris—lurked around in the darkness, no doubt in search of their clients. A Polish trio—the ship's only other musical entertainment—played quite undanceable music from their corner set on portside aft. Hal Carter sat at the bar talking with Barman Otto, already heavy into drink as his evening's reward for "pushing the old bags around the dance floor" for the last three hours. So this was late-night onboard *Sagafjord*, I thought. Certainly an unexpected yet convincing explanation for my retiring early.

So for us, clearly, the atmosphere in the Polaris was deadly; neither Vincent nor I was comfortable there. Together, we walked— first out on to the open Promenade Deck to enjoy an incredibly clear night under a crisp blanket of stars; then down to the pool area on Veranda Deck, and finally down even further to Upper Deck. We talked and laughed along the way, not really paying much attention to where we were or where we were headed—we just walked together and talked. It was clear that Vincent, too, was enjoying himself; it was clear that simply calling it a night had never entered his mind.

As Vincent spoke, I paid less attention to what he said, than to how he said it. I savored his voice; I was captivated by his movements. I was sorry Vincent would be leaving the ship in only a few days time. I knew we could become great friends—it seemed we already were well on the way—and I desperately wanted that to happen.

We continued to walk, and talk, as the night passed us by. And then, before I knew it, we were at Vincent's cabin door, somewhere aft on Upper Deck, portside. I guess we finally had to admit it was indeed getting late, and there was no real reason to stay up any longer. I knew I would see him in the morning, perhaps at breakfast, definitely ashore.

The ship was quiet—a sleepy silence I had never before heard. The walls creaked seductively as *Sagafjord* rolled slightly from side to side. It seemed that everyone onboard had already retired. It seemed it was only us.

"Why don't you come in for a while?" Vincent whispered. "We'll have one last drink together before Mexico. Besides" he joked, "if we stay up just a little longer, we may even get to see the sun rise over Acapulco harbor." He smiled and whispered again "Come on, let's see what I've got."

Vincent quietly unlocked his cabin door and glanced back over his shoulder. I hesitated, hushed, and stood nervously in the hallway not knowing what I should do. I knew I had to get up in just a few hours. The Acapulco tours were scheduled to leave quite early from the landing place, and the tender ride ashore, I was told, was at least thirty minutes in good seas. Vincent sensed my hesitancy.

"Come on" he said with a bit more encouragement as he stepped further inside his cabin. "It's too early to go to sleep."

"All right" I said as I followed him inside. "But just for a few minutes. I've really got to get to bed." I quietly closed the door behind me. I didn't want to awaken any of Vincent's neighbors.

"Sit anywhere" Vincent said as he took off his jacket and pulled off his tie. "Make yourself at home."

Vincent's cabin was extremely neat and orderly, and I liked that. As a member of the New York office staff, he was assigned a mini-suite during his time onboard—vacant until its passengers embarked at Los Angeles. The space was large and comfortable, and quite beautifully appointed. Quite different, I realized, from my very own A-54 just two decks below.

But with all the cabin's attractive appointments, I just couldn't seem to relax or make myself at home as Vincent had suggested. Suddenly, I was feeling very uncomfortable with this man—suddenly, being alone with him was almost unbearable—and I couldn't understand why.

I was confused by my reaction, and nervously fidgeted about—taking up some of the time insincerely, hopefully convincingly, inspecting the cabin's framed artwork of Norwegian wild flowers and picturesque fjord-scapes. Eventually though, I did sit, if you could call it that—slightly leaning against the edge of Vincent's writing table. I had to after all, I knew I couldn't stand the entire time. It was a commitment of sorts. Nothing formal, but a commitment nonetheless.

I forced myself to look directly at Vincent for the first time since entering his cabin, and as I did, I began to shiver uncontrollably; a tremor shot through my entire body. Suddenly, I was overcome with anxiety. What was it, I wondered. What was happening to me? Did Vincent notice? If he did, he compassionately didn't let on.

Why was I so nervous, I wondered, when just moments before, Vincent and I were relaxed and enjoying our time together? Perhaps it was simply the ridiculously late hour—and I was, after all, extremely tired. In fact, I was exhausted. Clearly, I needed rest. That's all it was. I'll have a quick drink with Vincent—it would be rude to walk out just then—stay just a minute more, and then off to my cabin, to bed and to sleep.

Vincent crouched down low as he searched deeply within his half-refrigerator under the bar—the glow of the small lamp illuminated his tanned face as he first opened the door; his contrasting white shirt seemed to self-radiate in its brilliance.

"All right—let's see here" he said. "What would you like? I have a couple of beers, some club soda, and . . . white wine—yes, I have some white wine left as well." His voice seemed different now that we were safely indoors, and protected from the endless dangers of the darkness and the open sea. Softer, more soothing.

"Anything" I said to him. "Whatever is easiest. I can really only stay a few minutes."

"Oh shut up and relax" he said with a smile. "Come on, what'll it be?"

"White wine" I answered. My voice cracked a bit, I realized just how stupid I was acting, and how ridiculous I must have looked. And even though I was not quite what one would call a drinker, I hoped that a bit more alcohol would calm me, and perhaps prevent me from embarrassing myself any further.

Vincent grabbed hold of the half-filled wine bottle, taking a beer for himself, and stood up, slamming the refrigerator door closed with his leg. Hastily, he filled my glass, and opened his beer; he turned, handed me the wine, and lifted his beer bottle high into the air.

"To the cruise" he whispered. "*The Great World Cruise.*"

"To the cruise" I repeated. Adding "Cheers"—a word I had heard Percy and Lar say so very often since coming onboard.

We lightly touched—my glass to his bottle—and sipped our drinks. There was an awkward stillness as we drank. The striking transition from our free-flowing conversations just moments before in the Ballroom, the Club Polaris, and again out on deck, was confusing, deafening—beautifully haunting.

"Aah, that's good" Vincent said. "There is only one first sip of the day. Too bad I've already had mine much much earlier—it would have been fun to share that very first sip with you."

How true, I thought. This one sip of wine was indeed exhilarating. It made my blood race through my veins unlike anything I had ever experienced.

Vincent then quickly broke the momentary silence.

"You know" he said, "when two friends toast each other like this, it is customary they look into each other's eyes while they drink—while taking that very first sip. It's an old Viking tradition" he continued. "Vikings were always fearful of their lives, fearful that their enemies—and sometimes their friends for that matter— might attack them; brutally murder them." Vincent edged closer to me and smiled as he spoke. "But by gazing into one another's eyes, one could be sure of not being stabbed in the back. Come on" he said. "One more time. Let's do it again, and let's do it right this time—the old Viking way."

Again, he raised his beer bottle, and I my glass.

"To the cruise" he repeated as I looked into his eyes and he into mine. Vincent's gaze was powerful, and once again I began to shiver—long and hard—from deep inside. This time, though, it could not be hidden.

"Hey, are you OK?" Vincent quickly put down his beer and lightly touched my thighs with both hands, rubbing them—perhaps in an effort to warm my blood. "What's the matter?" he whispered.

I froze for a moment, not knowing what to say, or how to react. Why was he touching me? Was he simply trying to calm me down? Or was it something more . . . serious? Could Vincent be a homosexual too? Maybe that's what I was sensing? Maybe that's why I was so surprisingly uncomfortable now that I was with him alone, in his cabin, when just hours before we shared the safety of others.

I couldn't believe it if it were true. And if indeed it was true, it curiously didn't repulse me the way as it did with Percy and Lar and Archibald and the others. Vincent was a guy after all; a real guy. He wasn't flamboyant like Percy or Archibald; he didn't speak with a lisp, like the outrageous bridge pro and the assistant cruise director. No one would ever assume Vincent was queer.

Yes I was frightened, yet it didn't cause me to want to withdraw. Rather, in a way, I was excited. The moment was exhilarating. I liked Vincent, and I wanted to be his friend.

No. I clearly didn't want to run. I wanted to stay with him. I wanted to know him better.

But this—this was something I just wasn't prepared for; something I clearly did not want to deal with.

"Calm down" Vincent whispered. "Relax." He rubbed my thigh just a bit harder, and straddled his legs nearer to my own. "Now doesn't this feel better?"

"Vincent" I mumbled softly as I put my wine glass down and began to move away. "I don't know what's going on here, but I do know we shouldn't be doing this."

"Why not?" he asked even more seductively. "It's OK. Just relax."

"Vincent." I attempted to move away once again. "Come on. I really don't think so. I've never done anything like this before."

My body trembled once again; I felt very much out of control. It was the trembling, I realised, of both fear and desire too. My mind told me to stop, but my body—intense feelings from deep within my soul creating emotions never before felt—hoped to God he would not. I wanted to leave, yet I wanted to stay so these incredibly warm and new and exciting sensations would continue, and hopefully would never ever end.

I was afraid. Afraid of what was happening, and afraid of what I was feeling. Afraid too that word of what was happening between Vincent and me would get back to the others onboard, and perhaps even to those in the New York office. Afraid of losing my job.

Vincent edged nearer to me still, and put his arms then around my waist.

"So . . . my new friend. Relax. It will all be wonderful, believe me. We'll have a great time together. It's OK" he whispered. "No one will ever know. Trust me." I was amazed at how much I believed him just then. At least I wanted to believe him. "It will just be between us."

By then, Vincent had one hand on my leg while the other edged up behind my neck—gently massaging my upper thigh, lightly stroking my hair. The heat of his body, and the strong touch of his fingers against my skin was overpowering. I had never been touched in that way before, and I was overwhelmingly excited by the feelings it aroused—sensations I was only just discovering; a thrill and a terror like the mysteries of a land still unexplored.

Indeed, I was stimulated by this man's touch, his handsome beauty, and most of all his tenderness. I felt dazed, bewildered—not knowing whether or not to act upon my feelings. I felt violently torn from the safety of the past—as a young chick is tossed from its nest—not wanting to go, yet yearning so much for the power and the freedom of flight.

Vincent embraced me then, fully and completely, pulling me yet closer to him. His arms were firm—strong and powerful. I could not move very much, nor did I want to. His masculine scent flashed a memory deep inside. As his hand brushed lightly against my lips, I remembered the faint smell of tobacco on the fingers of the barber who cut my hair when I was a child—an intoxicating drug I thought long ago forgotten.

Vincent's presence, warm and desirous, then so near to my own, made me feel unbelievably safe—open, and welcomed. With his face just barely inches from my own, I couldn't help but inhale the strong scent of his skin, and the sweet pungent remnants of his own cigarette, smoked just hours before.

After what seemed like long endless moments, he slowly and gently moved his lips to mine, and I was stilled. The warm wetness of his mouth pressing deeply against my own sent shivers again throughout my body—but now, held securely in Vincent's embrace, the uncertainty was gone, replaced by an astonishing excitement, a boyish ardor. His tongue gently parted my lips. His taste, the sensual sweetness, the probing, made my heart pound louder and louder, creating echoes which rang out deep within my soul. His kiss made my body tremble again and again, as a continuous surge of sensual excitement rushed through me.

At last, the trembling ceased; the shivering was no longer. The fear, the uncertainty, was transformed. Vincent was there. And that's all that mattered.

Yes, I thought, I wanted this to happen. I didn't really want to face that fact, but it was true. But what did it mean? What would it mean if I did let it happen? If I truly wanted it to happen?

"Vincent" I pleaded softly, passively attempting to pull away one last time. But he was too close, too sensually persuasive, too giving, and yes—too loving—to allow that very futile movement to even hope to succeed. I was betrayed by my actions. Vincent knew.

"Sssh" he whispered, placing his fingers gently over my lips once again. His left hand, now free from his embrace, moved slowly, and more intimately. His smile then was that of a child who discovers for the very first time a new wonder, or finally achieves his dream. "Now this doesn't seem to want me to stop, now does it?"

Vincent reached over and switched off the light, plunging the entire cabin into a blinding darkness. My eyes fought to see, and for a moment, it was impossible. But slowly, through the glow of only the night itself, it all became clear.

The radiance of the Pacific's transparent moon seemed sharply focused through his porthole, embracing us both in a shower of clear white light. Vincent kissed me again, a bit more passionately, a bit more deeply; and this time, I accepted him more freely.

I felt my belt being loosened and finally undone. And then my shirt. He undressed me there in the moonlight, witnessed only by the silent shadows our movements created. Within moments, Vincent stood before me with his clothes, too, thrown about the room. Naked, and with the incredible warmth of his skin pressing hard against mine; with the pounding of our hearts, we held each other closely, before finally moving to his bed.

The sound was loud and jarring, seemingly endless and abrasive; I tore from my bed in total fear and complete disorientation. The entire ship shook in violent steady cadence—pounding swiftly in time with the beating of my heart. And then, in an instant, it stopped—just as abruptly as it had begun. *Sagafjord* settled calmly back at peace.

I sat at the edge of my bed, my feet just touching the floor, still in the depths of a sleep-filled stupor. Passively, I laid back, surrendering to the warmth and comfort of my sheets. The still uncertain morning light just barely visible through my porthole.

My porthole, I thought. Or was it a dream? No—my eyes then opened wide. It was *my* bed I was in, and my cabin—I thanked God for that.

The anchor going down. That's what that roar and vibration must have been.

We had arrived at Acapulco.

The sun was growing brighter with the swiftness of my thoughts, as if in a race—who would win, I wondered. It washed gently across my body—the luminescence far too bright, I thought, for such an early hour.

"Shit!" I yelled as I leaped from my bed, this time running about in no clear direction, with no defined agenda; my heart pounding again furiously. I had to move fast—I had overslept. I had to get to the gangway as quickly as I could.

I stepped into a steaming shower, pulling the plastic curtain secure and tight, making sure to tuck the edge well into the ceramic lip below. The water poured down over me as I thought of the previous night. I thought about Vincent, and what we had done. I remembered only little of what actually happened. It seemed so illusive, so ethereal. A quick chill of panic and clear embarrassment made me hope to God it was only a dream.

But it wasn't. I knew full well what happened, and it was real. A feeling, a mood, and a wanting I could not escape. Even after a shattered night's sleep—however short it was—I could not ignore the truth. I smelled him near me still. I felt him. I tasted him. And in the shower's ever building mist, I again felt the spark, the intensity, the great passion of the night before.

I slept with Vincent. I had sex with another man—and as I drenched my body in the steaming hot spray, I felt dirty, and guilty, and disgusted for what I had done. I felt exhilarated too. And with it all, I felt whole.

Vincent had better keep his promise, I thought as I haphazardly soaped my body with panic and determination. I trusted that he'd tell no one about what we had done. I had no choice but to trust him.

He said it would be OK. He told me it would be just between us—as friends, he said. I'd deny it if word ever got out, I told myself. It would only be his word against mine, after all. I felt angry, embittered. The control was all his.

But was I angry with Vincent, or with myself? For a moment, I was unable see the difference. For the first time since meeting him, I was relieved that Vincent would be leaving the ship in a few days—not soon enough. Vincent knew my secret even before I did; in a way, I might have been party to its betrayal. Nonetheless, I could not, in all good conscience, face him again.

The water sprayed strong and hot; it felt good against my skin—symbolically washing away the deeds of the night before, my unthinkable desires. The hotter the water, I thought, the more I could cleanse away. A baptism, of sorts. Yet what was the belief?

What exactly was the new life I was initiating? Indeed, what was the faith?

I dressed as quickly as I could, and ran, quite uncharacteristically, down the A-Deck corridor, forward to the gangway area, portside. I had to concentrate on work, I kept telling myself. I had to think about my responsibilities. I had to occupy my time and my mind with thoughts of Mexico, of Acapulco, and of the day's tours ahead. I also needed to avoid contact with Vincent as much as possible until he finally disembarked at Los Angeles. Only then, would I be free once again. Only then—with Vincent gone and the haunting memory of our one night together a fading nightmare; the threat, then squashed forever, of his leaking word to anyone onboard—only then, would I feel safe. Only then could I relax.

For the first time in my life I was late. There was no question I had to skip breakfast that morning, something I never ever do. As I ran to the tender, I noticed our waiter Hans just off the A-Deck stairwell, no doubt peeking out just a bit to check the weather . . . what would the beaches be like, perhaps?

"I'm late" I shouted to him. "No breakfast today." Hans laughed and waved me off.

The view was magnificent as I stepped from the ship and stumbled down the shaky gangway to the bobbing tender below—the cool freshness of the morning air felt good against my face; the sun, quite warm. A cyclorama of brilliant color and shapes—the lush green mountains against the crystal blue sea; the other passenger ships at anchor in the harbor; and the city itself, quietly and magnificently perched in the distance—the scene filled my senses with a renewed enthusiasm for the day ahead.

The tender rolled quite heavily in the choppy waves as we quickly loaded tour supplies, and then those very few passengers always anxious to be the first ashore each morning. Eventually, we shoved off—the tender's flags flapped in regiment; my hair blew strongly back against my face.

Percy and the others were already onboard the tender when I arrived. They all sat huddled together on the lower level of the launch. Only Lar stood up front, alone with the chief officer of the deck—each straddling the helm as bookends do a literary work.

As the tender plowed ahead and began to pick-up speed, I donned my sunglasses to cover my eyes and I apologized to Lar for keeping them waiting. I edged further forward then, balancing myself as I went, trying to get as far away from the others as I possibly could—alone and up front, quite isolated from my colleagues. I didn't dare look into their eyes, or indeed let them see mine. I feared that Lar or Percy, or any of them for that matter, would instinctively discover what I so wanted to hide. Perhaps homosexuals had that inner sense, I feared. Perhaps, in their very own special way, they could tell if a man had just had sex with another man. That was it, of course. Percy, after all, always seemed to know when Per Sanders and his wife had had sex. How improbable would it be then if he could be just as intuitive when the sex partners were both men? Clearly, that would be of far greater interest to Percy than would the sexual escapades of Per and his stewardess wife Ilsa.

So I stayed clear, no matter how uncertain I was of homosexual intuitive abilities or sensibilities. I wanted no one near me. I wanted to forget what had happened between Vincent and me. I clearly wanted to move on.

Our tour-buses were already lined up, all in a row, as we arrived at the landing place. I was assigned to escort the *Acapulco City Drive* that morning which, in three hours' time, explored the city's tourist high spots, drove out into the countryside to view the beautiful landscape and popular beaches, then back again into the city to enjoy a piña colada while watching the famous cliff divers at the Mirabar Hotel's "La Quibrava" perform their uniquely athletic, yet quite theatrical, diving spectacular.

The drive to the Princess Hotel was strikingly impressive and afforded me the first opportunity to get lost in my thoughts, relax a bit, and escape even more. Passing along the splendid coastline, past small fishing villages and numerous rest stops and bodegas along the way, I was quickly aware of the very real lifestyle of these colorful local people; I had a vivid understanding of the culture which drives them.

Our tour guide that morning was an eccentric young man

called Jesus, who worked together with his pet cockatiel perched high on his shoulder—certainly an unusual conversation piece much loved by the passengers. We all took photographs with Jesus and little "Sam," and took bets on when the bird would actually "do it" on Jesus' shoulder.

The Princess Hotel, magnificently set along the sea, surrounded a huge open-air atrium lobby of soaring palm trees, native succulents and massive tropical vines and other foliage which hung quite symmetrically from the many floors above. I had never seen anything like it before. Its swimming pool, too, was a novelty—spectacularly designed with an underwater bar. Hotel guests could swim up to their very own barstool, sit, order, and enjoy their drinks—all while still in the pool, and very much under water. For the first time, I envied those who knew how to swim—something I feared since before I could remember. It would be fun, I thought, to simply swim up to the bar with all the others, and order a cold club soda with a fresh squeeze of lime.

The passengers on tour that morning were given one hour to explore the Princess Hotel on their own. Jesus told them they could do whatever they liked—swim in the hotel's pool or visit the beach; take some sun, or shop in the many boutiques along the esplanade. Some did swim, while others strolled along the beautifully landscaped walkways surrounded on each side by vibrant flowers of all colors and lush green ferns, still moist from the previous night's shower. Others sat under a splendid grove of majestic shady palm-trees.

Along the beach, children played as red flags flew from tall wooden poles in the strengthening winds. I could see that the waves were picking up; I dreaded another night of stormy seas and falling books—and most of all, of restless sleep.

Later that afternoon, when the tours had all returned and I was safely back onboard ship, I fell exhausted to my bed. The last twenty four hours were indeed draining, both emotionally and physically. I thought if I could just rest a bit before dinner, I'd feel better. It was just as I closed my eyes though that my telephone rang.

"Did you hear?" Percy said, with some nervousness in his voice. It was clear he'd been drinking.

"Did I hear what?"

"Hans. Our waiter. He's dead."

I was stunned. For a moment, I thought it was one of Percy's cruel jokes, and I wasn't much in the mood. But he continued, and by the tension in his voice—no matter how much liquor-induced it may have been—I just sensed the truth in his words.

Most of what Percy then told me was lost—my attention was elsewhere. Eventually, though, I forced myself to pay attention and I did manage to hear what actually happened—at least as much as Percy knew.

It was sometime after the lunch service that afternoon that Hans and a friend from the galley went ashore. They both knew they had only an hour or two before having to return to the ship for that afternoon's tea; but they wanted, at least, to say they had been ashore in Mexico. So off they went for a quick swim—ironically, to the Princess Hotel where we had all been just hours before.

Warnings had been posted. I remembered seeing the red flags earlier in the day. But not being a swimmer, I was unaware of their meaningt. So I took no heed. And apparently, neither did they. Perhaps in Norway, such warnings were different. Perhaps in Norway, red flags meant nothing at all. The Norwegian flag, after all, was red.

Our officer on watch was told by the local authorities that Hans' friend, a German cook named Rolf Habicht, had been swimming a good distance from the beach when he was overtaken by the treacherously strong underwater currents often found, I later learned, in these Mexican waters just off Acapulco. As soon as Hans heard Rolf calling for help, he immediately swam to his good friend's aid.

Apparently, the hotel's lifeguards saw the two men struggling in the waters, and raced to their rescue. But by the time they reached the swimmers, Hans had already been pulled well under. He was dead by the time they reached shore. Thankfully, Rolf was revived and sent to a local hospital where he would stay for several days to recover and regain strength.

Needless to say, I was shocked by the news. Again, I thought—even hoped—that Percy was playing some horrible cruel joke. But he wasn't. I kept hoping it was the drink talking. But it wasn't that either. Percy was coherent. His news was real.

Almost immediately, images of Hans and our times together in the dining room flickered in my memory like a brittle old movie shown for the very last time. I thought about missing breakfast that morning, and of running past him in the corridor. His sweet smile, and the innocent wave of his hand, haunted me. I liked Hans. He was my friend. Perhaps, I thought, he was my only friend; clearly I was his only friend at our table, only I doubt he ever really knew it. How sad it was that he never really knew it.

I didn't stop to talk with him that morning, I thought to myself. Not even to say goodbye, or to shake his hand. Little did I know it would be the last time I would see him. Why didn't I take the time? How selfish it was of me. Perhaps if I hadn't been with Vincent the night before, things would have been different. Perhaps if I hadn't overslept. Perhaps if I had indeed gone to breakfast that morning, just as I always did . . . I could have asked Hans to join us on the local tour; or asked him to meet me ashore for a drink afterwards. If I had asked him anything, that morning . . . perhaps he would still be alive.

If anyone bonds with anyone onboard a ship, it is with his waiter. He, after all, is the one you see three times a day, everyday. And for us, that would be for ninety eight days. Clearly, one's relationship with one's dining room steward is perhaps the most personal bond one can have onboard. In a way, it's the most intimate. It's clearly the most stable and consistent. So although it might seem odd how the loss of a waiter, however tragic, would create so much unrest; so much grief—the loss of that bond does indeed leave an emptiness as vast as the sea itself. And a need, in essence, to start over.

So naturally I was shaken, with a deep sense of loss—an emptiness, a hopelessness—as if I had just been punched in the stomach, then punched again. Such emotional pain was unknown to me;

this, after all was my first true experience with death, at least as an adult when I felt fully aware of just what it meant. Or at least I thought I was aware . . .

Years before, of course, there was Patricia Spellman—the girl who sat beside me in fourth grade. My mom and I were at Mass one Sunday. And at the close of the sermon, the priest quietly said "we'd like to offer this Mass for the repose of the soul of Patricia Spellman, who was killed yesterday afternoon in an automobile accident." My seven-year-old mind could not quite understand the impact of that statement, but I knew it was a terrible thing when I heard the gasp from the surrounding congregation. None of it seemed real, however, until the next school day. Patricia's desk was empty; the sadness in the eyes of the nuns and the lay teachers too could not be disguised, even to a seven-year-old. And when, just after lunch, Mrs. Fitzgerald announced that we were all going to walk the three blocks to Maher Funeral Home to visit with Patricia, I froze in panic. I wasn't sure what she meant. I wasn't sure I wanted to go. I couldn't imagine what it would mean to be in the same room as death. I knew death was something bad; Patricia was no longer here, after all. Where was she? Mrs. Fitzgerald said with God. Then why were we going? I wasn't even sure if I wanted to see her again. Especially now that she was dead. How do you say goodbye to someone who's died?

As we entered the chapel, I noticed her white coffin displayed against the far wall, surrounded by beautiful white flowers and burning candles. The twenty-eight students from Patricia's class were the largest group in the room. All was quiet, and dark—as if time had stopped and it was only those in that room who mattered.

Mrs. Fitzgerald walked us up to the coffin in single file, as a final farewell to our fellow classmate. And there she was—Patricia, forcefully sleeping, it appeared; her hands stiffly folded across her stomach; a white rosary strategically tangled between her fingers. A beige teddy-bear was warmly embracing her. She seemed fine, I thought. She looked fine, at least. She didn't look like someone who had just been run over by a speeding car should look. Why were we there? I wondered. Why?

And then just as quietly as we came—with the desperate cries of her anguished mother in the distance—we left. And that haunting image—that day—has never left my mind.

And now, it was Hans. Where was he? Where was *his* teddy bear to keep him safe?

Percy and I met at the North Cape Bar later that evening; we were quickly joined by the others—Archibald too. Screw the ladies, and screw the dancing, I thought. Hans was dead, and that's all that mattered.

We lingered together at the bar long past the dinner hour - none of us, I guess, really cared to face the dining room that evening. The memories of Hans at our table were just too painful; too indelible.

Philip Pound finally joined us; he was the last to arrive. My grief turned to anger as I saw him bouncing toward the bar. He walked with an arrogant air, a cockiness as if nothing at all was wrong. And all I could think about was Philip's constant mistreatment of Hans. Now, I thought, let's see what Philip has to say. Let's all bear witness to his no doubt guilt-ridden reaction to Hans' death, now that he too had heard the news.

"It's too bad" Philip said, as he shrugged his shoulders and lifted his Guinness pint to his lips. "Pity. But it's over, it's done with. Let's forget about it and move on. We can't bring him back, now can we?"

I hated Philip then. I wanted Philip dead as well. But then, I thought, he'd be with Hans.

The others were quiet; they just let Philip speak. They all knew, I guess, what a jerk he really was; how utterly stupid he was acting. So they all disregarded him. It was as if Philip didn't really exist.

Percy looked away, and stared out to sea. Even two or three gin and tonics couldn't obfuscate his sadness. Archibald quietly fiddled with the napkin under his wine glass—folding it endlessly in various shapes and angles. The emotion amongst us was powerful, pulling us together in a way I had never before experienced. But the grief, though—that was overwhelming. And I couldn't take much more. I needed to be alone. Finally, I broke the silence.

"I think I'll skip dinner tonight. I'm not real hungry. I'll see you all tomorrow." And with that, I abandoned them there at the North Cape Bar. It was their home after all, not mine. Where was I headed? I really didn't know.

I wandered through the empty Ballroom, then further aft on Veranda Deck. I felt I needed fresh air, so I stopped for a moment outside by the swimming pool. Clearly, I wanted to escape—escape from the news—escape from the nightmare and the tragedy of it all. Most of all though, I wanted to be alone.

Thankfully, the deck was quiet—free of passengers, at least; all of whom, I was sure, were well into their evening meal in the Dining Room below. Deserted, that is, except for Ingemar Heinerborg, a young Swedish deck steward whom I just barely knew. Ingemar was clearing the deck for the night, stowing deck-chairs and tables and umbrellas in suitable hatches and other safety areas for the sea time ahead. I had never been witness to Ingemar's duties so late in the day. I watched him work in numbed consciousness. Was he closing down, or preparing for another day? I couldn't tell which. To me, though, it was clear. At least in my present state of mind, I chose to believe he was clearing the decks; removing all traces of the day—so that tomorrow, we could begin anew. Starting over, I thought. I guess that's what it's about.

Just moments before, *Sagafjord* had pulled up anchor and began her journey north to Los Angeles. By then, the air was beginning to cool as the sun set off our portside. The sea breeze was strong as the ship's bow swung around a rocky promontory and turned northward. We were free at last from the confines of discovery—from the beauty and the horrors of Acapulco. I only wished we had never come.

Slowly, our speed increased.

I stood at the rail, and stared out to sea. Thoughts of Hans were all that were possible.

Ingemar had cleared most of the deck by then, working his way towards the area where I then stood. I felt his presence nearing.

It was this sea, I thought as I looked off the rail—the sea that I loved so deeply; the sea which had brought me so much joy and which had carried me so far in my life. It was this same sea which had taken Han's life. How could something so beautiful and so inspiring—something which had manifested so much joy and happiness in my life—be so fatal to someone else? And not just to any someone, but to my friend; to Hans.

I thought of Hans' parents and his family in Norway—his mother and his father, and perhaps even sisters and brothers too, none of whom I knew nor ever even heard about. I never saw a photograph. But I knew they existed. They must. And I sympathized with them. How heartbroken they will be when their telephone rings, I thought. How their lives will change when finally hearing the news.

But this wasn't only about them. It was about me. And I was hurting too.

We were well on our way by then, picking up speed. My heart pained to think we were leaving him there . . . leaving Hans in Acapulco—the lifeless shell of the young man we barely knew. My eyes leaked tears for a friendship unknown; a friendship that could have been. And the salty breeze made my eyes sting.

I thought of Hans' mother again, perhaps at that very minute cooking breakfast for her family. How sweet she must be. How happy and proud too, as she thought of her Hans, glamorously sailing the world on the beautiful *Sagafjord*—ship-of-state to many Norwegians. I couldn't bear the fact that I, a veritable stranger in his mother's life, already knew that Hans was dead, but she, safely at home somewhere in a Norwegian coastal village, did not. How would she hear the news, I wondered? Who would be the one to tell her that her Hans, her son, was dead? I heard the anguished screams of Patricia Spellman's mother . . . and just knew those screams were to echo once again.

I slammed my fist against the rail just then in momentary anger; salt crystals slapped my hand and splattered sharp against my face. I tasted the memories of Mr. Woodward's nautical interment just two short days before. In a way, it was all the same; it was always the same.

The moon was rising then. It embraced the sea in a shroud of white light and horrific shadows—incessantly moving, constantly aware. A now familiar light of which I was again a part, just as I was not too many hours before, somewhere far below in Vincent's cabin. It's the same light, I realized. Just different.

Suddenly, I felt free to re-live the great comfort and safety of Vincent's touch; the warmth and the intense passion we felt together. Those memories though were instantly shattered by a renewed sense of guilt. Where was Vincent, I wondered? Was he hiding from me just as I was avoiding him?

Grotesque images of Vincent and Hans—vividly reflecting the roles each played in my life—rapidly shuffled deep within my mind; the frames of a film abruptly cut, bursting from the lens of an aging movie projector seemingly on its last legs. Images of great fondness and sadness for Hans; of rigid shame and angry disgust with Vincent.

And I fantasized too about death, surprisingly glamorizing the process. I wondered where Hans might be at that very moment. What was he thinking? What was he experiencing? Perhaps in death, I thought, Hans had attained a magnificent ability; he had become all knowing. Death, I believed, was total awareness. The dead—their souls, their energy—were all encompassing. That was the heavenly state. There were no secrets left. There could be no hiding after all.

And if, indeed, my thoughts were true, then Hans knew me well—he knew what I had done with Vincent less than 24 hours before. How ashamed I was then. What must he be thinking of me? I hoped to God he wasn't disgusted—could he ever forgive me? Would Hans still, I wondered, be my friend—even in death?

"Did you hear? . . ." Ingemar asked quietly as he stood to my side, collapsing the last of the deck chairs left abandoned by the port rail.

"He was my waiter; we were friends" I said as I stared out to sea. "I just can't believe it."

I could not look at Ingemar directly. I didn't dare. I knew the tears would come and perhaps not stop if I did, and I could not let this young man, someone I did not know well, see me in such a state. Yet we continued to speak, gently and quietly, as Ingemar worked and I stared ahead, losing myself in the mutable sea. Perhaps it was our own futile effort to keep alive Hans' memory; to revere his spirit.

Although we were essentially strangers—two young men with only a few words spoken between us—Ingemar and I brought each other comfort that evening. It was a time of shared feelings between those who really shared nothing more than a common friend.

Darkness finally came—fitting, I thought, for such a day. Let it come, let it all end.

Ingemar moved on in silence—stalwart, considerate, just as he had come. I maintained my vigil at the rail deep into the night. I could not think of anything else I could do.

The Tour Office came alive the next morning with increased ticket sales and the usual operational inquiries. I would guess that the great success of the Balboa and Acapulco tours had encouraged passengers to inquire about the many other excursions we had to offer at future ports-of-call. Perhaps the passengers were beginning to trust us, and feel a bit more confident of our shipboard tour operation. Clearly, it was a positive sign of our skill and perhaps our professionalism.

Amid that morning's chaotic activity—just as the line of impatient passengers was queuing far down the hall, each of them anxiously awaiting their turn—I was called to the telephone. It was the chief officer from the Bridge.

"Captain Brookstad would like to see you in his office" the heavily accented voice commanded.

"Captain Brookstad?" I repeated in astonishment. "He wants to see me? What for?" I asked cautiously. "When?"

"Now. In his office. Can you come now to the captain's quarters?"

I was stunned, nearly frozen with fear. The captain found out about Vincent and me. I just knew it. Vincent must have told, that son of a bitch!

"Yes, of course. I'll be right up."

Quietly and somewhat nervously, I pulled Lar aside and let him know I had been summoned upstairs, although it mattered not how quiet or private I tried to be—everyone heard; the room was so small. Everyone knew—the ship, too incestuous. Eyebrows were raised. Yet God only knew what filled everyone's thoughts—God, and perhaps now Hans.

It had to be about Vincent, I thought as I hurriedly left the office. Why else would Captain Brookstad demand to see me? I was a nobody after all . . . just an assistant in the tour office. If it weren't about Vincent, then what would the captain want to discuss with me? What else could I have done to bring about such an audience?

Surely, I was in trouble. The captain wouldn't be wasting his time with me if I weren't. I was embarrassed. I was ashamed. I was sure to be fired.

I slammed aside the metal safety cage and stepped into the service elevator which offered direct access to the Bridge Deck and the captain's office two decks above.

Perhaps I'll even be put off the ship at Los Angeles, I thought—ironically, where Vincent was disembarking—the two of us just tossed ashore like ropes from a sailing ship; cast aside before ever having left the North American continent. All because of one very stupid thing we did together—one night only it was, when both of us were overly tired, maybe even overly intoxicated. How stupid I was. What would I tell my parents, and my family? What would I tell my friends back home?

I was perspiring just a bit as I knocked on the captain's door. To my left, on the bulkhead wall, was a small wooden plaque—"Sven Brookstad—Master, MS *Sagafajord*"

The captain's office was much larger than I had expected, and quite luxuriously appointed with dark woods and a thick burgundy carpet, and several comfortable-looking sofas and chairs. Leather bound books and elegant artwork was everywhere. A large vase of freshly cut birds of paradise stood centered on the sofa table.

Brookstad sat behind a circular mahogany desk, and wrote in a journal with a black fountain pen. His jacket was off, and for the first time since I had known him he seemed unusually at ease. There were a few moments of awkward silence before he finally looked up and acknowledged my presence.

"Come in" he said. "Have a seat." He pointed to a mahogany and black leather arm chair just adjacent to his desk.

Once again, another silent pause punctuated the captain's continued log entry. I sat as and where I was told, and waited nervously—like a naughty child just called to the principal's office—for the captain first to speak. Finally, the writing stopped, and the captain capped his pen.

"I'll get right to the point" he said firmly as he leaned back in his chair. "You were seen yesterday on Veranda Deck—by the pool, I believe—talking with a crew member. Is that not true?"

His accent seemed less affected then, somewhat softer—his English was indeed far better than I had thought.

"I believe it was, let's see here . . ." The captain briefly held his reading glasses up to his eyes, and looked over a small sheet of paper on which were written words I could not see . . . "last evening, just after sailing."

"Yes Captain, that's true" I stammered nervously. And yet I relaxed just a bit, relieved that the reason for this meeting with the Captain was not due to my sexual escapades or moral proclivities.

"I was standing by the rail last evening, around sailing time. And I did speak a word or two with the deck steward on duty. We were talking about my dining room waiter Hans and . . ."

"Young man" he interrupted in his usual arrogant way. "I'm sure you received the company's *Instructions of Cruise Staff* when you were first engaged to work onboard *Sagafjord*. Did you not?" He pushed a copy of the booklet towards me, across his desk. "And you—a bright young man, or so I've been told—should certainly recall the particular section which discusses social staff and crew relationships."

"We weren't having a relationship Captain. I had never even spoken with the guy before last evening." The captain's eyes widened with incredulity that I would even question his intimation.

"Nonetheless, it could appear so, couldn't it? What if a passenger had seen you? Now how would that look? Cruise staff must never fraternize with the crew. You know that. It's the number one rule onboard Den Norske Amerika Linje—Norwegian America Line." He paused a moment, apparently to allow time for his statement to sink in. "So will that be a problem for you in the future?" He looked straight at me, carefully waiting for my reaction, knowing full well what my response must be.

"No Captain, of course not" I answered. "That will not be a problem. I fully understand the rules. You see, I was just upset about the accident—about Hans' death—and didn't think that . . ."

"Well *think* from now on. I can't emphasize that enough. We don't want to give the wrong impression to our passengers, now do we? Never again must you be seen speaking socially with a crew member while onboard this ship. Do you understand? That sort of behavior cannot, and will not, be tolerated on my ship."

I was indeed surprised and somewhat dumbfounded by Brookstad's outburst. I simply could not believe it was a matter of such importance—to him, or to anyone. I was astonished too that my very brief talk with Ingemar was even noticed at all. Who the hell could have seen us, I wondered? But more importantly, who would turn us in?

"Do you understand?" The captain asked once again, this time quite firmly.

"Yes Captain. I do. I do understand."

"Will there be anything else then?"

"No sir."

"Good." He stood then, signaling that my very brief audience with him had ended. I hurried from his quarters as quickly as I had come; abandoning the service elevator this time, opting for the stairs. I couldn't wait to tell the others.

"He's that way, you know" Percy commented. "He's really an ass. Let it go in one ear and out the other." Percy and I spoke together over the luncheon buffet we shared at the Veranda Cafe that afternoon. Neither of us was very much interested in going to the dining room anymore—at least not just yet.

"Just don't let it bother you."

"Yeah, but it does bother me. I never get into trouble."

"Well get used to it then" he snapped back. "Look" Percy said as he paused and ate his hamburger with a knife and fork—as the French do. "Just go along with what he says . . . he didn't say 'don't do it' now, did he? He just said 'never be seen.' That's all there is to it. Now, shut up and pass the Dijon."

L os angeles—City of Angels.
 I looked forward to the rolling hillsides, the tall lush palm trees gently bending in the cool Pacific breezes; the glamour and the glitter of Hollywood, Mann's Chinese Theatre, footprints in cement, and sidewalk stars for as far as the eye could see. I remembered the lively sailings of Captain Huxley's glamorous ship from this beautiful southern Californian port, and imagined how our own arrival would be matched by equal pomp and streamer-strewn color and confetti. But when I arrived on deck that morning, just after 7:00 A.M., I witnessed not my fantasy at all, but what was to be the reality of our only visit to the Golden State. It was not the Los Angeles I imagined at all, but a somewhat industrialized Long Beach, with its surrounding maritime districts of San Pedro and Wilmington.

Giant smoke stacks set atop fading factories were scattered about as far as I could see; all angrily spewing thick black smoke into the noncommittal sky. I saw rusty freighters and container ships too sitting quite low in the water—aging vessels which, with the assistance of some equally corroded tugs and battered motor launches, were reluctantly edging themselves against dockside wharves, cautiously awaiting their unloading like a long over-due pregnant woman.

The port itself however—although not picturesque in the least; indeed, quite unattractive to the visitor's eye—was extremely busy and full of life, and that alone, to an avid ship lover like myself, brought great excitement to my first west coast visit. I became energized when a sea port lived. A rush of adrenaline; a surge of excitement. A driving pulse of activity which continually fed the heart. Ships coming and going wherever one looked. And I was fortunate. Such was the case that day. Indeed, it was a rare occurrence, even in 1973.

But unlike the great attention being paid the tankers and the freighters and the older cargo ships scattered about, there seemed little excitement or interest in us at all that day. There was no visible welcome for *Sagafjord*. No action from shore-side seemed to say anyone even cared. So it was nothing but silence which greeted us when we finally arrived at our berth and the first of our lines was thrown ashore. Longshoremen, no doubt bored and indifferent from years of tossing and catching heavily weighted ship's lines, seemed lethargic at best with their morning's duties. It appeared they cared little whether or not the line thrown ashore came from an aging and tired old cargo steamer, or from a glamorous ocean liner like *Sagafjord*—sailing on a world cruise no less. Nor could they appreciate the excitement they were missing. Let them service those rusty old tubs all they want, I thought. I was onboard *Sagafjord* after all. We were sailing around the world. And I knew just how special that really was.

I had expected to step ashore in downtown Hollywood; to walk off the pier and already be on the great Sunset Strip, or glamorous Rodeo Drive. But such was not the case. Clearly, we had tied up at a working port far from the true spirit of the city; any form of social life—residential or urban—was nowhere in the eye's view. We were an hour's drive at least from where I thought we should be—and I had no idea whatsoever how I, alone, could manage such a distance.

I was somewhat disillusioned with the betrayal of my dream; resigned to the fact that I wouldn't be going ashore that day. It seemed too difficult, too problematic to move about alone, with no clear direction.

Then Ornulf Johnson came by after his morning walk around the deck. Ornulf was the only Tour Office member who wanted to go ashore that day. Like me, he had never been to the west coast of the United States and he too wanted to experience its culture, its landscape; simply put, he wanted to see as much as he could, within our limited time ashore.

Ornulf Johnson and Per Sanders were the only members of the Tour Office staff who I considered to be normal—at least sexually, that is. Each was married to attractive Norwegian stewardesses. And I truly believed it was because of their heterosexuality that Ornulf and Per helped bring a sort of balance to the Tour Office environment. I could only imagine how sexually charged—homosexually charged, that is—the office atmosphere would be if Ornulf and Per were not with us.

Yet however normal I imagined their sex lives to be, it soon became clear to me that Ornulf and Per were in reality not unlike the others in at least one respect. They too seemed to have had nothing but the sex act itself continually on their minds. Maybe it was a cultural thing. Perhaps it was the result of being endlessly cooped up on a ship for so long. Whatever the reason, I was beginning to wonder if everyone—straight *and* homosexual—could perhaps be similar in his sexual appetite. Could it be then, that it was only the individual expressions which differed?

Of the two, it was Per who seemed to be the most sexually obsessed—and tried, and succeeded, in having sexual relations—whatever the physical extent or duration—with his wife Astrid wherever and whenever, and as often as he could. Nearly each and every afternoon in fact, following our extended lunch break, Per would arrive back at the office just as we were opening up for our afternoon session—just in the nick of time. He always looked a bit flustered, red and blotchy, with perspiration dripping down freely from his forehead.

"Are you OK?" I asked him one day when he looked particularly disheveled.

"You'd look that way too if you just fucked the hell out of your wife" Philip shot back with a grin and a chuckle—knowing full well, and taking pure satisfaction in, the fact that hearing such information would be, for me, quite uncomfortable.

And naturally, like the formidable fool that I was, I fell for it completely. It was clear that my visible reaction of pure disgust to Philip's piercing words gave him just the orgasmic satisfaction he sought. And as such, the verbal dissention between Philip and me endured.

I was unsure why having such knowledge bothered me so—knowing that Per and his wife had just had sex. It was something I just didn't want to think about, or deal with. It was strangely uncomfortable to think that perhaps just moments before, he and Astrid were naked together—he fucking her forcibly; she perhaps hungrily sucking his penis. And I was totally dumbfounded to think that he, Per, was not in the least uncomfortable with any of us knowing that he had, in fact, just "done it." He seemed boastful, in a way; almost proud.

What was it with these people, I wondered. Was all this open sexual behavior normal? Was I the only one who seemed so unnaturally prudish? Why was it that I found such solace and great comfort in remaining so private with the details of my own personal life? Was I feeling something I should not be feeling? Or more importantly and perhaps even more frightening—was I not feeling what I should, and could be feeling?

Whatever it was, I was clearly uncomfortable, perhaps even frightened, by the others' casual openness and blatant sexuality. And maybe even threatened a bit by it too. I wondered just why that was; just what was it that threaten me so. After all, it wasn't any of my concern what Per and Astrid did when alone together—he was with his wife after all. But did I have to hear about it continually, day in and day out, in explicit and all too predictable detail? Did I really have to have it pushed in my face?

It was clear that whatever the form or the forum, I did not want to talk about sex, whether it pertained to me or to anyone else. Maybe, I thought, if I just didn't think about it, it might not really exist. And perhaps if I just didn't react so prudishly to the others' comments and to their incessant teasing—perhaps then that uncomfortableness would all go away, and not torment me so.

But no matter how much I tried to alter or camouflage my outward behavior and what appeared to be my true innermost feelings, I couldn't help but think, and I couldn't help but be reminded, that it was me who seemed to be the one who was different. Per and Ornulf—both young and heterosexual—seemed quite happy and emotionally stable in their lives. Quite settled, they were; and in a way, I envied that confidence. And ironically, all the others—Lar and Percy, and Philip and Archibald too—all clearly homosexual—appeared quite content with their lives as they were. Or at least on the surface, that was the case. Even though they did not have "husbands" or "wives" or whatever homosexuals called their sexual partners, they were all confidently proud of who they were as people, as individuals.

I was the one who appeared troubled. I was the one who seemed confused. It was I, more and more often, who simply did not fit in.

The others were all refreshingly open with their thoughts and opinions. I was amazed at how willingly free they were from the judgmental fear of others—free from the concerns that others might speak ill of them; shockingly liberated from the social ramifications of their own sexual proclivities.

I was a young single guy, after all—traveling the world alone. I had no girl friend. I never had a girl friend. I had never even been sexually intimate with a woman. Such desire had not, until then, been a focus of my life. However sexually inexperienced I was, I knew I was unlike Percy and Archibald, or Per and Ornulf, or Lar or Philip. That one-time experience with Vincent clearly could not define me. But no matter how much I tried not to think about it, it haunted me still. I kept telling myself it was something that just happened; a meaningless act of no consequence. And the most important thing of all, was that it was over. Vincent would be leaving the ship that very day, in Los Angeles, traveling east. I was relieved at just the thought of his departure, and I hoped and prayed that I would never see him again. I smiled when I realized that I would soon be heading farther and farther west, far away from him—around the world in the opposite direction. And the further away from Vincent I could get, the better.

But the world is round, after all. And I did not yet realize that by encircling the earth completely—as one travels away from someone or something in one particular direction—one eventually gets closer and closer to that same someone or that same something as the voyage continues; and you eventually—inevitably—return to the very same spot from where you once came.

So I was really quite pleased when Ornulf—not Percy or Archibald; not Lar or Philip, or even Per—approached me on deck that morning and invited me to go ashore with him to see as much of Los Angeles as we could. He had it all planned apparently—we would have lunch together ashore, and still return in time for sailing.

"Crew Purser Olaf told me there's a shuttle bus which will take us directly downtown, near the Mexican area—Alvera Street I think it's called" Ornulf said. "I'm told there are lots of shops and restaurants there. Let's go" he said encouragingly. "It'll be fun." So off we went to explore a new city and a new culture; for tamales and colorful piñatas, embroidered shirts and some mariachi music too.

The Los Angeles Ornulf and I saw that day was far from my fantasy—no film stars, no crooked Hollywood sign, no blond-haired surfers lifting giant surf boards high above their muscled shoulders. Yet any initial disappointment was overshadowed by the wonderful experience of sharing that very personal day with Ornulf. For the very first time—away from the others—I was able to get to know this man not only as a colleague and co-worker, but as a friend.

And there was an added bonus as well. There was perhaps no better image of pure masculinity that I could have chosen to pal around with that day—to be seen with that day. Birds of a feather, they say. At least on the outside. At least that's what I had hoped.

We reboarded ship at 5:30 P.M., just barely in time for our scheduled sailing. Steinar, from the sailing crew, had already disassembled the sign posted at the gangway—

"At 6:00 P.M. — MS *Sagafjord*
Sails Promptly for Honolulu, Hawaii"

Quartermaster Jan was untying the gangway ropes just as we stepped onboard.

The ship headed west then; our transpacific voyage had begun. Two weeks had passed since leaving New York, and in that very short time my experiences onboard seemed overwhelming—the indelible scars of a life being lived.

The five-day voyage between Los Angeles and Honolulu became for me a time to think, to reflect. What was I really doing onboard, I asked myself, and how did I in fact fit in, if at all? Why was I suddenly so confused about personal identity and my life's own direction?

I began too to question who I was, and who I wanted to be? I was never so challenged when back home; never in my dreams of exploring the world. It was easy to dream; always protected by the comforting hands of unreality. But I suddenly realized I was no longer dreaming; I was living. Truth, it seemed, had taken hold swiftly, and somewhat unkindly.

Indeed, what was it about this voyage in particular, about these people specifically, which had conjured up—no, demanded—such dangerous and uncomfortable introspection? Perhaps I should never have come. Perhaps I should have kept things simple, kept them familiar—remained safely at home, unchallenged, just as my schoolmates had done—taken work bussing tables at the local diner, or pumping gas at the four-corners' Sunoco station. At least then, after all, I would have no options to challenge or confuse me; no gnawing anxieties of making lifelong mistakes. And no fears of failure, since what I would be choosing—or accepting—would be nothing really at all.

My basic instincts though commanded that I, in fact, had no choice at all. I could never have remained back home, passively content. I could never have played it safe as did all the others. That local diner and the four-corner's Sunoco held no interest for me. That person who dreamed—the young man who hungered all his life for free exploration and keen self-discovery—he, of all people, could never have made such a moribund choice.

Indeed, I found myself just where I had dreamed—thrust into an alien sphere of significant uncertainty and comfortless change—prolific with unknowns, guided by fear. Acceptance was key, I felt. But how, I wondered, could it be achieved? Would I ever be fully accepted for me—for exactly who I was?

The emotional inadequacies of childhood, perceived or otherwise—in contrast to the powerful histories of those who now surrounded and controlled me—seemed not just an embarrassment, but a burden; something to hide, never to reveal. I fully believed that in order to succeed—in order to be truly accepted in this strange new world I had discovered—I would have no real choice but to deny my simple, middle-class, suburban past. It certainly was not significant enough I thought, especially for the passengers with whom I was now traveling the world, sharing my life. How could I ever compete with their genetic sophistication, their quite enviable worldly experience—with their highly desired social status and intuitive appropriateness? To me, their superiority was clear. There was no doubt. They appeared to have much more importance in life than did I—than did my family and my friends back home. They appeared to have far more power and influence in the world than any of us back home could ever conceive of, let alone achieve. Clearly, I wanted to be like them. I wanted to have lived their histories; I wanted it all to be second nature.

I often fantasized about our passenger's families—about childhoods no doubt spent in lavish mansions and elegant country houses; schooling in only the finest of British tradition, with ivy-covered stone walls surrounded by sheep-dotted pasture-lands and misty countryside cottages; with an abundance of family money to guarantee every need or want. Old money too, as only Percy would allow it to be.

The more I dreamed, the more I shuddered with shame and embarrassment at my own family history and my own uneventful past—more for the lack of one, I guess, than for what it actually was.

I wondered how I appeared to the passengers. They seemed to like me well enough. On the surface at least, they appeared to accept me. They said I was cute—"just like their grandsons." But a dog is cute. I didn't want to be a novelty; someone or something to simply amuse them. There had to be more to the truth. I had to know what they really thought.

I sailed in fear of exposure; I believed that if any of them really got to know me; if any of them uncovered exactly what I was about; if they really knew where I was from and what little I ultimately knew about the world—I would never be accepted into their enviable society; I was clearly destined only for rejection. How devastating it would be to be abandoned by these people, I thought. I could never let that happen.

I scoured my mind for any impressive experience in my family's past which might just, I believed, boast a heritage of sorts—one, at least, a bit more fitting this society. It was these family histories after all, which they flaunted with every word and action. And it was just such a history I lacked. A history for me—either real or imagined, it didn't really matter—was what I felt I needed to be one of them; to be fully accepted onboard *Sagafjord*.

A past indeed. If only I had one.

Growing up in Pleasantville was all I knew. I managed as best I could. I was the last of three boys, each of us chronologically—and one might say culturally—separated by a very distant five years.

We were a typical family of the genetically prolific baby-boomer years with some strong, yet hazily defined, quasi-Italian traditions. Although my parents instilled in all their children the fact that we were of pure Italian blood—I had even heard the word "royalty" used once or twice in passing; but no one could ever say who, when, or where—it was a great disappointment when, as a young child, I realized that my parents had little, if any, real knowledge of our family's true origins; from a place somewhere near the great Bay of Naples. For whatever reason, my parents seemed quite reluctant to discuss the old country or our family history, or any of our Italian relatives at all. Yet, we seemed to hold on to our fading Italian traditions with desperate fear of letting go—for what purpose, I would guess, they did not even know. It was just important, that's all; even if those traditions' true significance was virtually unknown to them, and therefore meaningless.

No one in my family was truly conversant in Italian, and so from an early age, the cultural contradiction was clear. Italian words were rarely spoken in our home—only, it seemed, when we children were not to understand—during an argument let's say, or when a sexual reference simply could not be avoided. And when those few words were actually spoken, they were so bastardized that the language itself—Italian or English for that matter—was literally unsalvageable; it could rarely be deciphered. A dichotomy of cultures; a clash of identity. It was impossible for one to know which way to turn.

So we were not real Italians; we were not real Americans either. Yet even with such a confused heritage, we were encouraged at all times to socialize with Italians whenever possible. A security blanket it was. After all, as an aunt once told me, Italians might be known in some circles as the greatest mobsters the world has even known, but at least you could trust them.

It was understood too that when the time for marriage came,

the perspective bride's last name had not only better end in a vowel, but her family had better come from the same region of that boot-like country as our own. Never Calabrese; never Siciliano. Oh God no! Napolitano only. Nothing less.

I vividly remember the great familial display which occurred when each of my brothers began dating—the first with a German girl, the next with a Swede. The fallout was tremendous; a malignancy, seemingly never in remission. "She's no good for you" I would hear, as a facial smirk would punctuate the opinion. "Cafone"—peasant. So I decided back then that such would never happen to me. The answer came easily; the plan quite profound. After all, how would anyone be able to deprecate the person I might love, if they were never allowed to meet? So no one ever accompanied me home to greet my family, I made sure of that—except, that is, for my one boyhood friend Michael Conutto . . . Italian, of course. I was not a complete fool after all.

"People despise us out there" I remember my uncle Amerigo telling me one cold winter afternoon. "They always want to get us. And do you know why?" he asked. "Because we're Italian—il migliore—the best!" This was the same uncle, I might add, who when visiting Italy for the very first time in nearly forty years, was so used to his usual American habits, grandly ordered a bottle of imported wine, and received the finest California Merlot.

Yet to confuse matters even more, we were constantly being told that although being Italian was the very best one could be, if we truly wanted to succeed, we must become as American as possible; not be bogged down by archaic traditions or ethnic, if still charming, customs.

So even with the Americanization of our young lives paramount to our future, there remained great emphasis on the basic values and the pride of being Italian, so much so that I began to believe that the people of Europe—especially Italians—were superior. They seemed to have it all—magnificent good looks, winning charm, great intelligence, perfect taste and sophistication, not to mention being able to speak the most beautiful language in the world.

"Doesn't he speak beautiful Italian?" my aunt would ask when hearing a young waiter rattle off the dinner specials at a local Italian restaurant? No one ever said "doesn't he speak beautiful English?" when talking about me, or anyone else, for that matter. Why not? Certainly, my aunt made that waiter quite special in my young mind, and I wanted to be special—so I wanted to be like him.

So *Italians were simply the best* became our family credo. No matter what they attempted, I was told by cousin Josie one day, Italians surpassed all expectations. The best artists, the best chefs, the best Catholics, and yes—the best gangsters too. There, quickly stated, was her pride. Her ancestry. Her identity.

But where was mine?

Holy Innocents Roman Catholic Church was the nearest parish to our home. My parents liked attending that church, as did other relatives in the area, mainly because it had a heavily concentrated group of Italian parishioners. The clergy too were under the same ethnic influence—Father Materasso was pastor. His name, I later learned, meant "mattress" in that beautiful language we all spoke about, but rarely dared speak.

And so the personal conflict continued. I often wondered why priests, when saying Mass, would speak Latin—why not Italian? After all, weren't Jesus and the Holy Family Italian?—didn't everyone in the Bible speak Italian? Wasn't Italian the absolute best language in the world?

I attended St. Thomas Acquinas Elementary, the local parochial school taught by an insular tribe of Dominican nuns, assisted by a few token lay-women, overseen by the three or four priests who administered to the Holy Innocents parish. You've heard the stories I'm sure. So there's no need to duplicate them here. Back then, we were all taught by the same limited texts, under the same syllabus of discipline. Indeed, that discipline was quite strict and, in retrospect, often times unnecessary.

The sisters were mirror-images of themselves, dressed in creaseless black floor-length habits with just a trace of white in their bibs—designed, no doubt, to camouflage any semblance of their breasts—and just a bit in their highly starched headpiece too, deeply embedded within their foreheads, and attached to long flowing black veils. Even their arms were covered tightly with fabric all the way down to their wrists; not a trace of human flesh exposed to the public's eye. They wore a simple gold band on their left ring finger—"married to God" they would say. The piercing shrill of those rings slamming against our classroom's blackboard as the sisters called for attention clearly demanded our response, a sound which reverberated down the hallways, echoing hauntingly from classroom to classroom.

The sight of Tommy Heath's nose being smashed into a small chalk circle drawn on the blackboard hasn't yet left me even today. Tommy was caught talking while Sister Regina was out of the room. And Sister vowed to make a spectacle of the young Tommy that day, re-claiming her authority at the same time. So the dreaded circle was drawn and soon covered with the vivid red of the young boy's blood.

Across the hall, Sister Acquinas was slamming young Rodney Hanson's fisted arms into the cinder-block wall as his punishment for talking in an otherwise quiet classroom. He refused to punch the wall on his own—so by positioning herself behind him and using her own vicelike grip on little Rodney's wrists, Sister made sure that the chubby ten-year-old would get his true and just punishment before God, and his fellow classmates.

But it was Sister Rose Marie who was clearly the most intriguing, and perhaps the most disturbed. She continually ran up and down the aisles in agitated silence while she stared and poked and seemed determined to identify the one student who was creating a disturbance in her otherwise sanctified classroom. Fun was made of her by everyone. Many students took creative ingenuity to heart, and used her endless runs up and down the aisles to deliver notes to their fellow students—they would simply pin the note to her veil when Sister's back was turned. And when she again ran down the aisle, the recipient of the note would unfasten the pin, and the great communication was completed. Obviously, Sister soon became the laughingstock of the classroom; she never really knew what the commotion was all about.

One day, Sister Rose Marie rushed to the coat-closet at the back of the room looking for whomever it was she thought she heard talking. Two young boys approached from behind and pushed hard, locking her inside.

Another time, Sister ran down the aisle with such determination that her long strands of rosary beads caught on the edge of a desk—the beads broke free, and scattered and rolled about the room as the entire class laughed. For the first time in our presence, Sister Rose Marie cried—it seemed her deceased father had given her those rosary beads on the day of her vow-taking. It was then when I realized that she too had feelings, and for the first time I shared them. My laughter then quickly turned to sadness, and empathy for her sorrow.

Sister had another responsibility, other than teaching—although somewhat self-appointed, I believe. She would station herself at the urinals in the boy's lavatory each day during recess. She said she was there to ensure the boys did not do evil things with themselves, or with each other. At that time, I was unclear just what she meant. Today, perhaps, I wonder if she stood her vigil for her own very personal reasons. Watching little boys pee—was this what a parochial education was really all about?

Nonetheless, we felt special at St. Thomas—special to be Catholic and special to be attending a Catholic school. That feeling was never more real than on Thursday afternoons when we were released from regular classes to allow students from the local public school an opportunity for religious instruction—the heathens. We had God with us all week long; they only got him on Thursday afternoons.

I walked past them each week with downcast eyes as we were released to board our buses for the drive home to freedom. We played while they studied and learned about Adam and Eve, and St. Christopher—still a saint at that time—and all the good things which we instinctively knew. I wished them well—they would need it—the pagans!

My secondary education was taken at the local public high school, just minutes from our family home. I rejected a scholarship to attend the county's all-boys Catholic high school, or prep school as it was called—I certainly had my fill of Catholicism after nine years at St. Thomas. And so by deciding to attend the more socially popular public high school, I felt I would be better exposed to the realities of life—without having to wear morbid uniforms, or take even more religious classes, or be disciplined by more and more nuns or most likely by the younger men called Brothers of yet another religious order—certainly stronger and I'm sure a bit more determined than St. Thomas' Sisters of the Dominican Order.

But with all of my hopes of an excitingly active social experience at high school, the reality was somewhat disappointing. The years there continued to be quiet and lonely. I had few real friends, boys or girls, and spent a good deal of my time alone. I dreamed often of a future, my future—of being in a far better place, living a far better life—of travel, of meeting new and different people; I dreamed of great and permanent change.

I often fantasized about becoming an explorer—discovering new lands and exotic places which, until then, were quite unknown to me and perhaps even to the world. I would explore our property—under the evergreens and behind the weeping willows—deep within the darkened corners of our basement and creaky attic crawl-space too, imagining it all to be some great new land of secrets. And in a way, it was.

One day, I found something I had not seen before—oddly nestled between our Christmas ornaments and our Italian-style nativity set. A crystal it was, beautifully sphere-shaped—unscarred, like the world. No one knew from where it came; or who might have given it to us. In my mind, at least, it seemed to magically appear, and I felt proud to have been its discoverer.

It was destiny, I was sure. And since I found it, I was responsible for it for the rest of my life. I felt obliged to care for it, to protect it. I loved its natural texture and its solid weight—its touch was always cool and sensual; I stroked it compulsively, and held it often. It became my charm, if you will. And I vowed to keep it with me always.

From then on, imagination alone was my life's own catalyst. Fantasies about my crystal's origin and how it found its way into our attic were vivid and alive. It became a symbol of great adventure for me and of the unknown world I soon hoped to discover. I wondered from what part of the earth it had come, and if it ever knew that its true purpose was to be found by me; to lead me and to guide me through a life of personal growth and great adventure. Surely, it didn't. Yet I would hold that crystal tight with both hands whenever I dreamed of far away lands. It became my magic lamp; my magic carpet. With it, I knew, I could go anywhere I dreamed. With it as my companion, I knew I could be anyone or anything I wanted to be.

And so on this voyage, that crystal was with me—safely protected, well secured, deep within my top cabin drawer—snuggled between my tee shirts, wrapped lightly in the softness of my white cotton briefs. Whenever I was anxious or confused, I felt safe knowing my crystal was with me. And those days, it seemed, I often felt anxious and confused. Whether it was because of Hans' death, or my experience with Vincent—the emotional turmoil was real. And I held that crystal close and often—for utter protection, and for pure emotional strength.

Well out at sea, passengers quickly settled in to the routine of shipboard life—creating their own, very personal, social escapades. And inevitably, those gatherings revolved around alcoholic libation. It was soon apparent that private cocktail parties seemed to be all the rage onboard longer cruises, and *Sagafjord* seemed no different from the rest. Passengers were well focused on hosting one or two during their voyage around the world, and they quickly began the often-times intense preparations for an extensive series of themed soirees—each specifically designed to out do the other in size, and decor, and gastronomic display.

Most of the larger parties were held in the Club Polaris, as this room could most easily be closed off from public access and allow for the desired privacy, almost segregation, each of these gatherings demanded. A host would invite only one's "closest friends"; it became almost a game among the staff to see just how many invitations each of us would receive.

The parties were lavishly produced by the chief steward and his staff, and once a particular theme or decor was determined, it was up to the waiters and barmen to transform the room into the particular fantasy of that evening's host and hostess, and to also ensure its overall success. Scenic elements and props were obtained from the ship's very own storage locker, as well as from various ports of call along the way; some were even fabricated, by hand, by the service staff and their assistants. The results, at times, were breathtaking in the style and detail with which these artists accomplished their hosts' dream. The creativity was theirs, and money, of course, was of no object—the finished product, quite spectacular.

One afternoon, while getting ready for yet another formal evening onboard, I heard the *swoosh* under my cabin door. Something—some notice or staff memo perhaps—was being delivered. The envelope was handwritten—I anxiously tore it open.

Mr. and Mrs. John Stanton
requests the pleasure of your company
for cocktails — Saturday Evening
January 20th, 1973—6:30 P.M.
The Club Polaris.

The Stantons, I knew, were long-time repeat passengers with Norwegian America Line—well liked onboard, and quite well respected. Their reputation as impressive spenders preceded them, and great speculation followed about just how lavish this party—the Stanton's first for this voyage—would be.

Naturally, I was thrilled to be invited to my very first private social function onboard, and no doubt pleased it was the Stanton's. I did wonder, however, why they invited me. They didn't even know me—and in a sense, I thanked God they didn't.

Percy told me that staff members were usually invited to these parties—the Stantons in particular always included the entire social and tour staffs on their invitation list. Nonetheless, Percy's comments didn't lessen my excitement. Passengers as important and Mr. and Mrs. John Stanton thought I was special enough, and important enough, to be included on their invitation list—that's all that mattered. So I looked forward to that day, and gave considerable thought as to which of my two newly purchased tuxedos I would wear.

I arrived at the Polaris promptly at 6:30 P.M., just as the invitation had stated. And naturally, I was the first. Mr. and Mrs. Stanton, though already standing nervously side by side at the entranceway, were ever so gracious to me as I introduced myself. They quickly made me feel comfortable and welcome. I should have known it was considered "chic" to be fashionably late. But I didn't, so I was early—conspicuously so. And as I stood alone at the bar and waited for the other guests to arrive, I smiled to myself at my obvious innocence, and wondered if anyone really cared.

The theme of the Stantons' party was *Tales of the South Pacific*, and so the Club Polaris was transformed into a veritable tropical paradise of exotic and vibrant colors, and lush island splendor. Palm fronds encircled the room, with brightly colored orchids and hibiscus of pastels and earth tones adding just enough accent to give the room a warm and wondrous glow.

The hors d'oeuvres table stood at the center of the dance floor—a gastronomic island in a sea of theatricality; and it too was draped in lush green palm fronds, with white orchids and crimson hibiscus. The various food platters were presented with elegant flare, and beautifully displayed in a manner which offered guests the best of the best—from classic hors d'oeuvres like country patés and shrimp with garlic, to authentic and rather unique south sea island delicacies. Centered on the table—no doubt as conspicuous as I was at this party—but raised just a bit, sitting slightly at an angle, were three large tubs of Beluga caviar, elegantly surrounded by and decorated with the appropriate garnish, of course.

When Percy arrived, he immediately made his way for the bar. I knew he would. A freshly made gin and tonic was set before him by barman Otto even before Percy reached the railing. Although I wasn't sure why, I felt more at ease knowing Percy was there. At least I knew him. Whether or not I liked him was another matter altogether. At that moment though, it seemed unimportant.

"Thank God you're here" I said to Percy as he folded his pocket handkerchief and replaced it ever so properly in his midnight blue tuxedo's breast pocket. "I thought I was going to be the only one."

"No one comes on time, you twit" he said. "Everyone knows that."

Others were beginning to arrive by then at a very steady pace, and the Stantons literally had their hands full greeting everyone at the door. The decibel level of multiple voices and high-pitched laughter rose with increased intensity. Few of the guests actually danced to the live trio's music, but instead moved about the room purposefully and strategically, as if they had specifically choreographed their own individual entrances and exits; as if they believed that all the others in the room were looking only at them.

"This is amazing" I said to Percy. "I've never seen anything like it before."

"It's a bore" Percy answered quickly. He took his first sip, and Vincent's words replayed in my head. "You'll see." He sipped again, and motioned to the guests in the room. "After a few more of these parties, you'll wish you'd never get invited again."

"Well I think it's pretty wonderful" I said.

Percy quickly downed the rest of his gin and tonic and quietly ordered another. He looked anxiously around the room.

"Did you see her?" Percy asked as he leaned a bit closer and whispered in my ear. "Did you get a close look at Mrs. Stanton . . . at the door? That dress! And did you see her face . . . those wrinkles! Like leather." He took one last sip before his glass was swept away and a fresh one was put before him. "I have baggage in better condition than that. Vuitton, of course."

"Oh Percy, come on" I said as I laughed just a bit. "It's not her fault she has wrinkles."

"My dear, *everyone* is responsible for his face" he said.

I encouraged Percy to walk with me to the buffet table. I didn't want to go it alone. As we turned past the bar, I noticed Archibald sitting with three elderly women in one corner of the room. He looked asleep as they spoke to him, his glasses slightly askew on his nose.

There seemed to be some excitement at the door just then—Ted and Anne had finally arrived, making their usually grand entrance.

The caviar was my main interest, having never seen or tried it before. At Percy's instruction, I took up a small piece of toast and spooned out a generous portion, watching closely as Percy did the same.

"Not too much" he snapped as he apparently didn't appreciate my aggressive spooning. "No, we won't be doing that" he continued. "Just a petite portion, please."

My face reddened with embarrassment, I'm sure; but I balanced the toast as he instructed, and added the chopped egg and onion garnish just as Percy had done. I watched him then as he pushed his serving quickly into his mouth, savoring every last bite—rolling his eyes in gastronomic ecstasy.

In pure emulation of my tutor, I did the same. But before it reached my mouth, however, the caviar and all the garnish too, slipped right off the toast, and straight down my shirt sleeve. No one noticed—at least I hoped no one noticed, although I wasn't too sure about Percy. If he did, he gallantly looked away. Naturally, I acted as if nothing had happened. I was too embarrassed to admit to my inexperience. And the caviar, and the egg and the chopped onions too, stayed unacknowledged as well—settling deep within my shirt sleeve until I could comfortably and inconspicuously excuse myself off to the men's room—without further comment.

Later that evening, after dinner and all the usual shipboard festivities had ended, I walked out on deck and stood at the rail, portside. Again, as on most evenings, I found myself alone—choosing to be alone. Wanting it; savoring its safety. For reasons still unknown to me, I was beginning to feel trapped. And unsure. There was much going on around me—the personal pressure; the social pressure. There was so much I did not know, I realized. What I did know, however, was that I was feeling more and more uncomfortable; and I simply wanted to escape.

But that was impossible. Where would I go? Have I always been running and just didn't know it? And if so, just how much longer could I continue?

A cool breeze blew against my face as I looked ahead and out to sea—out towards the islands we were soon to visit. Hawaii. Who would have ever thought I would be traveling to Hawaii? That notion alone was exhilarating, and helped ease my fears.

Thoughts of Vincent still haunted me. It was reprehensible what I had done.

From my earliest memory of school days back home, I remembered how, when boys disliked other boys, they called them fags or homos, and everyone laughed and ran from them—they ran and ran, as far as they could.

I had seen photographs of them in Greenwich Village on the cover of *Newsweek* just after the Stonewall Riots of the late 1960s with the title *Homosexuality in America*. They looked seedy, and effeminate. They just weren't normal. They just didn't look as I had wanted them to look. Some had shoulder-length hair with purses flung over their shoulders, while others cavorted in dresses and make-up and high heels and beards.

I felt disgusted then after seeing those pictures; and I felt disgusted thinking about what I had done with Vincent. And I feared, if by just that one act, I had become one of them.

Yet at the same time, I was intrigued and exhilarated—for what, though, I was still unsure. No matter how much I tried, I could not get Vincent out of my mind; I could not forget the excitement—the beauty—of what we had shared. In a way, it was our own very special secret; no one needed to know.

I remembered a time when I was much younger—at home, alone. I was in my older brother's bedroom ruffling through his books and magazines which he kept securely under his bed. There, amongst his dated copies of *Playboy*, I discovered a tattered edition of *Everything You've Always Wanted to Know About Sex But Were Afraid to Ask*. Indeed, a gold mine for a child my age.

I found "homosexuality" in the index. And not surprisingly,

few kind words were written by that author about those very people; the author writing in quite off-putting detail about the debased life of a homosexual—lonely, sad, pitiful. He wrote of a nameless emergency room doctor who recounted the story of one young man who was admitted to his care—it appeared a foreign object was lodged deep within his rectum—a whisky glass it was. The doctor described how he carefully and skillfully had to flip the glass around so that it could be removed more easily, narrow bottom out first.

Queers they were called, and everyone willingly did. It seemed to be the only universal agreement among the people I knew. Queers, fairies, fags, homos, cock suckers, sodomites—on and on the name calling continued. People just instinctively seemed to know those words and how to use them derogatorily, without, I'm certain, ever really knowing a queer, fairy, fag, homo, cock sucker or sodomite—or indeed without really knowing the person to whom they were referring. They just did it; they just called them names. It was fun. It was cool. But why? From where did that hatred come? On what was such contempt really based?

Until stepping onboard *Sagafjord*, I had never even seen a homosexual, at least not knowingly. Yet I would never have thought of calling anyone a name with that much hatred, with that much violence attached to it, without first thinking about what I was saying, and to whom I was saying it; and why I felt the need to be so hateful and so degrading to another person in the first place.

What actually made someone a homosexual, I wondered? What did it really mean? Was he someone who spends his whole life in pursuit of other men with whom to have sex? Or was it someone who just once, and only once, had a sexual experience with another man purely for the sexual release—just to see what it might be like? Or was it someone, in fact, who simply preferred the camaraderie of other men?

I had read how commonplace it was for boys to experiment sexually with each other during early adolescence. That was normal, the article had said, and indeed quite harmless. But if that behavior continued throughout adulthood—well that, then, was clearly something else.

But what was it?

Percy and Archibald, and Lar and the others too, were not bad men. If they weren't so open about their sexuality and their numerous escapades, one would never know that they themselves were homosexual. And after getting to know them individually and in depth, who could ever even think of calling them such hateful names and shun them and embarrass them so, just because of their sexual nature? Would those same people call me such names after that one experience with Vincent? Clearly, I couldn't be categorized with all the others. I was different.

Yes, I was alone onboard, and perhaps a bit starved for companionship—having never really had the typical male fraternity that most young men undoubtedly enjoy from playing together on sports teams and from other scholastic organizations which unconsciously encourage and promote male bonding. Perhaps the sex I had had with Vincent was just a way to achieve that camaraderie. Perhaps it was way of getting to be his friend, to be close to him. Obviously, it was what he wanted. And if it meant having to have sex with him—as easy and as innocent as just a couple of guys getting together and masturbating, just as I'm sure they would do anyway, alone—well what was the problem? It wasn't that big a deal, after all. It certainly wasn't as serious or as complicated as having sex with a woman. We would just be fooling around a bit—just the guys. Playing together. Nothing serious. Getting to know one another a bit better. It would just happen. Like with Vincent. And it would mean nothing. Nothing at all.

The new waiter assigned to our dining room table was called Franz. And I could quickly see that he was a bit flamboyant—quite swishy, as Percy would say.

Oh no, I thought. I'm never going to escape this. Never.

But Franz was quite personable and pleasant—and, I must say, very good at his job. Luncheon that day was served hot and on time, and everyone at our table received exactly what he had ordered.

"He'll be gone soon" Lar said to us.

"What do you mean?" I defensively shot back. "He just got

here."

"He's too good. Once they see how good Franz really is, they'll pull him away and give him to the passengers." Lar then turned towards Franz and motioned him over.

"Would you do us a favor?" Lar asked. "You see, you're quite a good waiter Franz; I'm sure you already know that. And we'd like to keep you. Would you like to stay with us?"

"Yes, I think so" Franz replied. "I'd much rather serve you than the passengers. At least you're fun . . . and young. And I'll know what my tips are going to be." He rolled his eyes back and off to one side.

"Good" Lar said. "And we'd like to have you."

"Oh, would you now" Franz said with a smile, quite filled with double entendres.

"Now stop that Franz-y" Lar laughed with a chuckle. "You know very well what I mean. What we'd like you to do is to slow up a bit. You know, don't let the chief steward see that you're such a good waiter, at least not for now. You see, we're afraid he'll take you away from us. Off to the passengers, you know. And you certainly wouldn't want that."

"Heaven's no!" Franz said while he lightly placed his hand over his heart as if his breath had just been taken away. "Danke—thank you. I'll try harder to be lousy, if that is the English word?"

We laughed at the irony of it all as Franz then walked towards Ted and Anne's table offering second cappuccinos.

"He's been here before, you know—onboard *Sagafjord*" Per whispered to us after Franz was out of hearing distance. "He just returned to the ship. I'm told he had to take several weeks off to have some surgical stitches—is that what you call them?—sewn in his ass. Can you imagine the size of the last guy who fucked him?"

Laughter erupted from everyone at our table, except of course, from me. I couldn't believe they would joke about such things, even discuss them at all. And how did they find out these details about other peoples' personal lives in the first place? I certainly did not know. I certainly did not want to know.

I realized then, that at all costs, I had to insure that my relationship with Vincent was kept an absolute secret. I shuddered in horror at what could and would happen if it ever got out. I would be the laughing stock of the tour office, no doubt. I only hoped Vincent was being as discreet as I, wherever the hell he was.

And then I had a thought. A way to throw them all off the track. It was obvious just what I needed to do before any gossip could start up about me. I had to find a girlfriend onboard—perhaps a cabin stewardess not unlike my very own Bruni. Clearly, that would prevent them from thinking that I, too, might be homosexual, and it would certainly eradicate my personal guilt and disgust; it would certainly stop any more insecure thoughts —about me, and about my life. It was perfect, and I needed to do it soon, to retain and maintain my own good sanity.

One morning at breakfast, Archibald presented me with a copy of *The Emperor's Throne*—his epic history of the Moguls of India and the building of the Taj Mahal. The book had only just been published three months earlier. And it was clear that Archibald was very proud of it indeed.

I had seen the colorful volume quite often around the ship—in the gift shop, in the ship's library, and in the hands of many passengers out on deck too. It was required reading for both passengers and staff alike as a prerequisite for our upcoming visit to India. And whenever it was in view, Archibald found every opportunity to make it—and himself—the center of conversation.

I love books; indeed, I'm what you would call a compulsive reader; a hopeless bibliophile. So I was quite pleased to receive his gift. I had planned to purchase it myself—my knowledge of Indian history was extremely limited. I knew it would be a perfect informational source. No doubt, Archibald did as well. He knew I needed the support; and the education.

But yet, as I held the book in my hands that morning, I wondered if by accepting his gift, I would be falsely encouraging Archibald in some way. I didn't want to be indebted to him for anything, for fear that he may, at some time along the way, want to collect.

"It's a brilliant book, even if I do say so myself" Archibald said as I paged through it quickly. "I wrote it on my kitchen table you know, in my little monk's cell on 22nd street. I showed the first draft to my best friend Dick Asher—he hated it and said it was garbage." Archibald looked sad as he recounted for me what must have been a very traumatic time in his life.

"So I came right home and cried. And after that nonsense was all over with, do you know what I did? I became determined to prove Dick wrong. I threw it all away—the entire manuscript—and started again. Needless to say, I was thrilled when my agent called to say she had sold my book. Can you imagine that? *My* book!"

He was quiet for a moment as he, I'm sure, savored that thought.

"Do you like the dust jacket? Do you think it's too busy?"

I have to admit that I spent many a night onboard *Sagafjord* snuggled safely in A-54—bed covers pulled up closely to my chest—with *The Emperor's Throne* well in hand. And through it's pages, my respect for Archibald was further solidified. It was a remarkable book; totally engrossing. His words brought to life an entire world full of lavishly dramatic scenes and bigger-than-life characters previously hidden from my limited historical perspective. The more I read, the more I wanted to know about Shah Jahan and the magnificent Taj; about the spiritualism, the politics, and the cultural makeup of these very unique and mysterious people. The man who authored this work, I knew, was truly unusual—a master of words, a sorcerer of understanding. And here . . . onboard *Sagafjord*... we found ourselves, traveling the world together.

Our Pacific transit continued. We sailed on closer to the Hawaiian Islands, with the great Asian continent just over the horizon.

The nights that followed were long and silent, although Ted Jones and his staff did their best to produce what they considered to be an interesting and varied entertainment program. Of us all, however, the busiest seemed to be the dancing boys, who kept the ladies moving about the dance floor as best they could. They would entertain them with drinks, or some times just conversation; or with anything else the ladies might feel would be entertainingly appropriate.

And it was then that I realized that something had changed in our day-to-day responsibilities; and thankfully so. By this time in the voyage, it was somehow understood that the tour office staff would no longer be required to dance or to socialize with passengers when off duty. Lar made that fact quite clear, especially to Cruise Director Ted Jones, as well as to Captain Brookstad. Our main responsibility, Lar said, was tour sales, planning, and operations. Often, our preparation time was in direct conflict with cocktail hours and after-dinner dances. Whether or not this was the actual truth was not questioned, just accepted. And when once in a great while, we did assist with the socializing, we instantly became *Sagafjord*'s fair haired boys.

Information about the ship's nightly entertainment, and all other shipboard activities as well, was listed daily in *The Cruise News*—a simply written schedule of events and announcements authored by the cruise director or his assistant Hal Carter, and produced onboard by Swiss printer Bobby Venn. And one performance featured during this transit was *An Evening with Gennifer Gray—The Girl with the Velvet Voice.*

I knew little about Gennifer, having seen her rarely around the ship since sailing day from New York. Where she hid those last weeks, I never really knew. Although periodically, she would visit the tour office solely, it seemed, to giggle and to laugh in a never-ending private joke with Percy—something about having a long-lost "sister in Ceylon." Both Percy and Gennifer would giggle like school girls whenever it was mentioned, with Gennifer's long and harshly auburn hair bouncing up and down, and from side to side. She scrunched her lips together, and spoke the words over and over again, with a pinched sort of confinement—"my sister in Ceylon."

The only other time I saw Gennifer about the ship was one afternoon by the pool. I pulled a deck chair over to where Per Villand, Philip Pound, Gennifer Gray and Marshall Smith were seated. I had to. It would have been rude not to join them—although I naturally preferred to sit alone, nearer the rail. It was still lunch break, and the only free time—at sea at least—that the tour staff had to sit on deck and take some sun. I forced my eyes shut and stayed mostly to myself, not really wanting to enter into conversation with any of them. Yet I couldn't help but get swept up in their silly chatter and their nonsensical childish laughter. It became clear from the conversation that Gennifer Gray and Marshall Smith were far better friends than I had first thought—Marshall telling her about a small house just left to him by his recently deceased mother. He first described its quaint cottage-like design—then in somewhat greater detail, talked about its location in an area called the Pines on Fire Island—a place up until then quite unknown to me.

"Hey, Marshall" Philip yelled from across the deck. "Did you hear about the Martian who landed on Fire Island and got blown to bits?"

Everyone laughed—except me of course. I understood not a word. It made no sense.

Later that night, Percy told me that Fire Island was infamous as a summer retreat for homosexuals. "Blown to bits" then took on an entirely new meaning.

Gennifer Gray walked onstage after a brief overture by the Walesky Orchestra. She wore a simple white evening dress—its blousy effect covering her all too matronly figure quite well. She carried her guitar with her too. She always had her guitar with her—for all I knew, she could have been going to another staff meeting.

Gennifer's repertoire that evening contained mostly popular American folk songs of the time, and some easy listening music too—trying her best to utilize her coloratura soprano to its fullest.

But in an abrupt and quite unexpected turn of events, she set aside her guitar and began her finale—the magnificent aria *Un Bel Dei* from Puccini's *Madame Butterfly*.

Needless to say, Gennifer's voice just could not command the strength and the control needed for such a difficult and well-known piece. She got through it though, somehow, and ended her performance with a brief encore—a clap-along rendition of *He's Got the Whole World in His Hands*.

The polite applause she received would have subsided tastefully if Ted Jones hadn't milked it for all it was worth. Poor Gennifer came out for two additional bows, while Ted urged the audience on. Poor Gennifer. Poor us.

Although I had been interested in theatre and the entertainment arts since early childhood, the unprofessionalism of the shows onboard ship made them far from enjoyable. They seemed produced out of pure desperation and selfishness rather than inspired creative ability; all too amateurish for my tastes. So I avoided them as much as I could.

But it wasn't just the evening entertainment programs which seemed to depress me then, it was the contrived atmosphere in the Ballroom overall—the folksiness that Ted and his staff tried desperately to create. It all seemed tragically forced. As if he was trying to make us feel as one big loving family—and we were not. As if we were, in a way, all responsible for what he and his staff had created; and therefore, out of sheer politeness, we'd have to support the effort fully. It was unnatural. It was blatantly dishonest. And it never stopped. For me, and I'm sure for the others too, the social atmosphere onboard was becoming uncomfortably confining, flagrantly mendacious.

More and more, I found that I wanted and needed time alone, away from people, and away from work. So while most of those onboard spent their evenings listening to the illustrious Gennifer Gray or to some other such performer, I became a near recluse in A-54.

I read. I held my crystal and thought about my life. And I began a journal—not only to keep my mind alert and alive, but to record and to document these new and mysterious feelings I was feeling, and the unnerving anxiety which so oftentimes accompanied them.

My cabin, though, was not my only haven. I took many evenings on the open deck. Most often, I found myself at the furthest forward point of Upper Deck—the very peak of *Sagafjord's* bow. This area, just forward of the crew's swimming pool, was stark and open . . . fully exposed, naked to the world. It was an area well crowded with winches and cranes, and heavy ropes neatly coiled in circles like satanic serpents waiting to strike at our next port of call.

At night, at sea however, this area of the deck was deserted—dark and quiet, with only the indefatigable sounds of the Pacific as accompaniment. So it was mine alone. I claimed it. It stood as my promontory, mystically bathed in the crisp cool light of the moon. I would walk forward, to the very edge of the deck, carefully feeling my way as I went, to sit on the bulwark and stare out to sea. The intense pressure of the wind against my body was exhilarating. It gave me strength—something which I felt I desperately needed at that time in my life.

At times, I had to brace myself securely so as not to be swept overboard. Those moments were frightening; a thrill of terror, if you will. A thrill which brought me back again and again, night after night, to alone stand my vigil.

I searched the sea for hours—for what, I was not sure. But I knew I could not be bored or anxious there. The sea alone was calming. It continually changed, and yet it was changeless. I watched its movement and heard its sounds. The rhythmic pounding of the waves against *Sagafjord's* steel bow as it swiftly and sometimes silently, without announcement, sliced through the sea ahead, became a life-giving pulse; it stimulated me with an electronic jolt of unknown energy.

And as I sat there, night after night, I found myself surrounded by another sea as well—an ocean of stars, brilliantly perforating the endless black of night. An uncountable number of stars which I knew very well had always been there throughout all lifetimes, and yet seemed to reveal themselves only then, and only to me, on those very special nights, at those very special times. The darkened sky above would become a massive yet intimate dome of sorts, embracing me and the world. It sealed us together within a pocket of security; a universal serenity.

I wondered too about yet another world—the one deep below; beneath us at that very moment. Indeed that was a world incomprehensible to me, inconceivable. One looks out over the railing of a ship to see an endless sea stretching far to the horizon and beyond. But do we really know very much about those continually ceaseless waters—a liquid skin stretched over a silent body whose limits are limitless? Life within its depths was no doubt plentiful, and just as valid as anything we know in our own world—perhaps even as intelligent, and even, in its own way, as sophisticated. But we understood so little of that world. Most of us hardly even cared. But I wanted to know. I had to know more—because I never felt as exhilarated as I did when I was alone with the sea.

One night, I stood my post looking west, directly into our ship's path. I held my crystal firmly; the wind, unusually still. It created the illusion that the ship was stationary while the sea shifted about beneath her. *Sagafjord* existed merely as a speck upon the ocean; she was totally at its mercy. We were an insignificant and insular world of our own, creating our own existence and our own self-made importance as we continued along our way. The world could end, and there we would remain—sailing along, never again able to touch land. Essentially, we were cut off from society and civilization. We knew nothing of the world's reality, only our own, yet they both existed simultaneously.

I thought about time. How did we know that we were not transcending time, at least time as we knew it? Perhaps we were sailing into a different era, a different century, as so many films and science fiction stories have often depicted—and that the Honolulu we would soon visit would be the Honolulu of 1860, or perhaps 2050. These thoughts gave me a feeling of hopelessness and frustration; of total insignificance. They also gave birth to incredible feelings of strength and power—an endowment of the endless possibilities of beginning anew. Starting again. In a new time; a new place.

In a way, it was overwhelming. At one moment, I felt I was nothing—insignificant in relation to everything and everyone; yet at the same time, I became everything there was to be.

And suddenly, I sensed I was not alone. Behind me, I saw no one. Yet, indeed, the presence was strong. I knew someone was there. I felt I was being watched. I shifted my position and twisted around. I was frightened, but the sea gave me strength.

Yet just as I felt I should return to the safety of A-54, I heard his voice.

"Incredible, isn't it?"

The words came forth from the windy darkness. I was startled to hear but see no one near me. Instantly, I resented whomever it was who dared intrude in to my own private place.

"It's me—Arne" he said.

His figure, a bit clearer now, stepped around the deckhouse and out of the shadows. He laughed his Nordic laugh and quickly sat down next to me, leaning his back against the bulkhead.

Arne's closeness brought us both some warmth, a much welcomed protection from the cooler night's wind.

Together, hidden in the darkness, I learned a good deal about Arne that night. It seemed as if we had spoken for hours—and most likely, we did.

Arne Christiansen was from Denmark—a town called Roskilde, just one hour's drive west of Copenhagen. It was where he still lived, he told me, although he had—at twenty two—already left his father's home and had taken a small studio flat just minutes from downtown. Arne's father was curator of the Roskilde Cathedral and Museum—the Cathedral itself dating back to the late 17th century. His mom was a typical Danish house-wife—very giving and very caring, always cleaning—endlessly in the kitchen.

Arne's dream was to have an inn of his own. He had the spot all picked out too, he told me—an 18th century farmhouse in the city of Aarhus, located on the European mainland—the Jutland peninsula—just one quick ferry ride from Copenhagen. Arne's vision became grander as he spoke—at first, describing a quaint village café; and before we both knew it, his dream had expanded into a one-of-a-kind guest house with accompanying gourmet restaurant.

"You have to feature the 18th century look" he said. "Restore it well. That's the secret." And his eyes widened with childlike wonder as he described, in the smallest of details, his own Nordic dream.

Arne had signed onboard *Sagafjord* after seeing an advertisement in a Danish newspaper offering "worldwide travel and good pay." He was not disappointed, although the bulk of his "good pay" came not from Norwegian America Line itself, but from the very generous gratuities offered by the wealthy passengers onboard.

Arne told the story of Chief Steward Bjorn Anderson who, for several years, had been personal escort to Gretal Heckettson whenever she was onboard—which, as I've already mentioned, was most of the time. Mrs. Heckettson seemed most appreciative of Anderson's attentions over the years. On one particular arrival at Oslo in fact, a new Mercedes sedan awaited him on the pier, as a very special thank you from the grateful Gretal Heckettson.

"That's pretty unusual" Arne said. "I'm just hoping for my pay and the usual tips. That's all I expect. When I signed onboard, I figured I'd be able to save enough money for the downpayment on the inn in a year or two. I'm almost there. This trip should do it."

He sat quietly for a moment.

"But I do hope for a bit more. Especially now that I've been assigned to Mrs. Heckettson's table for the rest of the voyage."

I envied Arne as he spoke. He, after all, had a dream; a clear passion in his life. His little Danish inn was what he lived and worked for. And Bruni and Gerhard—they had their dream too. Where was my dream? What did I want in my life? What was my passion?

Since earliest childhood, my dream had always been to travel the world by ship. And here I was—having fulfilled that dream so early in life. How lucky I was, or was I really lucky at all?

The only thing worse than not getting what you want is getting it, Archibald once told me. And those words have haunted me ever since. I got it; and now what?

What happens to you once you've seen your rainbow; achieved your dream? Perhaps you create new dreams, because you begin to realize that your dreams—your passions—may not have been what you thought they were in the first place. And you want more; you want different. But what was the "more" and the "different" I now wanted?

Arne glowed as he spoke of his girlfriend back home. Liz was pretty, he said, and very sweet too; and she planned to move with him to Aarhus as soon as he returned home.

"And you, my friend? Do you have a girlfriend?"

Naturally, I panicked.

"Sure I do" I quickly answered, knowing full well that a hesitation of any sort would create doubts in Arne's mind. It would have tipped my hand. I was never a convincing liar, and I despised myself whenever I felt compelled or trapped into telling untruths.

"She's back in New York. Real pretty too. Her name's Donna" I anxiously searched for the name of a high school friend's sister in whom I was completely disinterested.

"That's wonderful" Arne said, and smiled—pronouncing his "w's" with the typically Scandinavian "v" sound. "I'm sure you miss her a lot."

Oh, yes Arne, if it were only true.

The night was clear and the air crisp. I shifted my direction a bit, to better shield the wind.

We talked about the ship, and life onboard, and of course the tragic death of Hans just days before. Arne told me about B-Deck—crew deck as it was called—and about life among the ship's crew.

"There's a recreation room for us with a record player in it, and a ping pong table too. Someday we'll sneak you down to see it—if you want. But other than that, there's not much to do when we're not working." He shook his head. "We're not allowed to drink onboard, so we can't even get drunk. Except when its smuggled in. That happens once in a while. But it's always found out, and the guys get shit. Sometime ago, some members of the cruise staff used to buy liquor for us, but they got into a lot of trouble and were put off the ship. Now, we're not allowed to talk to the staff at all, unless its business."

"But you're talking with me now" I said with a smile.

"Yeah" he said. "Screw them. Anyway, this is different. Besides, no one's around. And what they don't know won't hurt them." We both laughed.

The crew, he told me, bunked four to a cabin—the men were assigned the larger and more forward area on B-Deck, while the women were confined to the much smaller section aft. The cafeteria and crew recreation room separated the two sexes both physically and psychologically—a bunting board of sexual wills, protecting each gender from the other.

"You're lucky you can eat in the Dining Room" Arne said. "You should have a meal in the crew cafeteria sometime . . . just once. Nothing but fish balls all the time. I think that's all those square heads eat . . . fish balls."

"Square heads?" I said, not sure what he was talking about.

"Norwegians" Arne answered. "Don't you know? When they go for a haircut, its twenty-five cents a corner. It's a bit of a nasty term, I admit. I guess I shouldn't use it, since we're all Scandinavians and all. I learned it from some American guy."

Somehow, I was not surprised.

"But it's true" Arne continued. That's all it seems they to want to eat is fish balls. Doesn't that sound a bit square to you?"

Arne and I continued to laugh together; in fact, we giggled like children that night. We were as two boys at play—skimming verbal rocks over an imagined lake, mutually nurtured by our innocence.

Indeed, what does one do when one achieves his dream? My dream was right in front of me. A new friend. That's what it was.

That's what I wanted. It felt good to have Arne with me that night—even in my very special and very private place. He was fun to be with, and the more I got to know him, the more I liked him, just as I knew I would. It was becoming increasingly—painfully—clear that I wanted and needed friendship—perhaps *his* friendship—on this long voyage, more than anything else.

The next morning, I awoke early. I didn't want to miss a moment of our arrival. As I reached Sun Deck, the island loomed before us. A massive giant, asleep in the distance—the sun silently smiling from the east. It created a silhouette of sorts, and crystallized the mist into a shimmering glaze over the land and the sea.

Silently, *Sagafjord* moved closer to her destination—cautiously, pensively, as a tiger stalks its prey. The volcanic Diamond Head seemed a bit out of place so close to the edge of the sea; the pure white sands and the surf and the palms extended out from its base, offering the illusion of limitless vision.

Waikiki was its name, and its grand yet diminutive setting in relation to Diamond Head recalled a far earlier memory—the illusive Yellow Brick Road leading up to the majestic and quite distant Emerald City.

Downtown Honolulu filtered slowly through the haze. I saw modern high-rises towering above busily trafficked streets, surrounded by the lush tropical landscape I vividly imagined.

We tied up alongside Aloha Tower, the terminal usually assigned to visiting passenger vessels. I received my first "lai" as I disembarked that morning—beautifully woven from delicate violet and pink orchids. I kept that lai fresh for days after our visit—soaking in water in my bathroom sink. I didn't want it to die.

That first morning on Hawaii, I was assigned to escort the three-hour city tour *Honolulu and Environs*. The haunting opening tune from the TV show *Gilligan's Island* continually played over and over in my head: " . . . a three-hour tour . . . a three-hour tour."

The buses were loaded quite easily that morning, and off we went, very much on schedule.

The bus I was assigned that morning was quite full—every seat taken—so comfort was set aside. I began to see some unfamiliar faces on this one—those who had not yet toured in Panama or Acapulco. Although Mrs. Woodward was with us, as was a woman I recognized as one of Marshall Smith's bridge regulars.

The sun had quickly burned off the morning's mist, and the city now revealed itself in crystal clarity.

We first visited the Iolani Palace which, as our local guide explained, was built in 1882 by King Albert Kalakaua. Then, we were off to the Judiciary Building which encircled the famous statue of Kamehameha, still proudly wearing his yellow feather cloak. The cloak, we were told, was a replica however—the original was in the Bishop's Museum which, unfortunately, we were unable to visit.

We drove slightly out of town then to the famous Punchbowl, an extinct volcanic crater. One just had to stand in its center for an incredible view of the entire city, and beyond.

Just adjacent to the Punchbowl was the Pacific National Memorial Cemetery where many of the victims of the Pearl Harbor attack were buried. And surrounding us were endless fields of lush green grass, tightly dotted with plain-white crosses—far too many to make our visit pleasurable; a green and white quilt it was, stitched proudly with the blood of heroes. For the first time in my life, that infamous attack was real—not just a tale of excitement and valor found only in history books, safely read in the comfort of one's library. Standing before those graves, one couldn't help but be swept away by the emotion of that tragedy, by the enormity of it all. There was a silence from our passengers as I saw in their eyes the memories of family and other loved ones who may have been a part of the group those white crosses represented.

Back at the ship, with a full afternoon and evening free, I decided to do something special for my one and only night ashore in Honolulu. Although reluctant to venture off on my own, at night, deep within a city with which I was unfamiliar, I was willing to make a go of it . . . throw caution to the wind, if you will. But when Lar and Percy invited me to join them ashore for dinner, I was secretly relieved; I eagerly accepted.

We jumped in a cab at the pier's end, and headed south along the beach to dine at a local Chinese restaurant—a favorite of Percy's in which, I was told, he ordered only sweet and sour pork. Together, we spent a leisurely, and quite uneventful evening together. It was the very first time I felt at all comfortable in their company. And for once, and thankfully so, the conversation was nothing but routine, with discussions about the cruise ahead, and the longer overland tours still to come.

After dinner however, it was a different matter. Before returning to the ship, Percy and Lar suggested we stop for a quick drink at a local club they both knew. They wanted me to join them; I couldn't say no, even if I'd wanted to. I didn't know where the hell I was; I had no other way of getting back to the ship, unless of course, I wanted to make my way alone.

So together, we ventured off on foot further dockside, deep into an area of enigmatic darkness—quite reminiscent of the back-water port cities I had read about in exotic mystery novels, often portrayed in classic black and white films. I instinctively knew I had made a mistake when, as we turned a corner, Lar and Percy both acknowledged we had arrived. Actually, I think they too were relieved we were safe. I was sure no living creature survived in these alleys for long.

Harshly colored neon tubes—faded and degraded by time and the elements—flashed on and off as we entered the establishment; the shattered "H" from one in particular flickered uncontrollably, a spastic muscle awaiting release.

Once inside, it took a minute or two for my eyes to adjust; the air, clouded by a much heavier darkness, had been tainted, no doubt, by years of cigarette smoke. The layers were indelible, like a ripe onion's skin. Loud music blasted from an unknown source; tired spotlights were barely focused at a minute staging area on which two scantily clad women danced. A true sailor's retreat, if I ever saw one. It was such a cliché, after all. Why the hell, I wondered, would Lar and Percy—the oh-so-elegant Percy Hayes—want to visit such a sordid place?

We sat at the bar and I ordered a beer—drinking from the bottle as I recalled Vincent had done. For some unknown reason—important just for that moment—it was imperative that I show Percy and Lar how well I could handle being in such a bizarre environment; perhaps let them know I could even enjoy it as well. Who was I kidding? I was always a terrible liar.

The noise was so deafening we could hardly speak. So we stood together in silence—Percy, Lar and I—drinks in hand, searching the room with only our eyes.

Within minutes we were joined by Peter Steiner, one of *Sagafjord's* two wine stewards. Just about my age, Peter was Austrian, attractive in his very own way, and warmly personable—always pleasant and friendly—at least with me. As we spoke, it became apparent that both Lar and Percy knew Peter well, and had been out with him on other occasions.

Peter's presence was reassuring. Seeing someone else from *Sagafjord* in such an odd place made me feel a good deal more comfortable, a bit safer. At least we weren't alone. At least if we were killed—throats viciously slit, or brutally bludgeoned to death for that matter—someone like Peter Steiner, the wine steward, would be witness to our murder—no doubt in the alley behind the bar of course. At least he'd inform the ship. I didn't want to be left ashore in some unknown city, shut up in a steel drawer like they did to poor Hans. Thank God for Peter the wine steward, I thought. Thank God he was there.

A woman walked towards us just then; and naturally, she decided to approach me. Her appearance could not be misconstrued.

"Hey cutie" she slurred. I nodded to her, quickly turning my back to face Percy and the others. I became instantly nervous, her presence made me sweat. I didn't want to see her—I didn't want to look at her—let alone talk with her.

She stood to my left, brushing up against me slightly, perhaps a bit incredulous at my response of great indifference.

In the dimmed crimson glow, she appeared to be about thirty years old, with trawled-on makeup and glistening black hair which fell straight to her naval. A severly cut mini skirt just barely did its job; her blouse was cut low, hardly concealing her proudly displayed breats.

Slowly, the woman edged her way around my barstool, ostensibly dancing to the rhythms of the beat. Finally, she stood directly before me—cutting me off from Percy and the others. She spoke again, this time having to raise her voice a notch over the blaring musical riffs. Between her words, she seductively twirled a red swizzle stick over her tongue—moving it in and out; the moist invitation hidden deeply between her lips.

"Out for some fun tonight, cutie?" she continued, no doubt hoping to be provocative, clearly quite repulsive. "Hey cutie—don't you want to talk with Gina?"

I focused ahead and continued to ignore her, hoping to God she would just get the message and move the fuck away. Why wasn't she bothering Percy or Lar, I wondered? Why me? What the hell did I have that they didn't? It couldn't be youth—there were clearly many men of my age all over this club. Maybe she knew, I wondered. Maybe she knew Percy and Lar were homosexual. They wouldn't be interested in her, after all. So she zeroed in on me. She knew I wasn't like them. She just knew it.

The peculiar way Percy and Lar reacted to all this made me suspicious, and angry too. I wondered for a moment if this was just what they wanted—for me to be embarrassed; for me to be completely intimidated. Maybe that was the reason we were here after all. Maybe this whole evening was a setup. I truly hated them for it.

"Hey. I know"—she jumped up as she spoke. "How about a dance?" She grabbed my hands and attempted to pull me up and off my barstool.

"C'mon. Don't you want to dance with Gina? You look like you could use a good dance." I heard the others laughing as they passively looked on. Help was what I needed, not laughter. Get this woman away from me, I telepathically pleaded.

I was disgusted by it all. A whore—a prostitute, no doubt. I wanted to throw up. I couldn't believe this was happening. I didn't want her touching me; I felt dirty, and nearly as repulsive as she appeared.

The woman continued her aggressive advances—persistent little devil that she was—never accepting my stoic silence as a clear sign of utter disinterest.

In what might be considered a final attempt, and perhaps full witness of her futile tenacity, she grandly withdrew the red swizzle stick from her lips—now quite wet with saliva, gleaming in the shallow light—and rubbed it directly, strategically, against my penis. The action was quite obvious; the result, less so. No matter what her intention was, the last thing I could have achieved just then was an erection—big and strong, and ready to go.

"Just *what* are you doing? Get away from me." I said strongly, yet somewhat cautiously. I took my chances. I didn't quite know how she would react to such blatant rejection.

"Well fuck off then" she shouted angrily.

Done—I had gotten my way. She threw her swizzle stick down at my feet; its still wet tip shining like a star from the grimy floor beneath us. "You fucking faggot" she shot back as she turned and walked off. She flipped her hair while well enroute, no doubt, to her next unknowing victim . . . aah . . . client.

"What's the matter?" Lar asked sarcastically. "Wasn't she your type?" Percy and Peter laughed.

"Let's get the hell out of here." I pleaded. "This place is disgusting." I don't think I had ever been more definite in my life.

"Wait" Percy responded. "We can't leave just yet. We haven't seen the show."

"What show? I'm not staying for any show."

"Oh but you must" Lar shot back. "It's nothing like Ted and Anne's, I can tell you." I noticed Peter smiling from behind. "As soon as the show is over, we'll go."

"We promise" Percy added, as he slowly sipped his fresh pint of Guinness.

And then it began, as if on cue. It was a type of burlesque it seemed—sleazy women moving about the stage, removing bits of clothing with each musical phrase. A striptease; what the hell was going on, I wondered. Why the hell would Percy and Lar want to see women taking off their clothes?

The music continued loudly, abrasively, and the clothes came off—what little there was in the first place. I was angry and uncomfortable. I wanted to go home.

The patrons were into it though, no doubt. They whooped and hollered and cheered with enthusiasm—Percy and Lar and Peter Steiner too. Thankfully though, the artists seemed to be quickly building to their finale, and within minutes, the drum roll came. The women reached awkwardly behind themselves as they sleazed and slithered and simultaneously undid their tops. The finale chord sounded. The cymbal crashed, and off they came.

Nothing. No tits. The women were men. Damn it! I knew that Percy and Lar wouldn't have gone into a real men's bar. It was a drag bar, we were in. A homosexual bar.

Everyone around me screamed and whistled in full admiration as the performers grandly returned for their final bow. I wanted to scream too, but not in salute of their artistic accomplishment.

As the applause continued, I looked around the room and finally realized that all the women in the club were men. Even the woman who pushed her saliva-soaked swizzle deep against me. The perspiration came quickly, yet I stayed quiet. Yes, I hated them that night—Percy and Lar—for bringing me to that place. Why did they do it, I asked myself. What amusement did it really give them?

Later, safely back in my cabin, I showered with the hottest water I could stand—just as I had done after my illusive evening with Vincent—as if the continual flow of steaming hot water would cleanse me of the horrid memories of that place and those people. As I dried myself off, and slipped softly between my sheets, I realized we had already left port, the lights of Honolulu slowly drifted past my porthole.

Thank God for my lei, I thought—its fresh blossoms still rested peacefully and quite innocently in my bathroom sink; sweetly nurtured by an inch of fresh water. It was all that remained of a vivid Hawaiian visit; a symbol of a land I had only wished I experienced. The only pleasant memory of a day I wanted so much to forget.

The long and tedious crossing from Honolulu to Yokohama began and continued in miserable weather. The sea was an endless gray; rain fell intermittently during the entire twelve days. The ship rolled and creaked in constant motion, although not nearly as it had during our pre-Acapulco storm. Nonetheless it created an inescapable uncomfortableness; and naturally, our moods were greatly affected.

Archibald had made it a practice to visit the Tour Office each morning at sea before his scheduled lecture. He would gaily bounce up to the selling counter, working his way behind the waist-high separation for a brief chat with Lar. Any updated tour information Lar received by telex or cable during the previous night would then become a part of that day's port talk—itinerary and or schedule changes often arrived from the various local port agents along our route.

Archibald was at his best during morning hours; his conversation vibrant, frequently shot with color and enthusiasm. His words, however, often seemed immobile and out of place, as if he existed solely within his own insular world; his conversations taking place only with himself. Often, it appeared, his words seemed meaningless, unless one was fortunate enough to have heard the set-up, which, unfortunately and most often times, remained only within Archibald's mind.

"Did you hear about the female tourist who hailed a Boston taxi and told the driver she wanted to get scrod? The taxi driver said 'Scrod? That's the strangest use of the plus-perfect tense I've ever heard.' "

A rather intellectual taxi driver, no doubt. Archibald's humor was clearly not for everyone.

Tour Office duties became more intense as we neared the Pacific Far East—clearly one of the high points of our voyage for most everyone onboard. Archibald's lectures were the catalyst; passengers then flocked to the Tour Office to purchase tickets for the excursions which best suited their needs; which best supported their dreams.

There was great anxiety among the tour office staff concerning our tour-escorting assignments while in Japan. One excursion was particularly favored—an overload journey which featured a rare visit to the beautiful lake district. The tour was scheduled to depart from Yokohama just after our arrival, and rejoin *Sagafjord* by air, at Hong Kong, five days later.

Requests for specific tour escorting assignments in Japan were submitted to Lar the day following our sailing from Honolulu. Naturally, as I was not experienced enough to escort the longer, multi-day, overland tours, I left them off my list. I wasn't greedy. Let the others have their choice. I would be happy with any assignment at all.

After two days of anticipation, mostly by the others, the assignments were announced one night after closing. Philip was awarded the favored overland. Percy was indifferent, he being the more easy-going of the group; after all, he already had his hands quite full with Mrs. Heckettson's—and others'—private arrangements. But Per and Ornulf—well that was another matter indeed. They were outwardly annoyed at Lar's selecting Philip, and clearly made him, and everyone else, aware of their intense dissatisfaction. Each felt the overland tour should have been his. They snidely inferred that Philip must be sleeping with Lar. Why else, they asked, would the overgrown Australian be awarded such a prize? It should have gone to a Norwegian they felt, at least.

The official word came down from the bridge just after lunch. Sol Eisenman—a somewhat crotchety old man, and husband to the equally crotchety and particularly outrageous Edith Eisenman—had died during the night. A heart attack, we were told. Lar told me that sort of thing happens often on longer cruises.

"Let's face it" he said "the passengers are between eighty and dead. Some actually expect to die, in fact. Many of them even attach burial instructions to their cruise questionnaires and send them along with their final cruise payment." He told me there was a freezer onboard where the bodies were kept—safely chilled until the ship reached the next port. The corpse, then, could "disembark" and be properly transported ashore, and home. The freezer, he said, was right next to the one where the ice cream was kept.

Just before closing the office that afternoon, Maggie stopped by to give us the details. Thank God for Maggie; she always had the latest gossip on who was doing what and to whom.

That day though, she arrived a bit nervous and out of breath. She was clearly embarrassed, and none of us knew why.

Maggie had just come from Ted Jones's cabin. And being the assertive woman that she was, Maggie felt no need to knock. So she barged right in to find Ted and Anne totally naked—screwing—right there on Ted's fold-out sofa. Ted Jones never locked his cabin door, I was told—until that afternoon, perhaps.

Maggie sat with us—but only for a minute; she was always in a hurry.

Mrs. Eisenman had just telephoned her sister in Chicago, ship-to-shore. This, Maggie said, had come straight from the radio room officer, so we knew it had to be true. Everyone knew, after all, that Maggie Sinclair and Radioman Jarle Anderssen, had some sort of "understanding."

Apparently Edith Eisenman had told her sister that Sol had died, and that she was sending him home from Yokohama as soon as we docked. But since the cruise was already paid for, and there was, of course, a no-refund policy with Norwegian America Line, Edith asked her sister to fly to Yokohama to join the ship; to continue the cruise with her. Poor Sol would have to fly home and attend his own funeral, alone.

"Some die on tour you know" Percy later told me. "I once led a five-day trip to Egypt, Israel, Turkey and Greece. By the time we got back, six . . . *six* . . . of the twenty-four passengers had died—actually seven; one died later, come to think of it, after we sailed from Piraeus. It was a horror."

I couldn't believe Percy was talking about tours and death in the same sentence. That was all I needed to hear—being the fledgling tour escort that I was. As if I wasn't overly neurotic enough.

"So what do I do if someone dies on one of my tours?" I asked him, not really wanting to know.

"Always stay with the group" he said. "Don't leave them, ever. The local agent should take care of the body—or bodies; they should make all the necessary arrangements—you know, customs, immigration, shipping . . . whatever needs to be done. You can only worry about the living, not the dead, although sometimes I know with these people it's difficult to tell the difference."

Rock Hudson's mother was onboard, or at least that's what I was told. She joined ship at Los Angeles and was to stay till New York. She spoke often of her son, and how proud she was of his success.

"He's a fag" Archibald volunteered one day during lunch.

"I don't really care if he is" I snapped back at him, obviously annoyed that he found it important enough to share with us that very private, if true, information. As far as I was concerned, everyone in Archibald's world was homosexual, or at least he thought so. "Besides, how do you know that?" I asked him quite pointedly.

"I have my sources" he answered. "And believe me, he's one of the biggest queens in Hollywood." Archibald smiled.

I got up and left the table.

At the next day's pre-luncheon cocktail party in the Garden Lounge, I met Estelle Middleton—a rather unattractive but kind woman; supposedly quite wealthy.

"New money" Percy commented, as we entered the party through the crowded North Cape Bar.

"So what? What's the difference?" I asked him. "New money or old money. She's still rich."

Percy made a face as if he sucked lemons. "Oh, dear heavens" he said to me with a sigh. "You're so naive."

Mrs. Middleton greeted us just off the dance floor. Almost immediately, she began discussing her husband who, for some undisclosed reason, was not with her onboard; he decided to stay at home, alone, somewhere near La Jolla, California. Her husband seemed to be a key topic of conversation that day, especially his obvious absence. Percy told me later it was clearly a marriage of convenience. He winked, then. Edith Middleton always traveled alone.

"He's so handsome" Mrs. Middleton boasted. "Did you know he's an actor? He was in *Butterfield 8* and he kissed Elizabeth Taylor. Can you imagine that? My husband kissed Elizabeth Taylor!" And with that, she clapped her hands together in sheer delight at the thought.

Lar then joined us.

"Oh, Mr. Vandelis" Estelle Middleton said. "So *so* nice of you to come. By the way, Mr. Vandelis, do you know my husband? He's an actor, you know. And he kissed Elizabeth Taylor during a most marvelous love scene in *Butterfield 8*. Now, isn't that just wonderful?"

At that same party I also met Thelma Ledbetter—a wrinkled woman of considerable years, yet still with a lively step. Archibald quickly introduced us, then escorted her off to the center of the dance floor.

"Thelma Bed-wetter?" I asked Percy, while trying convincingly to suppress a laugh.

"No, you twit. Not bed-wetter. Ledbetter" Percy interjected. "If you want a bed wetter—check out Mary 'P' over there. They don't call her 'Mary P' for nothing. And whatever you do . . . don't sit next to her in the Ballroom after she's had a few drinks."

And I met Susie Snow—a somewhat younger gray-haired Floridian with a deep dark tan and icy blue eyes. Susie maneuvered around the party looking for her own particular type of action; we all knew what that would indeed be. It was clear she wasn't interested in our ship's aging dancing boys. It would seem that a much younger beau, whomever he was—wherever he was—might be far more to her own personal liking.

As the days went on, Percy began to tell me more about his long-time relationship with Elizabeth Bowen, the mother of his former lover Billy. It seems that after William Sr. died, Elizabeth became far more independent and began traveling the world in ships—sometimes specifically planning her voyages to coincide with Percy's own cruise assignments.

"She's very wealthy" Percy said boastfully. " . . . Very very old money." And now *I* made the face.

Elizabeth, it turned out, had given Percy the funds to purchase his very first townhouse on London's Smith Street just a few years before. Percy has had tenants in the property ever since—making quite a good profit to boot.

"She just recently purchased a home for me in the south of France as well" he boasted somewhat grandly. "It's in the medieval town of Valbonne, just forty-five minutes or so north of Nice. We're all very proud" he continued. "The village has just been designated a national landmark of France."

I marveled at Percy's life, and his lifestyle. How was he able to manipulate these women into giving him houses around the world? What indeed was that bond? One townhouse purchase in London apparently was not enough—Mrs. Bowen was now, in addition, giving him life estate at the Valbonne house.

It was the only thing for her to do, I learned. It was clear, Percy said, that if Elizabeth had bequeathed Valbonne to Percy in her will, her gift would most certainly be contested by her son who, by this time—through great jealousy and perhaps even infantile contentiousness—thoroughly despised Percy Hayes. Billy, in fact, was even known to leave a room at just hearing a mention of Percy's name. So upon Percy's death, the agreement stipulated, the house at Valbonne would revert to Elizabeth Bowen's estate. So if he outlived Percy, Billy Jr. would indeed get the house after all.

Clearly, Percy was more than pleased with these arrangements, and continually bragged to us all about his great good fortune.

"You must all come visit me in the south of France" he would say. "Stay for a month, or two if you'd like." And then he would laugh uncontrollably, and giggle like a child who's just gotten his way. One couldn't help but like the man when he was like this. No matter how one may have previously felt about him.

In fact, it was about this time in the voyage when my relationship with Percy began to change. With all his faults, the one thing he was, was positive. Always up. Always content. Percy brought humor to most every situation. And although I was still quite bothered by it, I tried not to think of his overt homosexuality. It seemed far less threatening to me now that I was beginning to know the man—to understand him for who he was. And I had to admit that I was beginning to like this Percy Hayes very much.

My days at sea usually began at 6:30 A.M. when early riser's coffee was served in a quiet corner of the Veranda Cafe, just forward of the swimming pool area on Veranda Deck aft. It was a simple service offering steaming coffee and teas, and a full variety of fruit juices and freshly baked scones and croissants. Only a handful of passengers took part—it became a sort of "breakfast club" more than anything else; with the same passengers present, day after day.

For me, it was a welcome respite. A place for a first cup of coffee to get the day started, and perhaps to chat quietly with a fellow passenger or two who, like me, appreciated and enjoyed the unique freshness of the early morning sea air, and the almost surreal quality of light only existent at sunrise, at sea.

For me, this was a special time. A private time. I felt as if the ship, with most of her passengers still asleep, belonged only to me and to my fellow early breakfasters. There was a peacefulness to that feeling, and a comfort too. If only for an hour—those moments were cherished, and I looked forward to the start of every new day.

While at sea, the more active passengers were able to occupy their time by choosing from a host of daily activities of varied interests. *The Cruise News* was full of such offerings—from complimentary dance classes conducted, of course, by Ted and Anne, along with the assistance of the indefatigable dancing boys; Archibald's inspiring historical and port lectures; Maggie Sinclair's expert shopping talks and needlepoint classes; Marshall Smith's bridge lectures, lessons, and tournaments; and the wonderful pre-luncheon concerts in the Garden Lounge, which featured the talented pianist from the Jan Walesky Orchestra.

Additionally, periodic arts and crafts classes were offered, and a full line of deck sports as well, such as ping pong and deck tennis, and shuffleboard too. Each day, after luncheon, a first run film was shown in the ship's theatre—a showing which was repeated at least one other time during the voyage—most likely in the evening, after dinner—giving passengers the opportunity to view each film without having to miss out on their own favorite lecture or deck sport.

Naturally, John Marratisch conducted his golf clinics each morning as well, encouraging passengers to drive golf balls directly into the sea while he expertly analyzed their swing. Just adjacent to John's golf platform on sport's deck aft, passengers were able to shoot skeet—an activity conducted, thankfully so, by the particular officer of the watch. It was he alone who professionally handled the firearms, and safely protected passengers and others from accidents or innocent misuse. How strange, I thought, that the noise of shotguns firing off and out into the sea, would not affect the serious golfers, trying to concentrate on their swing and the distance of their drive. Why, I wondered, couldn't these amateur marksmen just shoot the golf balls as they flew off into space? Naturally, skeet shooting and driving golf balls too, were only conducted well out at sea, and never while docking or leaving port, when land, and innocent victims . . . people . . . could be standing ashore in clear view of the ship—a time when "hitting the bull's eye" in either sport simply would not have been appropriate.

Although Ted Jones' and Anne Dickson's official role onboard was as cruise director and dance instructors, it was clear that their main interest was the production shows. When they were in rehearsal, everything onboard ship seemed to stop. Ted would secure the Ballroom daily from 3:00 P.M. to 5:00 P.M.—barring access for passengers and crew alike—so that rehearsals for that evening's show could be held in complete privacy. Passengers, then, wishing or needing to get from the Theatre to the Veranda Cafe or the pool area, for example, would have to walk down to Upper Deck, all the way aft, and then up again to Veranda Deck. Most were annoyed by such inconvenience. Some, even disregarded Ted's hand-written notice announcing that the Ballroom was "Closed for Rehearsal" and barged right in—much to the dismay of the performers and the other social staff too.

Cocktail entertainment began nightly at 6:30 P.M. in the Garden Lounge, the North Cape Bar, and the Grand Ballroom simultaneously—mostly easy-listening melodies played awkwardly by the Polish Trio, or theatrical show tunes performed solo in true cabaret style by our onboard pianist Tom Akron.

The North Cape Bar, the most popular of all, offered an intimacy not found in any of the other lounges onboard. It quickly became my favorite, with its soft chestnut leather armchairs and warm lighting. Hand-carved wooden etchings adorned an entire wall opposite full-length windows overlooking the sea.

Each night, areas of the Garden Lounge would be sectioned off for smaller private parties—as was done for Mrs. Middleton's pre-luncheon affair. The Club Polaris, however, was clearly the favorite for the larger private functions, especially those hosting 100 passengers, or more.

In addition, off in a secluded area of the Ballroom on portside aft, Maggie Sinclair hosted the *Dutch Treat Club*. It was at Dutch Treat where the ship's single passengers, mostly female—especially those not invited to a specific private party—would meet for pre-dinner cocktails, and hopefully for a dance—most likely with a member of the ship's social staff. The atmosphere here was hopelessly desperate and all too predictable. An awkwardness of silence kept most of the women to themselves—hands folded on their anxious laps; a foot tapping here, a head bobbing there; a sip between musical beats only added to the tranquil syncopation. The fortunate ones might be spoken to by a male staff member as they breezed through the room enroute to yet another private party. The dancing boys made their rounds however—indeed, that was their job after all—and as each dance climaxed, they moved along to the next available female—no doubt still sitting alone, patiently awaiting her turn. I did visit Maggie's *Dutch Treat Club* whenever I got up the nerve and strength to do so, but I wasn't at all comfortable with the feelings I felt there. I often dreamed up bogus excuses—tour-related or otherwise—in order to justify my absence.

There was no doubt though that my favorite activity onboard was afternoon tea, served daily—both in and out of port; 4:00 P.M. sharp—in the Garden Lounge. It was difficult for me to attend most tea times however—its mid-afternoon schedule usually conflicted with our own office hours. Yet I did attend as often as I could—when in port, or any other time the Tour Office might be closed.

The service at tea time was romantically lovely and very European in style and finesse—it was what I had always dreamed or imagined an old-world tea service would be.

The Garden Lounge itself created a superb atmosphere within which to hold such a service, with its deep rust hues and other earth tones, accented by lush tropical blossoms and green leafy plants. And the service by the European crew was impeccable. Afternoon tea then became the perfect time to sit quietly with a book, or to become valiantly lost in the sea while gazing through the soaring picture windows which surrounded the room on all but one side.

The Earl Grey was served steaming hot in individual china pots, accompanied by tiny finger sandwiches and cookies and sweet pastries too. I had never before seen sandwiches so small—so petite, nor had I ever tasted any made with crispy cucumber or crunchy watercress. But they were indeed delicious. And if there was one thing I was learning onboard, it was that I should be more open to experiment. I quickly found myself doing just that—and the more I tried, the more I truly enjoyed.

Afternoon tea also became an opportunity for me to become better acquainted—although somewhat discreetly—with several of the dining room waiters who were assigned to tea duty in addition to their regularly scheduled hours of daily service. Due to its somewhat relaxed social atmosphere, afternoon tea became an unexpectedly convenient place for us to meet and talk together, without the grave feelings of guilty exposure. In this respect, tea time became a social time for me, and perhaps for the waiters too.

Thankfully, no one patrolled the area as much as I'd feared—if they did, they would clearly have realized that I spent more time talking and joking with the dining room waiters than I did with any of the passengers. We—the guilty parties—would certainly have gotten into serious trouble. No doubt a second and perhaps very final visit to the captain's office was in the cards for me. But they didn't notice, and I was glad.

"Oh no. For God's sake. Don't chomp ice" Archibald exclaimed. "I can't bear it when people chomp ice. Stop it—stop it, for God's sake!"

Archibald, Percy and I sat together near the pool. We had opted once again for the less formal luncheon buffet on deck. Archibald was speaking, of course.

"First of all" he shouted to me "it's bad for your teeth. I couldn't do it when I was your age. I had thermal-sensitive teeth."

Somehow I wasn't surprised by Archibald's disclosure of having thermo-sensitive teeth. If anyone would have thermo-sensitive teeth, it would be Archibald. He always had something—a bad leg, an oncoming cataract; it all set Archibald up to be far more of a hypochondriac than even I thought I was. Yet Archibald had a way of thriving on his hypochondria. He seemed nourished by his physical ailments; seemed to wallow in their uncomfortableness. Any illness—real or imagined—was milked by Archibald for all it was worth by cleverly played-out histrionics.

It was at that on-deck luncheon buffet that Archibald Hannon first began to tell us about a young man he had met just one year before. Matthew was a college student, nineteen years of age or so, living in Boston. And not surprisingly—perhaps because Matthew was young and no doubt handsome; perhaps because he was unusually gifted, or so we were told; most probably because he was simply male—Archibald found him irresistibly attractive, and a relationship of sorts quickly developed. He spoke of Matthew at length that day in painful memory, in vivid detail; and it was clear to us all that Archibald's new friend was a very troubled young man.

Matthew's parents were divorced; his relationship with his

father nonexistent. The parting was a bitter one, the sorrow far from sweet. It gave birth to frantic in-fighting, hostile money concerns, and a vicious custody battle too. And Matthew was the pawn, doomed to live out the bitter results of his parent's mutual rage and revenge.

Three years before, and well into his parents' marital separation, Matthew informed his mother that he desperately missed his dad—the young man, having uncomfortably settled into eruptive adolescence, wanted to know his father better; wanted to be a part of his father's life. He even dreamed of living with his father for a while.

Matthew's words that day, however, sent his mother into an uncontrolled rage—a condition Matthew knew well by that time in his life. She was determined to crush her son's dream in an instant; ensure that the boy and his dad would never again meet. She screamed at Matthew viciously, maliciously, even becoming physically violent with him. Under no circumstances, she told him, would she ever allow her son to be shared by the man she hated and so despised.

Matthew's mother had withheld one trump however; she had no choice, she felt, but to finally play it through. So one summer afternoon, she pulled her young man aside, and told him her truth of the separation; the blinding rationalization which forced their divorce—and indeed, it was Matthew himself.

When he was just five years old, she told him, Matthew was forcibly taken by his father, and violently raped.

Whether for custodial revenge, or for mere sexual kicks—and whether or not it was even true at all—Matthew's mother's motive in sharing this horried secret with her son was impossible to know. But in a way, it was irrelevant. By utter proclamation, his father became the bogey man in Matthew's young life; a phantom figure who spoke to his son only in his dreams. Matthew understood nothing of the incident; he had no recollection whatsoever of the unconscionable act which his mother had finally chosen to share.

Naturally, Matthew was shocked and angered by his mother's revelation. And there was no turning back. Once that information was known, the young man was doomed—permanently scarred. Matthew's emotional health and sexual performance deteriorated drastically from that moment on, never to be reclaimed, never to be blessed.

Throughout our conversation that day, it became clear that Matthew and Archibald's relationship—however it could be described—was indeed a volatile one. Clearly, the young man was seriously disturbed. He often lashed out at Archibald in a violent rage—like father, like son, one would say. And perhaps like mother as well. And such vivid projection was thrust upon others too. Archibald was his father after all, or quickly became so early in their relationship. In Matthew's eyes, it was time for revenge—sweet, vicious, lovingly angry. At last, a man of mature years with whom he could vent his orgasmic rage had come into his life.

Archibald, quite oblivious to such deadly emotional scars, must have seen in Matthew a wounded young man who was intellectually gifted—someone with whom he might share a simple life on West 22nd Street—and by so doing, could somehow ease Matthew's psychological pain. Sex—of any kind—was purely a bonus—for Archibald; perhaps for both. The nearly thirty years difference in their ages apparently was not an issue.

"I'm becoming an old man" Archibald said to us. And as he spoke, he became his words. He seemed weak, and passive—not at all in control of the calendar he hated so. For the first time, he seemed to be speaking honestly, from his heart, about the realities, the practicalities, of his life as an aging homosexual. "Matthew may be my last chance at romance" he cried. "My last chance at happiness."

"You've fallen in love" Percy observed.

"Yes, I guess I have." He smiled sheepishly as soon as the word was mentioned. "So what's wrong with that?"

"It's the first step to destroying the relationship, that's all. Is he attractive?"

"He's nineteen. Anyone at nineteen is attractive to a man nearing fifty. Besides, the older one gets, the more one is willing to let beauty be."

He paused for a moment, then continued.

"After all, I have a good deal to offer him. My intellect to start. You know, I'm very bright. And I'm a gourmet cook as well—I could easily picture the two of us; Matthew studying, and me—preparing filet mignon with crispy snow peas and broiled potatoes—just the two of us." He paused long enough for his romantic scenario to become as fixed in our minds as it already was in his. "I'm not just a pretty old face, you know."

"Would you rather have been born with high beauty, Archie?" Percy asked him, slightly getting off the subject.

"And that's all—just high beauty? Or with my own self and intellect too? . . . And don't call me Archie!"

Percy chuckled. So did I. Having known Archibald Hannon for as long as I had, I could not even dream of anyone ever calling him Archie.

"No. No. Without your own self and intellect. Just the beauty."

"Then no" Archibald answered. "And you?"

"I'll take my beauty as it is" Percy said with a curious smile, and then paused a moment as if in thought. "But enough of this talk about beauty and this young man called Matthew . . . what about that other young man you were telling me about . . . the one you met on the *France* World Cruise last year? Didn't you have a love affair with him too?"

"Oh, Creighton. Creighton Wright III— from Wood Fork Plantation; Chalottesville Virginia." He smiled as he remembered the young boy in question.

"No. I never said I had an affair with him" Archibald answered emphatically. "I just gave him a couple of blow jobs—you know, while his grandmother was in the casino. That was all. Besides, he wasn't even gay."

"Well I'm glad about that—because if he was gay, you'd have had an affair with him. And if you had had an affair with him it would have ended, because you wouldn't have been able to stand the fact that he was a nice young kid without problems."

Percy ate one of his crispy potato chips—tiny crumbs fell like snow flakes onto his bright Hermes scarf.

"Perhaps" Archibald said calmly, after a thoughtful pause. "Perhaps you're right. Love affairs are unending only when they begin."

Percy turned for a moment to watch Ingemar moving deck chairs near the pool—shifting them gently, more in line with the sun.

"You know Percy, your hair is thinning" Archibald commented as he looked Percy's way. "When you're forty you'll have a bald spot."

"When I'm forty, I'll deserve a bald spot."

"No one deserves old age" Archibald said.

There was a lesson to be learned that day—a master's degree to be sure. Both Percy and Archibald revealed a good deal about themselves and I began to appreciate—intellectually, at least—their challenging witticisms and downright honesty. As Archibald and Percy volleyed back and forth with their clever one-liners, I observed an openness between the two of them which I began to greatly admire and willingly envy.

As I'm sure you've already understood, I have always been successful at hiding from others my true and inner most feelings; camouflaged emotions were indeed my middle name. But suddenly, I began to wonder if the reason I may have been so eager to hide my entire life—*for* my entire life—was out of fear. Perhaps I felt that if someone really knew what I felt—if someone really understood what I thought—he would think me foolish, or silly, or totally unintelligent; he would, out of pure necessity, reject me—quick, easy, out-of-sight, over the side. They would clearly have no choice after all. So what better way to prevent such opportunity, than by not letting anyone in at all; repudiating my true self completely from the world.

It was the pure honesty of Archibald and Percy's friendship which fascinated me most. That very blatant upright integrity of these two men—a truthfulness which I, and everyone else it appeared, seemed to hold irresistibly dear. I had none of that honesty,

I realized. It was something totally missing from my life. I began to wonder if by withholding my true self from the world, I was not also withholding it from me as well.

As our lunch continued, the three of us began to talk about the latest shipboard gossip—the scandalous affair between the lustful Susie Snow, and a young French waiter called Bernard.

"I'm sickened and shocked" Archibald commented with great emotional passion. "How could such a mature and obviously aggressive woman go after a man almost thirty years her junior? Personally, I think it's disgusting."

I simply could not believe what I was hearing. I could keep silent no longer.

"Wait a minute" I said. "What about this Matthew you've been telling us about? What about that vast age difference?" Percy looked at Archibald and smiled. He paused a moment. He knew I had caught him, finally.

"Homosexual relationships are different" Archibald snapped back with a devilish smirk on his face. "Besides, a stiff prick has no conscience."

"No conscience indeed" I shot back, "whether that prick is straight or gay. No difference in my book. Just ask waiter Bernard."

The clear double standard within Archibald's philosophy made us all laugh out loud—the three of us together. It was at that moment, I believe, that the proverbial ice between us finally broke; the great barriers dropped. A wall had been lifted; the burdenous weight lessened. From then on, it became far easier to talk openly with Archibald and Percy about—well, just about anything at all—although still mostly relating to *their* lives; not mine just yet. I wasn't enlightened enough to even contemplate such raw personal exposure. The fear of their scrutiny was still too much to bear. I couldn't imagine what would happen if I attempted anything as blatantly open as that.

Nonetheless, we were finally able to set aside the mundane trivialities which, up until then, had been the basis of our conversations—indeed, our relationship. Clearly, I was fascinated by these two older men. I was intellectually stimulated by them both. They were unlike any I had met in my lifetime. And like an addict addicted to heroin or cocaine, once I had my first taste of their intellect and their humor and their worldly sophistication, I knew I could never have enough.

Passengers marveled at the clever design skills of Roger Rolande when, on the evening of Friday, January 26th, he created his spectacular environment Casino Night. The Ballroom was virtually transformed into a Las Vegas gaming palace—with dice tables, chuck-a-luck, roulette, craps and blackjack. Lights flashed, bells rang, and pretty young Norwegian stewardess, dressed as unusually modest Las Vegas showgirls, eagerly took drink orders and handed out complimentary cigarettes and cigars to our mock casino's "high rollers."

Passengers were asked to contribute five dollars to the kitty—the proceeds of which were to go to the Norwegian Seamen's Fund, of course. In return, they would receive $2,000 worth of *Sagafjord* Money. It was with this bogus money that the games were played. Prizes were offered to passengers with the highest winnings at a special awards ceremony scheduled for tea time, the following afternoon.

I volunteered to host a roulette table—although a skilled croupier I was not—and was teamed with a young Italian waiter called Marco. Crew members were allowed to volunteer their services for this event—Roger needed a fairly large staff to operate his casino, and just those of us from the social and tour office staffs were clearly not enough.

So I was teamed with Marco. We wore white frilly shirts with red and black garterlike arm bands and head visors too. We both got into our characters quickly and easily—slick, professional, never trusting the dealer.

"You're Rivellino, aren't you?" Marco asked me even before the doors to the casino opened. "Do you play football too?" I didn't know what he was talking about, however it really didn't matter. Any attention I received from the crew I accepted willingly, and openly.

Marco told me about a world-famous Brazilian soccer player—"football" to all un-Americans—whose name was Roberto Rivellino.

"He's the best in the world" Marco told me. "Rivellino and Pele are the two international legends of World Cup Soccer. They are rivals; and they are the best. Just say his name—*your* name—anywhere in the world, and I'll bet you'll be treated like a king."

As Marco spoke, I remembered my father telling me about his father, Felice Nicola, and his two brothers, Gino and Sergio. All of them boarding ships to immigrate to the Americas at the turn of the century. It was perhaps the only story my father ever related about the old country, about his family—the only family history I could recall. I'll take it, I thought. It's all I had.

The brothers, I was told, sailed separately westward—each on different ships; each it turned out, to different destinations. Felice Nicola, my grandfather, sailed directly to America—obviously, landing and settling in New York; Sergio sailed north to Canada, to Montreal; and the last brother, Gino, the youngest of them all, sailed off to South America, finally settling in Rio de Janeiro. Brazil. Of course. Could this world-famous soccer player indeed be a relative? Our name was far too uncommon for it to be mere coincidence. He would have to be my cousin if it were so. How could I find out, I wondered. I was determined to know. I had to write my father immediately with this irrefutable familial discovery.

Yet until I could confirm or deny the facts, I savored the fantasy and the spotlight. Just the name association with the great Rivellino—this powerful young soccer player who now lived only in my imagination—was exciting to me. And with that association, I became my own star with the European crewmen onboard. Once they realized that I was indeed "a Rivellino"—that I was closely related to the great Rivellino, Brazilian and World Cup football star—they became more and more friendly with me, more relaxed. More frequently, they initiated conversation. It was as if we now had a common bond, a common understanding. The once standoffish cultural separateness—American to European; staff to crew—was instantly eased.

I thoroughly enjoyed my new celebrity status onboard—even if it was by proxy. I felt proud of the new name recognition my phantom cousin had brought me. I dreamed that night of someday visiting Brazil, of meeting this world-famous athlete, my long lost cousin—real or imagined—face to face.

That night was memorable for another reason as well.

I felt like a child on Christmas Eve, anxiously awaiting Santa's arrival. For it was that night you see—the exact moment completely unknown to me—that *Sagafjord* would sail across the International Date Line, a memorable benchmark of our westward trek across the Pacific.

Archibald told us it was for uniformity in calendars that the International Date Line was established in 1839. On a map or chart, it coincided with the 180 degree Meridian—with 0 degrees at Greenwich England. When it was noon at Greenwich, it was midnight on the date line. A new day then had begun. And when it was 11:59 P.M. January 2nd on the International Date Line for example, January 1st was just beginning on the eastern side. One minute later, it would be January 3rd. A vessel, then, traveling west, would skip a day; just as those sailing east would enjoy two days of the same date. As obsessed with time as I certainly was, I became fascinated by these concepts. Confused a bit, yet fascinated nonetheless. I would go to sleep Friday night and wake up Sunday morning, just eight hours later.

The next morning at breakfast—Sunday morning—Lar asked if I had heard the bump in the night as *Sagafjord* sailed over the line.

Chapter Four

"Youth In Asia"

At sea, all seas are the same. Sailing the Pacific seemed no different than sailing the Atlantic, or the Caribbean for that matter. On a clear day, with the sun shining brightly and the seas rolling gently, no real distinction could be made from one to the other. You would be hard pressed to actually identify the vast sea before you.

To a nautical novice, the maritime approach to any port-of-call seemed similar as well. From a distance, at sea, there appeared no difference whether one were to land on St. Thomas in the Virgin Islands, or on Bali in Indonesia. The approaches appear the same. And although intellectually I was aware that we were sailing westward, across the Pacific, and would soon be arriving in Japan, intellectualism and reality are not necessarily synonymous.

So it was only on that frigidly cold January morning that I finally began to understand exactly where I was, and where I was going. It was the first time I actually felt the reality of sailing around the world. The very first time I believed it. For this approach—psychologically, at least, seemed far far different.

Yokohama is the main port of access for Tokyo—at least it was for our arrival. It is situated just seventeen miles west of the Japanese capital. This active port city is beautifully set against jagged rising cliffs—its vastness quite remarkable, sprawling on and on for distances far greater than the eye could see.

As I stood on deck that morning, I could see through the vapor of my breath in the air the magnificent Mt. Fujiyama towering tall in the distance—solidly standing watch over the harbor and its patchwork villages. The unusually clear sky that morning allowed the mountain's pristine snowcap to sparkle like a jewel in the rising sun. I heard a tug boat's whistle, then another far off in the distance. We slowly entered the inner harbor, pulling gently alongside.

That day, I was on my own—completely tour-free.

And for some unknown reason, my confidence was building. I felt strong. I was more adventurous in Japan than I had been on Hawaii or even at Los Angeles. And so I set off, alone.

I was struck, at first, by the wondrous look of the land itself and the proud intensity of the people around me—the busy-ness and the diligence with which they all worked; and the beautiful, magnificent, architecture everywhere I turned.

The people I met that morning, although none spoke English with any familiarity, were helpful and courteous, and their kindness offered me the courage and the confidence to explore even further; to continue on my own to the nearby village of Kamakura—the traditional and historic enclave which Archibald, in his talks, had highly recommended.

At the Yokohama station, while I waited for the high-powered bullet train to whisk me off to Kamakura, my attention was drawn to a group of Japanese school children—from first or second grades at most—and their teacher too, obviously on a class outing. The children's innocent laughter was infections as they saw me watching them. They covered their mouths lest I see their smiles. Unusually polite they were for children of that age, uniformly dressed with dark pants and lighter jackets, and beanielike caps atop their heads. I watched them for a while longer as their teacher rushed about making sure all was in good order. Indeed, I was struck by their discipline—they were certainly unlike the students I remembered from my very own St. Thomas elementary, I thought.

And so they became the subject of the first photograph I took that morning—I wanted to capture them before they disappeared on to the next passing train and out of sight.

One little boy, carrying a tiny blue pennant was the last of the group to step onboard. He turned and giggled as he again covered his mouth and waved his blue flag high into the air. His teacher pulled him away just as the coach's automated doors slammed shut.

As their train departed, mine arrived. And just as quickly, I too was being swept in yet another direction, to the wondrous world of ancient Kamakura.

I felt as if transported back in time. The villagers, many of whom wore traditional dress, were quite unlike those I had seen running about the open air markets at Yokohoma. Here in Kamakura, they appeared less structured, less concerned about contemporary commerce and big city business. They moved about, at least in my view, solely for their own day-to-day needs; their personal tasks and pleasures.

Many gardens surrounded the village square just adjacent to the railway station. All of them were beautifully designed and maintained. Indeed, just as Archibald had said, those gardens were in themselves works of art. And as in a museum of great stature and sophistication, many visitors, I noticed, would sit within the garden's simplistic beauty to do nothing more than admire them; to think perhaps, and to dream.

It was quiet. It was filled with peace. How wonderful that these people could enjoy these gardens so, and find solace in this basic yet remarkable setting. Remarkable, indeed, that these people could abandon their daily problems and traumas at any time they wished—surely problems must exist for them as well—and find transformational serenity and calming tranquility in the sanctity that these inner-village gardens inspired. How I admired that self-power, their great self-control. And yes, their discipline too. No doubt, there was something special here. I could feel it. And I longed for its greater understanding.

I walked across an arched bridge painted a shade of orange as bright as the setting sun—on to an island green with exotic flora, gray with the reality of the earth's own rock. There, I discovered a shrine—small, focused, strategically placed within a particularly austere setting of flattened stones. I too sat and thought, and envied again these people. What did they know that I did not, I wondered? Clearly, there was something. But what they knew and what I did not no longer mattered as much as the fact that I was there that day, with them, in that marvelously inspiring environment. Time seemed obscured. How much of it all I understood then, was really unimportant.

Speaking English in Kamakura was virtually impossible. And so ordering lunch, then, became a pantomime of sorts—physically pointing to the desired dishes which were beautifully displayed in the restaurant's front window showcase. Was it real or plastic? Before I was able to determine the answer, my lunch arrived, hot and steamy.

And then, the obvious; something I did not consider. Using chopsticks proved a fiasco. Many of the shrimp landed in my lap. The other diners around me shyly giggled. I too, had to laugh. I was happy, and thrilled to be there.

I came upon the Buddha—the Diabutsu, as it is known—quite unexpectedly. Cast in bronze in 1495, my guide book told me, the image stood nearly forty-two feet high. It was an awesome structure. I thought about this Buddha, and what it was about him that influenced these people, and so many others around the world.

This was all so foreign to me—not just the Japanese people and their rich culture, but their spiritual beliefs as well. My parochial education purposely avoided any discussion of other religions and other worldly beliefs. Why? Was there something Catholicism did not want us to know?

Nearer the Buddha and off to one side was an area of many trees—a park perhaps; a miniature forest of sorts. And from their branches hung tiny strips of paper. They fluttered together gaily in the crisp breezes which seemed so eager to embrace them. As I watched from a distance, religious worshipers and other visitors too were busily attaching their own strips of paper to the branches. Each was inscribed with a wish or desire—a hope for the future.

When the wind finally came, I saw them smile—for the essence of the message they'd just written was swiftly swept up within the energy of the universe. Their wish, their hope—the desire they so longed for was becoming true; its spirit, finally reaching its ultimate destination.

I scribbled my wish just as the others had done and nervously walked to a tree of my own. I looked about quickly to insure no one watched. And to an empty branch—which no doubt stood out strong and sturdy, just for me—I attached my note. And so it was done. I didn't wait though; I was too self-conscious. But as I turned to walk away, I felt the breeze at the back of my neck.

The crowded gift shop offered the expected novelties and souvenirs—I had to return with something, after all. So I purchased a miniature wooden statue of an old man—bald with an excessive forehead—the symbol of wisdom, I was told. In addition, I purchased a small book; it was simply bound in black, entitled The Teachings of Buddha. Perhaps, I thought, this held the secret.

When I returned to the ship that evening, I told Archibald about my experience ashore, and thanked him for his suggestion of visiting Kamakura. I told him about the "wish tree" and how fascinated I was by the simple concept of the wind carrying one's dreams and desires deep into the universe—creating its own energy, its own power.

Archibald smiled. He clearly thrived on my newly born interest in such philosophical matters—indeed, it was right up his alley. He told me then about an old Sufi tale which he knew I would enjoy.

Later that evening, as I undressed for bed, I heard a *swoosh* under my cabin door. And this is what I found:

The Tale Of The Sands

A bubbling Stream reached a desert, and found that it could not cross it. The water was disappearing into the fine sand, faster and faster. The Stream said aloud "My destiny is to cross this desert, but I can see no way."

The voice of the Desert answered, in the hidden tongue of nature, saying "The Wind crosses the desert and so can you."

"But whenever I try, I am absorbed into the sand; and even if I dash myself at the desert, I can only go a little distance."

"The Wind does not dash itself against the desert sand."

"But the Wind can fly, and I cannot."

"You are thinking in the wrong way; trying to fly by yourself is absurd. Allow the Wind to carry you over the sand."

"But how can that happen?"

"Allow yourself to be absorbed in the Wind."

The Stream protested that it did not want to lose its individuality in that way. If it did, it might not exist again.

This, said the Sand, was a form of logic, but it did not refer to reality at all. When the Wind absorbed moisture, it carried it over the desert, and then let it fall again like rain. The rain again became a river.

But how, asked the Stream, could it know that this was true?

"It is so, and you must believe it, or you will simply be sucked down by the sands to form, after several million years, a quagmire."

"But if that is so, will I be the same river that I am today?"

"You cannot in any case remain the same stream that you are today. The choice is not open to you; it only seems to be open. The Wind will carry your essence, the finer part of you. When you become a river again, at the mountains beyond the sands, men may call you by a different name; but you yourself, essentially, will know that you are the same. Today, you call yourself such and such a river only because you do not know which part of it is even now your essence."

So the Stream crossed the desert by raising itself into the arms of the welcoming Wind, which gathered it slowly and carefully upward, and then let it down with gentle firmness, atop the mountains of a far-off land. "Now" said the Stream, "I have learned my true identity."

But it had a question, which it bubbled up as it sped along. "Why could I not reason this out on my own? Why did the Sands have to tell me? What would have happened if I had not listened to the Sands?"

Suddenly, a small voice spoke to the Stream. It came from a grain of sand. "Only the Sands know, for they have seen it happen; moreover, they extend from the river to the mountain. They form the link, and they have their function to perform, as has everything.

The way in which the stream of life is to carry itself on its journey is written in the Sands."

The following day, in Tokyo and on tour, I was surrounded by a city not unlike New York; certainly the antithesis of Kamakura. Everyone hurried about, paying little attention to each other. They pushed and shoved in order to move along their way, and never did I hear an acknowledgment of disturbing others, or a simple "excuse me"—or whatever the phrase might be in contemporary Japanese. Preoccupation seemed the mode—with what, I was not sure. But I was not at all impressed with what I saw and what I experienced, and with whom I met that day.

The three-hour bus tour that morning first visited the Tokyo Stock Exchange, and then off to the top of their World Trade Building for a panoramic view at the city and the surprisingly congested commercial harbor surrounding it. A haze of pollution obfuscated our view, and any photographs I took were nearly indecipherable because of it. The bay, the river, the ships tied at anchor, all appeared as if seen behind a scrim.

I did marvel, though, at a special luncheon performance of the all-female Kokosai Revue which was staged in a lovely downtown theatre, beautifully decorated and elaborately ornate. Lavish, the show was, with glittering scenery and thousands of lights which helped to create an unforgettable theatrical magic. The production quality was first rate—rivaling even New York's Radio City Music Hall—making, at times, that art-deco palace's great stage performances seem more like a local community theatre. Some might say it was "over the top"; I loved every minute.

Percy joined us at the performance. He carried with him an overly large shoulder bag—Louis Vuitton, of course. By now you must understand that Percy always had his Vuitton with him when ashore.

"Look" Lar said as he pointed to the insignia logo on Percy's bag. "L.V. My initials. Didn't you know? They designed it just for me?"

Louis Vuitton was completely new to me—Percy's matching set being the first I had seen. I didn't particularly care for the design, and I couldn't figure out what all the fuss was about. Percy said they were the only kind to own.

"A complete set, naturally" Percy emphasized. "Never just individual pieces."

With Japan behind us, my attention soon focused on our visits to Hong Kong and Bombay—*especially* Bombay.

Although still weeks away, I imagined stepping ashore at Victoria's Gate, and eventually standing before the great Taj Mahal at Agra. Reading Archibald Hannon's book no doubt nurtured this desire, as it helped bring to life the very human drama which resulted in the creation of that famous mausoleum. That book became indispensable for me as I prepared for our visit; it once again made me realize just how fortunate we were to have Archibald with us. Who better than he would be able to introduce us all to the history and the wonders of that mysterious Indian continent?

Before sailing from Yokohama though, two new staff members joined the ship. Carmella was a continental chanteuse, I was told, who billed herself as *The Chilean Nightingale*. She was rather short, and slightly overweight; pudgy, if you will—perhaps that's how Chilean nightingales were. She was never seen about the ship without her cream-colored turban, meticulously wrapped, and tied securely around her head. A heavy, sometimes unintelligible Spanish accent was prevalent whenever she spoke, and also when she sang. Its inconsistency, however, made me wonder if the accent was indeed authentic, or just grandly affected. Carmella's closing number at her debut show onboard was *The Impossible Dream*—sung with an accent so indecipherable, I doubt Don Quixote de la Mancha himself would have been able to understand but one word.

And Clifford Deetlefs joined us in the Tour Office. He was to be the additional support greatly needed for the more complex overland tours still yet to come. Clifford worked permanently in the New York office as shore excursion coordinator. It was his job to arrange and pre-book all tours before sailing, and prepare the proper paperwork and ticket stock accordingly, which he delivered to the ship on each sailing day. South African by birth, Clifford was a handsome young man of about thirty years, with very short brown hair—almost crew—and crystal-blue eyes, the color of the sea at its deepest. When we first met, I could tell by his warm casual smile and his very easy manner that I liked him. I knew we'd get along just fine. I was glad he was with us—if only for a few weeks.

In a funny way, Clifford's arrival brought near chaos to office communication—for me at least, it was like working at the United Nations, with Percy's very very proper British accent, Philip's Australian drawl, and now Clifford's native Afrikaans. Not to mention Per and Ornulf's very broken English.

Clifford and I got along exceedingly well from day one. He was witty, and quite straightforward. And so Clifford and I quickly struck up a friendship. "Young REB-el-lino" he would call me. And although I knew him for just days, I began to turn towards Clifford as an older brother if you will—for confidence, for guidance, and at times for strength.

Two days out of Yokohama, while enroute to Hong Kong, I found the Tour Office door a jar when I arrived just after early breakfast; lights ablaze. It startled me. I was the early riser of the group, and have always been the first to arrive each morning.

Percy was there, already seated behind his chosen area of the selling counter. He was unusually lively that morning, heavy in conversation with an Austrian waiter named Dieter whose dining room station was quite near our own. It was obvious that Percy had been drinking, even at that early hour of the morning. And as always, Percy was doing most of the talking.

"So last night I decided it was time, and I went to see him" he told Dieter. I stayed quiet and out of the way so Percy wouldn't think I was listening. Yet I was. And I quickly figured out that the "him" Percy was referring to was the young Swiss boy who worked onboard in the Sundt Gift Shop. Rene was blond, and no doubt Percy's type.

"We were in his cabin" Percy continued. "We talked for a while—he kindly offered to translate a letter for me from French into English. You know—what with my new home in the south of France and all. It's in Valbonne—by the way" Percy said to both of us both. "You must come for a visit.

"But enough of all that" Percy continued. "I knew I wanted to have sex with him. I always thought Rene was attractive . . . and since he wasn't responding very much I took on the role of the aggressor."

Dieter smiled and listened with intent as Percy continued his story, neither of them seemed bothered in the least that I was present, hearing every word.

"So I tossed the letter aside, and we kissed; we kissed for quite a while in fact—we were already lying on his bed. The Swiss always like to do that, you know; they like to kiss for some odd reason. They think it's intimate. But God, those crew bunks are small.

"But it was a strange thing though—everytime I made a move to undo his belt, he'd pull away. He just kept pushing me aside. Can you imagine that? Why would he do that? Why wouldn't anyone want to have sex?" Percy was incredulous. He seemed shocked and amazed by his own words.

"He said he didn't know me well enough to have sex with me just yet. He wanted to get to know me better. He said he wasn't the type to sleep around with everyone on the ship. Admirable, don't you think?" Percy made a face, and then continued. "Well who, pray tell, was this Swiss boy kidding?

"So we continued to play back and forth like that for a while longer—he was very strong-willed I must say, and I was getting very very hot, if you know what I mean. The more I couldn't have him, the more I wanted him. So I stood up and took off my pants—stripped naked, right there in front of him. Well, that certainly did the trick. Will-power out the porthole! He reached for my dinker and we fell back onto his bed. Believe me, he needed it just as much as I did."

Dieter laughed, then ran off to work. And I just sat there, stunned and embarrassed, and quite amazed that Percy would discuss this—his most recent and private sexual escapade—as openly as he did, in front of Dieter, and me. Why was he so proud of all this? Is that why he made it a point to tell us? Pride? Conquest? Shock?

Percy, of all people, knew very well how much that kind of talk was upsetting to me. Yet he continued to do it, on and on—over and over—with seemingly no regard for me or my feelings.

And what about Rene? Within minutes, I was sure—now that Dieter was back in the dining room—the entire ship would be aware of his last night's encounter. Percy, apparently, had no regard for his latest lover's privacy either.

"Oh, come on" Percy snapped with just a little but of annoyance. "What's the big deal? Why don't you just relax and let go a bit? Why not tell us about the last time *you* had sex?"

The others were just arriving. My face reddened, I'm sure. I stayed silent. I knew they had heard Percy's comments as they entered the office; there was no way they could have missed it.

"No, thank you Percy" I finally answered to break the unbearable silence. "Perhaps I hold these things just a bit more special than you do."

Lar had just come in from the Purser's Office.

"I've got to leave for a minute; I'll be right back," I said to Lar, "if that's okay." And I quickly ran up to Sun Deck to get some badly needed fresh air—if only for a moment, to be in what I considered to be an unthreatening and very safe space.

Attitudes in the office became uneasy as the seas picked up and Percy continued to drink. He could be "on the wagon" for months, I was told, and never touch a drop. But when he began to drink, Percy drank to excess for a week or two without stopping—a time during which he was not only totally useless in the office, but a difficult and quite unpleasant companion.

Clearly, Percy was quite difficult when he drank. One could sense his condition even before he spoke. You could see it in his eyes, and by the embarrassed little-boy smile and the flushed-like pallor to his skin. It frightened me, and it hurt me too, to see him like that. All our moods were effected; there was really no escaping it.

The seas remained heavy for the next several days. I found it difficult to sleep. I wondered if my newly felt depression might simply be caused by the consistent and sometimes violent motion of the sea. I thought about the still uncomfortable atmosphere among us in the Tour Office. It seemed more and more, we were getting on each other's nerves. Going to work became a challenge, and increasingly unpleasant.

In addition, the anxiety I felt about escorting my first overland tour in India was beginning to haunt me. Was I experienced enough, I wondered? Would I really be able to do the job?

The actual itinerary for my particular tour was still uncertain. The flight times were continually being changed by the local tour agent at Bombay. Lar decided not to reveal that information to the passengers just yet—at least until the tour was about to depart, or even enroute. That way, he told me, we would prevent passengers from canceling due to the un-Godly flight times.

The latest schedule set the Delhi/Bombay return flight to depart at 3:30 A.M., which would mean a 2:00 A.M. motor coach pick-up from the hotel. Images of passengers dying kept filling my mind. While I attempted sleep that night, I was able to count only dead passengers—sheep were nowhere be found.

I was nearly asleep though when the telephone rang. It startled me, with that incredibly loud and piercing ring which only European phones seemed to have. It was Arne calling from his late night duty in the Polaris. I was surprised—this was the first time he had telephoned my cabin. A friend of his, another Danish waiter called Bent Anderson, was having a party, and Arne thought I might like to come along. But before I could even answer, he abruptly hung up. I didn't know how to call him back, so I rolled over and turned back to sleep. And then, just as I was drifting off, the telephone rang once again.

"Sorry" he whispered, as he laughed just a bit. Muffled dance music nearly drowned out his voice. "The chief steward came by. I had to get off the phone."

"Do you ever *not* work?" I asked him. It seemed that Arne, and the other waiters too, worked any or all of the additional service shifts, from early breakfast on deck, to mid-morning bouillon, to afternoon tea, to private cocktail parties, to midnight buffet, and even late night service in the Polaris, if necessary—all this in addition to their regular assignments of breakfast, lunch, and dinner in the Saga Dining Room. They not only needed the extra money; there was simply nothing else for them to do.

We chatted just a bit before he again asked if I'd like to join Bent's party.

"I don't know Arne. I'm a bit tired" I said. "I'm already in bed."

"Alone?" he asked as he laughed.

"Yes, of course alone" I laughed too. "I'm just not up for a party tonight. But thanks for asking."

As I dropped back into bed, settling my head deeply within my two down pillows; pulling the warm comforter up to my neck—I felt good that Arne had called. As I switched off the light, I realized I hadn't seen Arne in several days. I missed him. I wondered if I had made the right decision. Perhaps I should have gone to that party after all.

Dick Dichosian — although long married, with his wife safely ashore — had for years been living onboard ship with a Norwegian stewardess called Gro—a close friend of Ornulf's wife Ilsa and Per's wife Astrid. Gro was a true Nordic beauty indeed, with classic facial features, crystal blue eyes, and glistening golden-red hair. Together, they shared Dick's tiny staff cabin on Main Deck forward. Cruise Staff rules aside—Dick and Gro's relationship was not only overlooked throughout the years, but actually encouraged by Captain Brookstad—no doubt because of his, and Dick's, deep personal friendship; you remember—golf buddies. A clear double standard, it was. It apparently was perfectly fine for Dick to "fraternize with the crew"—yet for all of us "other" staff members, of course—if we did anything thing like that, we would be tossed off the ship in a minute.

Yet, in an odd sort of way, Dick and Gro's open relationship was encouraging. Perhaps, I thought, if I could find a way to get on the good side of the captain and his officers . . . or even Dick, for that matter—then perhaps any future friendships and relationships I might have onboard could—would—be overlooked as well. If Dick could do it, then why couldn't I?

I convinced myself that as time passed, and I had indeed paid my dues—I too would eventually be allowed to establish and maintain such onboard relationships as Dick's relationship with Gro; and my good buddy Captain Sven,and I, would laugh about that very first scolding I received. But what on earth would I have to do to get in such good favor with Captain Brookstad and his team? Golf was certainly not my game.

Gro walked passed our breakfast table each and every morning on her way to her assigned cabin area on Main Deck aft. Often times, she carried an armful of fresh sheets and pillowcases from the storage pantry forward. She always smiled, and greeted us warmly with a nod; with a kind of curtsy too, in true Norwegian fashion. Gro seemed to like Percy best—apparently, they'd known each other for years.

But one morning, Gro appeared, but she did not smile. In fact, she withdrew from any contact with us at all. And as she walked past our table that morning, she tried her best to camouflage an obviously bruised right eye.

"He's at it again" Percy said after she'd gone.

"What?" I asked. "Who's at it again?"

"Did you see Gro's eye?"

"How could you not? Archibald said. Boy, he's unbelievable."

"What happened? What are you guys talking about?" I demanded to know.

"Dick. He hit her . . . again."

"What do you mean he hit her—*again?*" My voice was raised a bit; to those around us, it could have appeared as if I was shouting.

"Aaah . . . would you say that just a bit louder." Percy shook his head and laughed. "They didn't *quite* hear you at the next table." Percy paused a moment to sip his coffee. "Oh, don't be so shocked" he finally said, realizing quickly that the content of our conversation was clearly quite disturbing. Percy's indifference to it all seemed nearly as disturbing.

"It happens periodically. He's very jealous you know. And Gro, well she's a beautiful woman, and very strong-willed. Dick doesn't put up with Gro even talking with another guy, no matter how innocent it may appear or actually be."

"Why would she allow such a thing?" I asked. "Why doesn't she just leave him?" Percy smiled again and tilted his head.

"Who knows?" Archibald slammed back. "Big Dick's big dick?" I smirked, and merely shook my head. Archibald always had the sexually-related response or comment ready as needed. He would disappoint us all if he did not.

"No, really." Percy jumped in. "Who knows why she stays? Besides, where's she going to go? Move to another cabin?—try not running into Dick on this ship? Impossible." He paused. "And even if she did complain and go right to the captain—whose side do you think he'd take?"

"It's true. We've all wondered why she didn't leave that jerk years ago" Archibald added. "But then again, maybe she likes it. Some women do, you know. At least that's what I'm told."

"How could anyone enjoy such a thing?" I asked in utter disbelief at Archibald's comment. "How could anyone like being beaten up?"

"Perhaps it makes her feel needed—makes her feel that some-one is so much in love with her—so concerned about her and her safety, that he would go to such extremes to keep her, to protect her."

"I don't call that protection" I said. "In fact, I think Gro's out of her mind."

I recalled Dick's aggressive behavior with passengers, and understood how easily that behavior could be transferred to his relationship with Gro—and progress, or *di*gress, into such a vio-lent act.

But what I could not understand, however, was the violence Dick aimed at someone he supposedly loved. How could such a gentle and giving emotion as love itself become—through its own innocent expression—such a horrid evil?

"Violence is a kind of passion" Archibald continued, "just as love is a passion. Both are extremely powerful emotions. In fact I could easily see how they can sometimes become indistinguishable." He then posed a question which at first made me wonder if Ar-chibald was again changing the subject, no doubt back to him.

"Have you even been tickled?" he asked me after a very brief pause and an even quicker sip of his coffee. "We all know that tickling is essentially the feeling created by a certain gentle stimulus upon the surface of the skin; by slightly touching the body where the nerve endings are sensitive. Most people think it's a pleasant sensation, and they laugh uncontrollably. But other's do not. Oth-ers are disturbed by such sensation. But what many of us don't know" he continued, "is that the sensation one feels from a tickle is actually a form of pain—yes, pain—an unpleasant sensation caused by the manipulation of certain nerve endings. The same nerve endings that respond and transport the painful images to the brain, respond and transport the tickling or humorous response as well. It's the same thing. While one sensation is pleasant, the other is most definitely not. And they both could be caused by the same stimuli, and perhaps even for similar reasons."

"Oh dear God, help us all!" Percy said in true exasperation. "I'm sorry you asked." He looked at Archibald then, somewhat incredulously. "What the hell was all that? I didn't understand one thing you said."

Whatever the basis of Archibald's somewhat convoluted logic, his analogy was acute. I understood how one might misinterpret another's actions or desires, or the manner in which those desires are achieved. I wondered if I could ever be guilty of such confusion or misinterpretation—actively, or passively. I wondered if I could be confusing my particular goals in life and my particular dreams, and might I perhaps be acting more on impulse—for the moment—just as Dick apparently was in his relationship with Gro? I wondered if my biggest fears in life might in reality be my dreams after all—just misinterpreted; misunderstood. Where was the careful thought and planning in my life—planning, which my father had always taught me was essential? Why couldn't I see all this clearly? What was holding me back?

But no, I thought. My goals could not be so confusing as to miss them completely. My dreams were simple after all. And the longer I remained onboard ship, the more I felt confident that I was indeed doing what I felt was necessary to achieve them—indeed, I was living my dreams. At least that's what I believed.

For the next few days, I thought often of Arne and his own dream of opening a Danish inn on Arhus with his girlfriend Liz; and I thought of my own. I compared them often to discover whose dream held the most merit. Was Arne's dream better than my own? Was my dream too shallow, or too irrational, or preposterous in fact? Would Arne literally laugh out loud if he ever found out that my dream was fully confined within the limits of the steel hull of this very ship? In essence, Arne was using my dream to achieve his own. What value then, could *my* dream have? Working on a passenger ship—a dream that just a few years ago seemed so unusual . . . so special . . . *now* seemed so mundane. *Now* had little importance to it at all.

As a very young child, I knew I wanted to be on the sea. And that the sea was to be my own true gateway to the world.

As I grew—the more I discovered about the world, the more I wanted. The more I realized how frustrated I would be—how unfulfilled—if I was unable to pursue my journey and continually expand my search. For what was I really searching? I really didn't know. But I knew, at least, that it had to continue.

It was a great adventure, after all. *The* great adventure. And it was just that simple. I began to understand that perhaps my great desire to travel, to explore . . . was perhaps far more important than the destination itself. The destination, in a way, might actually be irrelevant.

The people I had met so far along the way had encouraged my vulnerability—inspired me to understand and appreciate a fascinating new reality of the world, and of myself—an existence which had previously lived only in my dreams.

And personal recognition too; indeed, that was key. Recognition not only by others, but by myself as well. If I had stayed at home, safely in school, I would never have experienced what now shaped my life. I would never have been stimulated by such love and such hate; by soaring exhilaration, by devastating grief. I would never have had the very simple opportunity to know what the world had to offer. Indeed, I would never have known how simple it really was.

I guess it was true after all—what one doesn't know, one doesn't miss. But I couldn't help but wonder what more there was to know; to experience and to learn. I was exhilarated, because it was all ahead of me. And it was infinite.

I rarely thought about a career anymore, nor did I feel any pressure to do so—a pressure ever constant back home, and most notably in academia. I felt comfortably at ease with shipboard living—day-to-day; indeed, at that time in my life, I could not conceive of living anywhere else; could not imagine another place

I'd rather be; could not speculate on another life I'd rather live.

I was pampered by the effortlessness with which my life then flowed. There was no cause to worry about rent or utility bills; nor was I ever concerned with cleaning my room, or handling my laundry or making my bed. It was all done for me, it was all taken care of. And to complement it all came a salary—more money than I had ever dreamed I could earn.

Insecurity though faded in and out like a ship in a fog—briefly seen, then mysteriously lost again out of sight. My moods could get quite low; and at times, they soared. At times, I wondered if I was even more special a person than I ever thought I was; I just had to look at what I had achieved in such a short period of time. I was pleased with the choices I had made. I was finally getting the support, and the friendships too, from many onboard—most of whom seemed intelligent and wondrously remarkable. If they saw such value in me as a person, then indeed there must be something there after all.

I recalled several friends from high school who were then off fighting somewhere in Vietnam. Clearly, they had not been offered the choices I was handed. Or perhaps they were—they just didn't act on them; not seized such opportunity. Who really knew? Who really knows if the choices one makes are ever really right, until they are?

I thought of those school friends, somewhere southwest of our cruising position; I realized how close to them we were. I realized too, for a very brief moment, just how fortunate I was—comfortably safe on a classic ocean liner, traveling the world in a luxury perhaps never to be seen by those same young men with whom just two years before I had shared a morning homeroom, and a steamy gym shower.

I could have—perhaps should have—been ashore with them, somewhere off in a Vietnamese jungle. I wondered if they might just then be staring out to sea in a brief moment of peaceful respite; perhaps watching a passenger ship—ablaze with light—majestically sail on by, uncaringly dismissing all in her wake. Was it luck? A government lottery? Or was it fate—whatever that was? Was it my personal success in moving out on my own; in achieving my goal so early on in life due to obsessive dedication, basic hard work, and unyielding persistence? Was it all a game after all? And if so, who gets the next move?

Although I rarely thought about what I would do when I eventually decided I had had enough, and finally disembarked—what happens to you when you've realized your dreams?—I never honestly believed that working onboard ships was all that I would do in my lifetime. I didn't think that far in advance. I thought, and acted, from day-to-day. That's how I functioned.

Each morning began with the shocking serenity of the sea itself, which inevitably evolved into an inescapable adventure—a remarkable journey ashore for example; or by just being onboard, with my daily work to drive me, with shipboard activities to breed stimulation.

This Pacific period became for me a virtual palette of change; change not only in attitude and basic self confidence, but cardinal change too in my honest response to the world, and to the constant events bombarding me. Change, indeed. For it was at this time, that my attitude towards the passengers was dangerously increasing to a level of sheer cockiness, perhaps even bordering on arrogance. Those passengers who just one month before were quite intimidating to me, I now treated equally with the rest—no different. And, as I got to know them even more, they seemed far less desirable a people than others whom I would have originally considered to be of a much lower life stature.

In blatant contrast to the soaring heights of the world's great mountain ranges and the bruised depressions of its remarkable canyons, it was clear the sea had a pure and very basic mission of placing each of us on an equal and quite similar plane—the rich, the poor; the educated, the intellectually wanting—there is just no escape from it. We become the same after all. Yes—indeed, with all of life's great superficialities stripped away, the sea has a marvelous way of reducing everyone to his lowest common denominator.

Indeed, at sea level, we are all equal. The glamour days of the early transatlantic liners had died long ago—that time when first class meant just that, and tourist—well that took on an entirely altered meaning. No matter how much one tries to appear to be different—to be not what one truly is, but rather what one wishes to be—with make-up and new costumes, and a script of re-writes to satisfy the most difficult of thespians—it all becomes meaningless. No matter how much we try, our true and only image can't help but be reflected in the great seas of the world; reflected and enhanced like a tiny pebble dropped into a pool, with its endless concentric rings growing larger and away.

Naturally, there were the special ones—passengers whose lives one couldn't help but admire; those who offered me great encouragement for growth and discovery; those who openly received the respect they so deserved, not only because of their extraordinary lifetime achievements, but simply because of who they were.

But others, I'm afraid, showed true to their colors—no amount of money, as my father would say, could change a leopard's spots; colors which faded like an overly laundered sheet—thinner for wear, somewhat frayed at the edges.

I was saddened by those passengers; the despondency, at times reaching deep into my soul. Was it pity? Or was it fear that I too may become as they had become? The answer was unclear. The overlooked achievement of some, the lost opportunity, seemed overtly tragic to me. Their youth sailed by surreptitiously, without a mark. Now, they were old; and the physical limitations of great old age seemed to viciously betray them—transforming them all into empty shells with little imagination. Their desire to sail onboard a great ocean liner like *Sagafjord* was less, it appeared, for adventure after all, but because they perhaps really didn't have any other place to go; because they had perhaps little interest or ambition to really do anything else.

I observed the many elderly couples onboard, and some singles too, as they carefully chose their land excursions with an overly cautious eye.

"Does the ship anchor at the Seychelles, or do we dock?" They would ask.

"We anchor" I'd answer.

"Oh dear, then we'll be forced to go ashore in tenders, won't we? I'm afraid we can't take that tour then. You see, my husband's in a wheel chair. I'm afraid it would be too difficult for him."

Or others would ask, "Is there a good deal of walking on that tour? I'm afraid it will be impossible for me. You see, my leg . . ."

And then, what I felt to be the saddest of all—a woman who was traveling alone asked me one day if there were many steps on the Delhi/Agra overland tour.

"Would it be strenuous?" she asked. When I answered affirmatively, she seemed let down, deflated, as if I had punched her hard in the stomach.

"I'm afraid I'll have to pass it up then" she whispered. "I've wanted to see the Taj Mahal all my life. My husband and I saved our entire lives so that we could afford a trip like this. But he died last year you see—I'm afraid I'm a bit too frail now to take on such a strenuous journey on my own."

For the first time in my life, I wondered what it would be like to no longer be nineteen years old, but perhaps three or four times that age, perhaps even older; to no longer have the strength and the ability to do whatever I desired, but to be lost in a sea of frustration—to willingly accept the next best thing. And what might be worst of all . . . to no longer have the desire.

I began to realize that many passengers onboard were not inherently rich, but people perhaps like you and me. Those who had worked hard all their lives in order to be able to afford such a voyage around the world—their once-in-a-lifetime experience. And because of their ages, or an illness, or other such natural limitation, they were prevented from its full enjoyment.

I thought of my parents—my father and mother who worked hard their entire lives in order to obtain and maintain our comfortable home in Westchester County. And I thought of how tragic it would be if they were unable to fulfill their innermost dreams and personal desires—none of which, I realized, I actually knew. I made a pledge then to do all that I could to prevent that from happening; and by so doing, I would also insure that it would never happen to me. I would live a life of no regrets. I would live my life so that I could never look back and wonder about where that other path might have led. I would do whatever I felt; what my own personal instincts told me. And I thanked God that so far, I felt—I knew—I was on the right track. At nineteen years of age, I found myself circumnavigating the globe—doing what many of the passengers had taken an entire lifetime to achieve. Just the thought of that made me blush with pride.

During this time of intense introspection, I began reading through *The Teachings of Buddha*. I was intrigued by its simplicity and obviousness—its profundity. And unlike the Catholicism with which I had been raised, *The Teachings of Buddha* instilled within me a greater power to pursue my own life, and to act naturally within the universe. I could no longer say it was just God's will—because I now knew that it wasn't. It was ours—our own. We were the source of that will. We controlled that very simple, yet incredible, power. And what power, what awe, that very simple concept presented.

Percy and Archibald spoke often of their time together onboard the *France* World Cruise two years before.

"It was the ultimate" Percy said. "I still believe the Chambord Dining Room onboard *France* is one of the finest restaurants in the world."

Their talk of that beautiful liner excited me greatly, recalling warm memories of a frigid New York morning long ago. I quickly realized that the liner *France* had indeed become a passion of mine over the years. I simply could not get her out of my mind. Although I loved ships of all kinds and all sizes, it was really onboard *France* that I wanted to sail.

In a way, I felt like an aging man who cannot forsake the passion and the beauty of his first sexual experience—was she really so great? Or was it so, simply because she was his first? It really didn't matter much after all. In my mind at least, *France* was the ultimate liner—the height of luxury and worldly sophistication—far surpassing the great style of *Sagafjord*. So such praise of that ship—especially coming from Percy and Archibald—only confirmed my feelings and solidified my fantasy.

France rarely cruised. She was built solely for the North Atlantic passenger service—perhaps the last of the great liners. With the onset and increasing popularity of the transatlantic jet race, her owners—Compagnie General Transatlantique—soon realized the necessity of alternating her transatlantic crossings with periodic cruise excursions to more interesting and increasingly exotic ports-of-call. Most of those special voyages occurred during winter months when sailing the North Atlantic can be somewhat uncomfortable, if not downright treacherous.

A one-time-only cruise to Rio de Janeiro early on in her career was designed purely to test the waters. And because of its immediate success, the South American and Caribbean communities soon found themselves welcoming *France*—returning year after year—during her transatlantic winter hiatuses.

But it was her annual *Voyage Imperiale*—the ship's grand voyage around the world—for which *France* was best known; certainly the reason she was most often in the news. The television press, and print press too, eagerly featured her grand midnight sailings from New York, commenting rather cynically about the excessive fares escalating to numbers which—until then—were quite unimaginable. One woman, it was reported, booked not one but three staterooms for the voyage—the loveliest suite for herself of course, and the two adjoining as well . . . one for her luggage; the other for her maid. If one were sailing around the world onboard *France*, one certainly must be properly dressed.

"Hillary Margate was onboard you know." Percy beamed. He spoke of this woman as though any identification or any additional information about her was clearly unnecessary. I certainly had no idea who she might be. But I was beginning to realize that with Percy, such information was really superfluous to the point of his story.

"Of course she had the very best accommodations possible. But still, the dear was uncertain about it all. She was unsure as to whether or not she'd feel confined. You see, she was unaccustomed to sailing the world with other people. She preferred the comforts of her own private yacht."

"How could anyone feel confined on the *France*?" I asked in utter disbelief. "She's the largest passenger ship in the world!"

"Nevertheless" Percy continued in constant cadence, as if giving a lecture to eager students of the well-to-do. "You know the rich. Rather whimsical, to say the least. So she telephoned the captain of her yacht—over three-hundred feet I think it is . . . at least that—I forget what she's called just now . . . *Morning Star*, or something like that. Yes, that's it. *Morning Star*—like the beach. Beautiful, that; simply beautiful. And she instructed her captain to follow *France* around the world. Sort of insurance, I guess you'd call it. You know, in case she got bored with it all, and wanted to disembark. And so that's what happened. *Morning Star* followed *France* completely around the world—always at a distance, always in her sight."

The excessiveness of it alone made me gasp. Percy enjoyed my reaction, I'm certain, as he continued his story.

"She only used the yacht once, though. In Bombay, I believe. She threw a lovely luncheon onboard for six of her very dear dear friends. Naturally, my friend Elizabeth was among them."

"Naturally" Archibald commented rather sarcastically. "But I really think she's too big—the ship, not your friend."

"Yes she is. Remember Archie what a horror it became?"

"I told you never to call me Archie!"

"Yeah, yeah, yeah—Archie, Archie, Archie." Percy turned to me and continued his story. "Because she's so . . . enormous, she's unable to dock in most ports and therefore must anchor off shore quite a distance. You can't imagine the incredibly long tender rides we all had to endure. And to top it off, her tenders only had a capacity of one-hundred; the ship's capacity was nearly two-thousand. It was endless." Both Archibald and Percy laughed a bit as they each silently remembered their experience.

"On our first visit to Moorea" Percy continued, "we had to anchor so far out—we were still loading the morning tour at one fifteen in the afternoon. The passengers were furious. I, of course, was simply exhausted—I just had to get to a gin and tonic as soon as I could. I took to my bed as soon as the last bus pulled away.

"Now don't misunderstand. I certainly loved the sheer luxury of *France*. Grand, I'd call her. But working onboard was hell—a lot more work than I was willing to accept. I couldn't wait to get off that thing."

"You always can't wait to get off" Archibald burst in. "But there was another and even bigger problem too Percy, if you remember correctly. One which is clearly causing her rapid demise."

Archibald looked at me quickly then, and went on.

"When the ship was still in pre-construction—1960 or so I'd imagine—Charles de Gaulle was still President of France. De Gaulle—never really America's fondest supporter—was in fact against the ship ever being built. He wanted nothing to do with America—he loathed the fact that the ship would be sailing between Le Havre and New York, often with American passengers. Nevertheless, with French nationalism as it was—and still is, mind you—de Gaulle felt compelled to construct the finest ship of the time, perhaps the finest ever built. Clearly, such a liner would quickly become a tremendous object of French national pride. Remember, at around that same time, we had just introduced the *United States*, a ship which quickly—on its maiden voyage no less—became the fastest and most modern ship in the world.

"De Gaulle was a stubborn man" Archibald continued. "If the ship was to be built at all, he would insure that she would never have to pay the United States government one franc more than necessary in tariffs and tolls and docking and maritime fees. So he ordered the ship to be designed and constructed several feet longer than the longest lock of the Panama Canal—virtually insuring that she could never make the transit and therefore never pay canal tolls to the United States.

"What was the result? On our world cruise, the ship had to steam completely around South America, taking up an incredible amount of time, not to mention an exorbitant amount of excess fuel at a time when fuel prices were constantly rising—going through the proverbial roof in fact. That's why the French Line is in such trouble today. There's even talk of pulling her from service. De Gaulle built a white elephant for the onset of the jet age, and all because of his stupid national pride. All to prove a point. But that's the French for you. You know what they say, don't you? The French? 'Hell is other people.' They only want to deal with themselves. They truly believe the world revolves around Paris."

"Pity. It's such a beautiful city. It's just a shame it's French. Elizabeth lives there you know. Numero huit, Rue de la Paix."

At 5:30 A.M. My telephone rang.

"Are you awake yet? It's Arne. Get up."

"Ah . . . yes, of course I'm up." I lied. I wasn't awake at all. In fact I was still in bed, still asleep. I tried desperately to sound convincing. I never let people know I was asleep, or even in bed, when they called at extremely early or late hours. I didn't like being put in what I considered to be a compromising position. I always had to be up early and ready, and would never let them know that they may have caught me with my proverbial pants down.

"Look out your porthole" Arne said.

"Why? What's out there?"

"Just look."

I threw the sheets back and stood with the telephone still in my hand. I glanced through the narrow steel casing which housed my only porthole.

A Chinese junk was peacefully floating past.

"Arne?"

"Welcome to Hong Kong" he said. And then he hung up.

It was raining gently as I arrived on deck—the morning light already brighter and far more nurturing than when Arne had first called. Hong Kong harbor was busy—exhaustingly brisk. Somehow, I knew it would be. It was always so when Nugent and Captain Huxley and Miss Pomeroy visited; why not for me?

We quickly pulled alongside at the newly remodeled Ocean Terminal, and I was ashore even before the announcement was made that the ship was cleared and passengers could proceed ashore.

Hong Kong was the essence of the orient for me; second only to mysterious Shanghai. It symbolized the orient—the clichés, of course . . . seedy back water streets, hustling street vendors, rick-shaws and coolies—where angry Chinamen wearing miniscule skull caps as dark as the night chased unsuspecting felines with razor-sharp meat cleavers held high above their heads; where open-air markets offered snake and pig, and eel and shark. Espionage and murder were no doubt just around the corner; where investigative agents in overly long trench coats and colorless fedoras would frequent smoky harbor-side bars in search of incognito-ed informants. The air heavy with fog; a lone whistle hauntingly droning out its very own call from across the dark and obscure waters of Hong Kong bay.

Or at least that's what I expected to find; at least that was the Hong Kong of my grand poetic dreams. It's what films and television can do to a young man's imagination—paint a dramatic picture by a director's hand, quite often without any semblance of reality. Thank God for imagination—for allowing those seeds to grow and to flourish in one's own mind. But the reality—well, I'm afraid that's another case all together.

I stepped ashore into what appeared to be an immense shopping arcade, crowdedly built within the ship terminal itself. It was hard to see the distinction—hard to determine if this was a passenger pier with shops, or a busy shopping mall which also offered ships docking privileges. Shop after shop lined the vastly broad walkway between *Sagafjord*'s gangway and the busy street below. I must have visited them all as I stepped ashore that morning—one simply had no choice. Hong Kong, after all, was a shopper's paradise; at least that's what I was told. I was obliged, if not compelled, to find a bargain—as many as I could, in fact—and display them proudly back onboard; back at home. It was a badge of consumer pride and shameless esteem after all—boasting to friends just what you found, just what you purchased, and just how little you paid.

I remembered seeing television quiz shows when I was a child—you've got thirty seconds to fill this shopping cart with as many items as you can within the allotted time. And if you're lucky enough to toss in that very special mystery prize, you too will receive the washer dryer, and the elegant silver tea service specifically designed for you by the Michael C. Fina Company of Chicago, Illinois. So there I was, albeit in Hong Kong—ready to go, with a shopping cart of obsession well in both hands—wheels spinning, strategy already planned—waiting for the count off—"ready, set, go!"

I just had to have the jade ring as soon as I saw it—a simple band it was. It seemed to say Hong Kong—just by being jade and all. I thought it the perfect remembrance of my time ashore, although it had only been less than twenty minutes, and I wasn't yet sure what it was I wanted to remember.

The Nikon cameras called out too—a new 80-200 zoom lens for me, and a Nikkormat for each of my brothers back home. Nikons, I was told, were the very best. And this was the place to get them after all—at least that's what Dick told us at dinner. Although I was only still a fledgling photographer, I wanted, and had to have, nothing but the best. A lesson well learned from Percy and the others.

So on I went—from store to store and from shop to shop. Like a kid in a candy store I was, vulnerable as ever. With American cash in hand, I was the darling of the merchant Chinese. Clearly, they saw me coming.

Archibald soon found me on the pier, and quickly released me from my shopping frenzy.

"Are you crazy?" he asked. "We're going to be in Hong Kong for five days. You'll have plenty of time to shop. And never—ever—shop in these tourist traps if you're looking for real bargains. Come, I'll show you where you should shop."

So that morning, Archibald and I went off together to walk the streets and to browse the markets. Hannon had been to Hong Kong many many times before. He knew where to go and what to see; he knew which streets to take, and which ones to avoid. I was in good hands that morning, even if they were Archibald Hannon's. Indeed, I was pleased he found me.

The streets nearest the pier were filled with large wooden crates piled high above our heads. Colorful rickshaws where set in a row, and around them lurked a host of exotic seaport types—dark and

degenerate . . . in a way very much fitting my fantasy of the infamous British colony. I was disappointed to learn, however, that
the rickshaws were not for native use at all, but rather to gratify
tourist expectation, not unlike my own—hired for independent
city excursions, or for simple taxi-like service. There, they waited
for our passengers like spiders stilled; until just the right moment
to pounce upon their unsuspecting prey.

Everyone, it appeared, moved about in his own little world, under
his own secret plan. Their cacophonous voices—somewhat abrasive,
clearly annoying—were jarringly loud and aimed in no particular
direction. I noticed hundreds of street vendors—agitated, so they
seemed—and the remarkable swiftness with which they transacted
business; one eye, naturally keen on their wares, and their profits.

"They have an interesting law here in Hong Kong" Archibald
said as we walked. "Unwritten, at least. If someone is caught
stealing, they simply cut off his hand." The image of the meat-
clever-carrying Chinaman came to mind after all. "Very few thieves
steal a second time" he continued. "And no one, for quite obvious
reasons, attempts a third. I think they may have something there,
don't you?"

"Sounds a bit severe" I said. "But I guess it stops the problem."

"I'm sure it does just that."

We turned and walked up Nathan Road. The crowds grew
denser, nearly impenetrable, with each additional step.

"Come with me" he insisted. "I want you to meet my tailor.
Percy told me you could use a new suit or two."

Clearly, I was embarrassed. What did Percy mean—I needed
a new suit? I was quite happy with my wardrobe as it was. Perhaps it was simple, certainly functional. Obviously though, Percy
felt otherwise. Who the hell was Percy Hayes, after all, to make
such comments about me and my wardrobe? The pompous ass, I
thought. Just because his clothes were custom-made in Tangier...

The following silence was telling, but useful. For when I
thought about it a moment longer, I realized that perhaps Percy
might indeed be right. I laughed then at his frankness; fully ap-

preciated his honesty. Of course I could use a new suit. Why not? I was in Hong Kong, after all. And if someone was to travel around the world on *Sagafjord*, one should certainly dress for it.

As we continued along Nathan Road, Archibald began to share a bit more about his young friend called Matthew. It was apparent the boy had been on his mind; Archibald seemed unusually uneasy the previous days. There had to be something causing it; and it simply had to be Matthew.

Almost immediately, I sensed the sadness in his voice, the gnawing despair. Archibald's deep concern for his young friend was clear and openly apparent. His love, undisguisable.

He spoke softly, with a whisper so low I could barely hear its pain. The contrast between the caustic shrill of a busy Hong Kong street, and the potent intimacy of an aging man's dreams was shocking. So fitting and representative, I thought, of where our relationship had evolved. And as Archibald spoke that morning, I experienced a transformation before my very eyes. The Archibald Hannon I knew, or at least thought I knew, became quite another person indeed—someone who freely ripped open the very flesh of his soul. Someone so willing to reveal the honest vulnerability which, up until then, had been purposely hidden and curiously suppressed; someone who seemed far less cynical and far more nurturing and loving than the Archibald Hannon I had grown to know over the past five weeks.

I witnessed too the softening of the pompous intellectual image he usually donned, and the surfacing of a gentle and loving and surprisingly sensitive human being. And through it all, it was clear that the young Matthew of which he spoke that morning was not just a sexual conquest for the older Hannon—a sensual talisman to grab and to own for a brief moment in time, and then discard without ever a trace, without ever a care. No, Archibald Hannon genuinely did care for the boy. He loved him deeply, in fact. That simple revelation hit me like a thunderbolt.

We crossed the road to the other side.

"So what can I do?" he asked, his voice nearly breaking. "You're his age. I need your advice." Archibald sounded desperate. "Why isn't Matthew able to respond positively to me—to our relationship? He seems to fight it, and me, all the time. He wants to push it away."

I was flattered that Archibald was not only confiding in me, but asking my advice. Can you imagine that? Someone as bright as Archibald Hannon asking advice from someone like me? What the hell did I know about it all? What did I understand about love and relationships? Especially those homosexual in nature?

"Does he know why you want to be his friend?" I asked Archibald, quite amazed that—instinctively—I had such an insight.

"What do you mean?" Archibald shot back quickly, somewhat curious, somewhat defensive. I hesitated. I wasn't quite sure just what I had meant myself, or why I had even asked the question. If my insight surprised me, it certainly surprised Archibald as well, and quite possibly had taken him uncharacteristically off guard.

"Well, let me ask this" I continued. "How and where did the two of you actually meet?" I wanted to know the history partly out of curiosity, and partly because I couldn't really explain my previous question very well at all. I had to divert the conversation until I knew better what to say. I was pretty good at that—diversion, that is. This, after all, was my first and perhaps greatest opportunity to give and to share advice with someone as intellectually gifted as Archibald Hannon. I didn't want to blow it. I didn't want to appear stupid and shallow after all.

We settled in to a steady pace by then, and Archibald Hannon began his story.

"We met at a dinner party in Lawrence Kansas; that's where Matthew was attending college. I was visiting my dear old friend, Jeanne Atridge—she was hosting an informal dinner in my honor, of course. Jeanne, being the great intellectual that she is, is quite actively involved with the local university, so she invited a few of the more gifted students to join us. And Matthew was one of those students.

"Matthew was already at Jeanne's when I arrived. He stood when we were first introduced, towering over me as he shook my hand strongly. 'Finally' he said, 'I get to meet the author of *The Emperor's Throne*. A magnificent work.'"

Smart guy, I thought to myself. Matthew certainly knew what he was doing—to flatter Archibald Hannon, taking total control. Archibald continued.

"All during dinner, I sensed an intensity from Matthew—whether it was strength or vulnerability, I couldn't really tell. Yet he watched me assiduously all evening; he seemed to hang on to my every word. Naturally, I savored the attention—drank it all in if you will—especially when it came from such a handsome young man as Matthew Scott. It's not everyday that someone with his looks and his sensitivity and his intelligence shows an interest in an older man like me.

"The conversation at dinner was quite esoteric. We discussed everyone from Geothe to Kirkegaard to Russell to Wittgenstien; and Matthew fell right into it all, actively keeping pace with the rest of us. And let me say that it's not every young man these days who can intelligently discuss Goethe and Kirkegaard, let alone know who they were."

Indeed, Archibald was right. I certainly didn't know who the hell they were, but I couldn't let on to Archibald. So I encouraged him to continue his story—never a difficult task.

"At the end of the evening, as we stood to leave, Matthew offered to walk me across campus to the guest house in which I was staying. I sensed a certain exigency in his eyes as we put on our coats; a compulsion whose soul I could not bear. Each of us kissed Jeanne goodnight, and left quietly on our way.

"You must know that Matthew clearly fascinated me—right from the start. It was hopeless. I guess I was doomed.

"The cold air was refreshing. It awakened my senses to the realities of the night. The tension, though, continued to build between us as we followed each other's lead. Finally, Matthew spoke."

"'You intrigue me Archibald Hannon' Matthew said. 'I like that. I'd like to know you better.' I looked at him and trembled.

We stopped walking for a while. I wasn't sure where Matthew was going with these powerful and revealing words, but it excited me greatly."

"'How old are you Matthew?' I asked him."

"'Eighteen. But it's all right.'"

"By then we had come to a secluded area near the athletic field. Was it Matthew who led us there, or subconsciously did I? I wasn't certain. All I knew was that it was intensely dark. The uneven ground caused me to stumble. Matthew reached out to help steady my footing. And then it just happened. Simply. Naturally. As if fate had directed, and given us the cue.

"I felt his lips on mine as Matthew eased his body against me. My heart echoed powerfully; his warmth reaching deep within my being. I embraced him strongly right there amongst the trees, buried within the bushes. I felt his erection press aggressively against my leg—I felt it right through his pants. I knew then that it was safe. I knew then what had to happen. And I fell to my knees as his pants dropped to his.

"It was over quickly, somewhat telling, I guess. But I wasn't yet ready to let him go. Until then, the warmth of his closeness and the heat of the moment made us both oblivious to the night's frigid chill. But soon, however, it briskly embraced us. I held him though as long as he allowed, until, in silence, his adolescent fidgeting let me know that we had better move on.

"It was silence then that escorted us the remaining distance to my door. The crunch of frost underfoot was our only conversation. One light only glowed brightly overhead to welcome me home.

"I looked at Matthew; he smiled. He said he wanted to keep in touch with the author of *The Emperor's Throne*; perhaps we could correspond.

"The despondency in his eyes was magnetic" Archibald continued. "I wanted to take him into my arms once again right there, at the door to my campus home, but I knew how inappropriate and perhaps even embarrassing such a gesture would have been. We shook hands, and he was gone, off somewhere into the darkness.

At dawn, I left for New York." Archibald then fell silent. We continued our walk.

"And that's it?" I asked him.

"What do you mean 'and that's it?'"

"That's what you're basing this entire relationship on? A blow job in the woods at midnight?"

"Of course not." Archibald snapped back, somewhat defensively. "Do you think I would actually fall in love with an excruciatingly handsome eighteen-year-old, to whom I gave a blow job during what seemed to be an intensely exciting one-night-stand in a romantically wooded area of the University of Kansas, Lawrence campus, athletic field?"

"Yes. I do."

"Well—you're right" Archibald said. We looked at each other for a moment and began laughing uncontrollably. It was a moment of pure honesty, of genuine understanding. When we finally stopped laughing, Archibald raised his hand. "But no, no. Really, there's more."

Archibald continued, telling me about their subsequent correspondence and Matthew's periodic visits to his "little monk's cell" in Chelsea. What was remarkable, at least to me, was Archibald's willingness to express his great feelings for the boy. It became clear that Archibald's very innocent desire to establish a close relationship with the young Matthew was no different than those very basic desires of anyone else who searched for a loving relationship with another person—heterosexual or homosexual. It was the same, I realized. And each was certainly and equally valid. What was important, I realized, was the love the two people shared. How that love was expressed was not what should be at issue.

The neurotic fears of a month ago—perhaps of a lifetime— seemed already ancient and long forgotten. I laughed, first to myself and then again openly and out loud, as I understood just how unfounded and unnecessary my initial fears had been. Archibald and Percy and the others weren't a threat to me at all, unless I allowed them to be. And perhaps it was the fear itself which proliferated the deeper fear—not the men, at all. Not these people who were really quite harmless, and who were basically very loving and considerate human beings.

There, in Hong Kong, I found myself with an amazing man. I was proud to be with him, and for the first time in my life, I really didn't care what other people thought, or what others might say.

Archibald continued talking but I paid little attention to what he said. I walked with a renewed smile on my face—a smile I had not worn before. I felt the release of a burden which seemed to have always been a part of my life. I looked at the others along the streets, and felt a soaring exuberance—unparalleled knowledge. I finally knew something they didn't know. When would they, I wondered, understand how simple and how basic it all really was?

The colorless buildings lining Nathan Road seemed to move past us far faster than we were walking past them. Hong Kong was unimportant to me then. I was riveted to this man called Archibald Hannon and to his story more than I ever imagined was possible. It was a strange attraction I felt—more towards his sincerity and his enviable ability to care for another human being, than to the man himself—a feeling, I had never felt before.

And surprisingly, in an odd sort of way, I felt I knew and understood Matthew Scott as well. Because like Matthew to Archibald, I was greatly intrigued by the man with whom I walked.

As the road forked, and we began scaling the steps up to Archibald's tailor shop, Matthew lived as vividly in my mind as he clearly did in Archibald's life. I was energized by being a part of their lives. I became excited by the feeling it gave me.

While at Hong Kong—undoubtedly due to the extremely low cost and great availability of local labor—*Sagafjord* was to be painted from the top of her mast right down to her water line; from stem to stern. The ship was to undergo a complete external make-over—a transformation if you will—or at least that's what Quartermaster Jan told me as I left the ship that next day.

They began early that morning armed with scaffolds, and rope, bosun's chairs, and brushes and paint and rollers on long poles, and drop clothes too. Well equipped they were for the huge task before them, and within minutes it seemed as if they descended upon the unsuspecting ship in a frenzy.

I watched from ashore. They hung from *Sagafjord*'s massive soot-soiled funnel on scaffolds, with paint rollers in hand. They dropped over the sides of her rusting gray hull, and from the top of her white superstructure, on ropes and from bosun's chairs too. They appeared to engulf her—suffocating her—as a mass of angry insects overcome their prey; as bees swarm about their hive in a desperate attempt to protect their queen. The men, purposeful as they were, moved over the ship quickly. Hundreds of them there must have been to progress with such swiftness and with such intent—first scrapping the rust-stained hull, then applying a fresh coat of the trademarked NAL gray and white paint generously and routinely up and down, and from side to side.

As I watched them work that morning, I thought about our sailing day from New York just one month before, and I remembered how majestically proud the ship looked that day—as she stood there gleaming fresh in the crisp light of a winter's morning, safely tied to her pier, ready and eager to take on the world. She had strength then, and a powerful determination.

That strength and determination seemed gone now—lost somewhere I did not know. Was it really her strength which had gone? Or was it just my newly realized ability to see clear through it?

She looked tired, if a ship could indeed look so. She was calm, with a certain peacefulness somewhat reminiscent of that cold January day. The scars of the world we had sailed thus far—deeply etched within the paint of her gray hull—were being wiped away by a quick brush stroke; a chance for a new and fresh beginning thusly given her.

As I sat on a hill just off the pier, I watched the harbor live its life. I listened to its sounds. Ocean freighters, wooden junks and fishing boats too all seemed to hold firm on certain collision courses, yet none occurred. They all had their place to be, they all had their individual routes to take, and they effortlessly proceeded—one boat's movement necessary for the next one's advancement.

Percy came by and joined me—an Hermes scarf wrapped

casually around his neck, carefully tucked deep inside his shirt. He was off shopping for antiques he told me; his Vuitton bag, already half-stuffed with Hong Kong specials no doubt acquired in little-known shops somewhere off in back alleys perhaps known only to him.

"Always buy in pairs" he said. "I just found the finest porcelain vases; apple-green—they'll look fabulous at Smith Street. Come along."

But I didn't want to go with Percy just yet. I wanted to sit for a while. With Hong Kong Island just in the distance, the view of the harbor was remarkably beautiful—and I wanted to think, mostly about me and about my life, and about what being in that incredible city actually meant. I brought my crystal ashore with me—only I knew that. I needed to hold it. I needed the comfort. I needed the security; it always made me feel better.

Indeed I was pensive, yet at the same time exhilarated. What was it?—the crisp weather, the panoramic views, the excitement of Hong Kong itself?—who knew? Percy sat with me for a brief moment, quite curious, I'm sure, as to what was going on.

I was happy to be where I was, I told him, and to be doing just what I was doing. Nonetheless, I feared getting stuck. I didn't want to become a cruise bum like Hal Carter or Marshall Smith, or John Marratisch and his dancing boys. I didn't want to be fifty or sixty years old and coming back to the sea over and over again like so many of those I had met on this voyage. I didn't want to get stuck in this wonderful yet totally unrealistic world, and have no other choices offered me in my lifetime. Has-beens, I called them that morning. I didn't want to become a cruise ship has-been.

"So don't" Percy said as he laughed at what he perceived were nonsensical thoughts. "You're nineteen years old, for God's sake. What's all this talk of has-beens?

"You can change things, anytime you want" he continued. You've only just started." Percy was by then becoming impatient, I sensed, wanting to get back to the shops. And I knew I was keeping him from doing just that. Yet, surprisingly, he stayed.

"I'm not too sure it's that easy, Percy. I don't have the initiative or the drive that others seem to have. And that, I'm afraid, is apparently necessary to be successful."

"Success. What the hell does that mean?"

I fell silent. I really didn't know how to reply.

"What the hell are you talking about?" Percy asked, finally choosing to let his impatience show. "Why are you doing this to yourself? You're so . . . uptight."

"What's *that* supposed to mean?" I asked him. Now I was becoming a bit annoyed and a little embarrassed by his frankness and his honesty, and by the self-revelation that I really didn't know what I was saying; that I really hadn't thought any of this through very much at all.

"Well" he continued, as he finally took his Vuitton bag off his lap and placed it on the wooden bench next to where we sat. I guess he realized he would be staying a while after all.

"To start off with—who got this job for you? No one. You got it for yourself. You went out and wrote those letters; you pushed your way in to meet Robert Brooks in New York; and you sold yourself to him, convincing him you were right for this position. No one else did that. No one gave this to you. You did it.

"Now I think that's pretty amazing if you ask me. I think that's pretty remarkable. Do you know how many other nineteen-year-old boys are sailing around the world on perhaps the finest cruise liner afloat, and making money at the same time? Not many, I can assure you of that." Percy settled back into his seat, and looked ahead as he awaited my response.

"Yes, but that was easy" I said to him. "This—working on ships—was an obsession with me from as far back as I can remember. A passion, sort of. It was easy to pursue that passion. Perhaps I had no other choice."

"Aah . . . passion" he said as he smiled. "It's *only* about passion. Don't you see that? And the exciting thing is that you've got it." He paused a moment to let that sink in.

"Most people never really take a look at themselves—our passengers, for instance, let's look at them. Yes, they're rich—some of them, at least. And they may seem successful and worldly and sophisticated too, but what about *their* passions. Do you think experiencing the world like this is their idea of fulfilling their dreams? I doubt it. Most of them are here just so they can tell their friends back home they sailed on *Sagafjord*; that they wintered around the world. Yes, they may be onboard an affluent world cruise liner, but what are their real dreams? Have they ever really lived their dreams? Their passions? ...as you are doing right now... Think about that.

"Don't you see how exciting that is? To have a dream and to have a passion about that dream? Just stop for one moment, and think. Just look at what you've been able to accomplish so far in your life."

I did as Percy asked. I thought long and hard. I felt refreshed and enlivened by his suggestion, yet I felt overwhelmed and disenchanted at the same time. And I really didn't know why.

"Well, maybe so" I said. "But how will I know what to do next—if this is all there will be; how will I know if I can still do something else, something better?"

"Who cares about something better? That's not what this is about. It's about doing what you like to do, or perhaps just liking what you choose to do.

"First of all" Percy turned to face me, "stop living in the future; don't worry about the future. You're nineteen for God's sake! The future will happen soon enough, believe me. And if you just take care of now, the future will be healthy, and it will be right."

He waved his arms around in a flippant yet loving way.

"Life is moments. Moments like this one—with you and me sitting here together on a bench in Hong Kong—watching life go on around us. *Its* life becomes *our* life. It becomes us. Don't you see that?

"And if you do—don't ever forget it. This—this right here is all we really have. Nothing more, and most definitely nothing less, unless we choose to make it so.

"And another thing, my dear boy. Continue to take risks in your life. That's why we're here. And when you do, don't then spend your time worrying if you did or did not do the right thing. You'll be so preoccupied . . . you'll be so confused . . . you'll miss out on the wonders of the risk you *did* take. You'll miss it all. And there's nothing worse than that—than missing out. Believe me. Taking risks is what life is all about."

Percy became quiet for a moment and stared ahead at the harbor traffic.

"Do you see all those ships out there?" he asked. "Well, it's very safe for a ship to stay in its harbor. No harm can come to it there. But remember—a ship is not made to stay in its harbor. It's made to go to sea."

A tug's whistle blew just then, as if on cue in a fast moving play; our sleek white rival, Swedish American Line's *Gripsholm* was arriving in port. I wondered if that very confused passenger—the one who complained about not getting her time changes straight—would take this opportunity to actually jump ship while she had the chance.

"Now" he said as he stood dramatically and picked up his Vuitton, slinging it widely over his shoulder "can we please go shopping? Like life, shopping is moments too."

That afternoon, I took the Star Ferry across the bay to Hong Kong Island and wandered around on my own. The weather was perfect—crisp and cool—and I felt good to be alone. At one point, I glanced back towards Kowloon where *Sagafjord* was then moored; she looked beautiful there. She was perfect.

Percy's words echoed in my mind. If it were true, and I had the entire world ahead of me, open to me—a world of opportunity to experience and to choose from—I would be fine. But it was frightening too. Daunting. The whole world, after all. And I was alone.

I often thought it was better to have little or no choices at all. The more choices one has, the more one torments oneself to insure that his choice is indeed the right one after all.

Several months before our arrival at Hong Kong, RMS *Queen Elizabeth*, the then retired world-famous Cunarder, was purchased by Hong Kong financier C.Y. Tung. His intention was to transform the historic ship into an accredited floating university which would continually sail the world—offering students the opportunity of extensive world exploration along with their usual classroom studies—not unlike what I was doing, but clearly a bit more academically formal. He renamed his ship *Seawise University* and the refurbishment began in earnest, right there in Hong Kong harbor.

But late one evening, while the ship sat safely at anchor just off shore, Seawise University mysteriously caught fire, burning and capsizing; a total loss—just a mile or so from where *Sagafjord* stood. The cause was unknown—although sabotage by Tung's business rivals was actively speculated.

I had to see her, there was no question. So Arne and I chartered a harbor-cruiser and set out to the site, cameras in hand. It was mid-afternoon, and by the time we pulled away from the dock, thick gray clouds had already begun to form overhead.

From our vantage point we could see the wreck just ahead, portside; the sea grew choppy as we made our approach. The sight of that once magnificent liner—now nothing more than a burned-out twisted hulk of steel, lying helplessly on her starboard side—was overwhelmingly sad. Degraded, and debased, she was openly exposed, naked there for all to see.

I stood silent, as if in memorial, as our launch slowly circled the wreck. Arne too seemed emotionally moved by the sight; and he, clearly, had little passion for ships. In a moment, the great liner's history flashed vividly in my mind, and I fantasized about what she must have been like in her heyday, when she grandly traversed the North Atlantic with great pride and glamour. I mourned for her that day, and for an era of shipping history that was gone forever as well, never to be reclaimed.

It began to drizzle as our launch slowly turned to starboard and left the great ship in our wake. I would see her never again.

That night, several of the staff were invited to a special dinner arranged by Archibald's Hong Kong tailor—no doubt to promote future sales. Of course, Archibald and Percy were invited, but so were Lar and Maggie and Clifford too. Ted and Anne were invited as well, I was told, but they graciously declined. Perhaps they had their own tailor's dinner to attend.

We taxied to a street not far from the pier, and walked the remaining distance, down a short alleyway, to an alcove leading to a long and narrow stairway. Chinese characters in bold red neon adorned the sign just adjacent to the entrance. The name of the restaurant therefore was a mystery to us all—except perhaps to Archibald. I wouldn't at all be surprised if he was fluent in Chinese as well. Twenty-two Nathan Road, the invitation said. And that was all we knew.

The restaurant was filled with locals of all types. The room was brash and loud, and constant activity seemed to fill the space. We were quickly escorted from the entranceway to an adjoining private dining room where our host waited. Mr. Chen was his name—of course. He stood as we entered; his grin made his already rotund body seem broader and a bit squat.

He greeted us all personally, one at a time, shaking our hands with a little nod of his head. He had met each of us before, when we had first visited his shop for fittings and measurements for our new wardrobes of fashionable clones. I was impressed, though, that Mr. Chen correctly remembered each of our names. It was all the English he knew however, so conversation, however willing, was quite stilted throughout the evening.

We were all seated together at a giant circular table—the only one in the room—the center of which had a large turntable built right in; a kind of Chinese lazy-susan, I guess you'd call it. All serving was done from this center section with great ease.

There was lots of laughter that night, and lots of drinks too; and the shipboard pressures and anxieties seemed long forgotten. There was no ordering from a menu. Our host saw to that. And so we shared each dish presented to us—eagerly sampling what was offered without really questioning or knowing what it was we might be eating. My chopstick skills had improved just a bit since Kamakura, and I proudly manipulated them for all to see. A lost shrimp here—a dropped bamboo shoot there—it all mattered little in the face of experience.

I thoroughly enjoyed the shark's fin soup, served hot and steaming from little porcelian cups. The main course was a freshly killed, specially prepared duck—with head and feet still attached. It was strategically placed on the turntable; its dark and glazed-over eyes staring directly into my own.

"Could we turn this just a bit" I said as I eased the duck's head just slightly to the right and over toward Lar. "Does it have to look directly at me?"

Philip Pound and I were assigned to escort Tour 27—*The Island of Macao*. Together—with over one hundred passengers in tow—we took the Star Ferry's short ride across Hong Kong harbor to Victoria Island. From there, we boarded a hydrofoil for the ninety-minute crossing far across the channel to the island of Macao—the oldest European settlement in the Far East.

The island's Portuguese influence was quite evident in its colonial architecture and classic grand design. We visited the Temple of the Goddess of Mercy that morning, the Penha Church, and the great Bishop's Palace. Naturally, the tour stopped briefly at the casino where I lost twenty-five dollars on roulette—a fortune to me at the time. But at least I lost it on Macao, and that was something special.

When we were ready to return home though—quite tired and dirty after a long hot day of sightseeing, and busing, and touring and gambling—Philip and I were told by our local agent that the hydrofoil on which we had come to Macao was having mechanical difficulties, and would not be able to make the return trip. Instead, we were all to take the local ferry, then only minutes away from departure.

The ferry, the *Macao Star* it was called—quite easily forty or fifty years old—looked to be in quite a dangerous condition, with so much rust splattered across her hull it was impossible to decipher what color she may have originally been painted. The boat's once white superstructure looked faded from hundreds—if not thousands—of round trips; blemished too from the thickened black soot exhausted from her aging funnel. Her open decks were already crowded with people—six or seven hundred of them it seemed, clearly more than *Sagafjord* carried to capacity—on a boat perhaps just slightly larger than the average fishing trawler.

Macao Star's passengers rushed about from open deck to open deck with what seemed to be a crazed desire to be somewhere they weren't. With voices raised, they pushed and shoved, making it quite clear that they belonged there, and we—the non-Asians—did not. Babies cried. Chickens and other animals in cages squawked and madly fluttered about to make us all aware of their presence too.

It took nearly four hours of pitching and rolling in fairly rough seas to sail the same route the hydrofoil traversed in only ninety minutes. There was no possible way any of us could have enjoyed the trip. I stood by the rail in silence, and in fear. All I could think about was that the *Macao Star* would capsize in her overloaded condition, and we would all be killed. I saw the newspaper headline clearly in my mind—*Passenger ferry capsizes in rough seas off Macao. No survivors. Many Americans among the dead.*

We made it through though, arriving back at shipside at 9:20 P.M. Chief Steward Anderson held the dining room service open especially for us that evening.

A freshly painted *Sagafjord*, and cabin A-54, never looked so good.

On the last day of our Hong Kong visit, I escorted *Kowloon and the New Territories*—a half-day tour venturing north to the colony's mainland boarder. Standing atop Lok Ma Chau and looking beyond the infamous Bamboo Curtain and on into mainland China was clearly a thrill for me—a thrill of terror. In a way, I felt as if I shouldn't be there—shouldn't be seeing what I was then seeing. I felt like a naughty adolescent who's been caught peeking at his showering brother or sister. I knew I was safe; I was on an organized tour. I was an American citizen, after all. But still,

I was frightened and uneasy.

I imagined being violently captured by the communist Chinese and dragged screaming and yelling across the border, never to be seen or heard from again. That's what one gets—and perhaps deserves—for being where one shouldn't. In an odd way, that prurient feeling excited me. And it rekindled a fading memory of a similar excitement which haunted me still. Reckless excitement, it was. Total abandon. Romantic. The one night I spent with Vincent I was also overcome with unimaginable excitement. Then too, I felt as if I shouldn't be doing what I was doing, and yet wanted it all the more. But it was okay, I thought. I felt it now. I believed it.

Returning to the sea after so many days ashore was as comfortable as stepping into an old shoe. The usual day-to-day onboard activities picked up right where they left off—Hal Carter conducting his daily-at-sea walkathon around Sun Deck, while Anne Dickson held her morning "stretch" classes poolside. John Marratisch continued his golf clinics too, although by this time in the voyage, he seemed far more interested in dazzling the wealthy single women with his bleached smile, than by impressing the more sports-minded men with his skillful golf swing.

Clifford Deetlefs seemed immediately at home in the Tour Office environment; it was clear that he had done this work so many times before. It was good to have Cifford onboard with us—not only for the added support in selling and escorting, but because it was he who had planned and organized all of our land tours back in New York. Clifford knew, then, the history and the background of our entire tour operation, and that, in itself, was a tremendous help to us all.

I liked Clifford's manner; always a gentleman—proper, polite, and very very intelligent. He always smiled, and never let the others, and their sometimes very childish nonsense, get to him.

Clifford was a loner, something else I admired. He seemed to keep most people at distance. And there was a power in that; a strength I envied. A confidence, too, in not being swayed by others' judgments or opinions. Yes, what I admired most about Clifford was his great respect for privacy.

When he did agree to join us for a meal on deck—although he contributed well with conversation—he never seemed to thrive on gossip or propagate negativity as the others so eagerly did. Indeed, I liked that about Clifford very much. And I respected him for bringing such needed balance and order to our increasingly insular and somewhat fragmented world.

Yet eventually, as he became more comfortable with us all—perhaps even a bit more relaxed now that New York City's energy-driven neuroses had faded far behind him—Clifford too began to open up, discussing his personal life just a bit. Most of those conversations took place while he and I shared deck lunches together in the Veranda Cafe, sometimes even joining together with Percy and Archibald too.

Having sailed with NAL for several years prior to moving ashore to work in the New York office, Clifford was well known onboard not only for his tour office skills and keen business acumen, but for his artistic abilities as well. Clifford was very creative; he made things—centerpieces, greeting cards, paintings and water colors too. But he was best known for his traditional Norwegian dolls—a craft no doubt learned during the long winter months he spent working as an apprentice in Norwegian America's Oslo office.

One day, while still at sea, Maggie asked Clifford to show her how his dolls were made—she wanted to use his technique in her Arts and Crafts classes, which were held most afternoons in the Veranda Cafe. Clifford invited me along.

"You take the Styrofoam ball and carefully glue it to the cone, using the cone as a base—like this." Clifford explained as he acted out his own instruction. Maggie and I watched diligently as we too created our own.

"Now drape the cloth over the cone like this, and layer it with glue" he continued. And on Clifford went, explaining just how to attach the arms; finally demonstrating how to paint the doll and how that, in itself, was what really brought it to life.

"I'll tell you a secret" he confided to me later that day. "Those are really angels . . . Christmas angels actually." "But don't tell Maggie. Without the wings and the gold paint, they can be anything

Maggie Sinclair—or anyone else for that matter—wants them to be. Isn't that right, my new friend? Things are not always what they seem."

We laughed together then. I liked having a secret with Clifford, however insignificant it was.

Ted and Anne hosted their popular Champagne Hour our second night out of Hong Kong. It was a long awaited evening onboard; most ladies displaying almost childlike eagerness to be the very first to dance with the Cruise Director himself. And let there be no doubt, Ted loved the attention; so did his pocketbook. You see, as a pre-Champagne Hour incentive, Ted Jones offered private dance instruction in preparation for this very special night—for prices quite unknown to us—with only the wealthiest and only the loveliest of the single female passengers taking part. Champagne Hour was their recital of sorts—the one night his very special students could display what they had learned throughout the voyage.

But Champagne Hour was not the real prize actually; just the idea of being alone in the dance studio with the handsome and charming Ted Jones . . . What more could any woman ask for, after all?

Publicly at least, Anne seemed to accept Ted's extra-curricular activities, or at least tossed a blind eye towards them. It was expected after all; part of his job, perhaps. Clearly a part of the cruising business. But I could sense that she really wasn't pleased about any of it. Anne Dickson was totally and completely in love with Ted Jones—that was clear to anyone. Yet true to her nature, Anne remained silent, and she smiled approvingly that night; selflessly handing out chilled bottles of champagne to the winners, without a word.

Chapter Five

"Realities"

The word came during breakfast, directly from the radio room. After years of bloody and vicious fighting—after tens of thousands of dead, and even more thousands maimed and injured for life—the horrific conflict in Southeast Asia appeared to be ending. President Nixon or Secretary of State Kissenger or Defense Secretary MacNamara—who really knew?—had arranged a midnight ceasefire, we were told; the first positive news in years. Perhaps a treaty was soon to be signed—to be followed eventually by the total and complete withdrawal of American troops. The details were sketchy. But that, of course, was what we heard; that, of course, was all we wanted to hear.

Whether true or not, we grasped hungrily at the news. Everyone onboard was euphoric—passengers and crew alike. It was the magic one feels on Christmas morning; the exhilaration one gets as the sun finally peeks through after a long intensive storm.

The passengers held great anticipation of what the days ahead might bring. They spent most of the day seeking out more and more news of the long-awaited cease fire; when would the troop withdrawal actually begin? Indeed, the only thing that mattered was that the men and women who had been cast by fate to fight in Southeast Asia might finally be coming home. And many many lives would be saved.

I walked out on deck after breakfast that morning and looked westward from Sun Deck, starboard side; Vietnam was just over the horizon. How ironic to be so close, I thought—to be right there—when such great news was announced.

I imagined the soldiers whooping it up in massive celebration. They, of all people, knew firsthand what it meant to be finally free from that nightmare called war. I thought about those soldiers, who, perhaps even yesterday, were out in fierce battle; and those who were injured or even killed. And today, it might all be over. Twenty-four hours too late for them. How could we allow them to die just yesterday, when peace would come as early as today?

I thought of their families back home who were no doubt tearfully exuberant at the news that the war might indeed by ending and their sons and daughters would be coming home. And how they would react, no doubt with anger and utter disbelief, to the news they would receive in just a few days time, that their sons or daughters were among the unlucky ones, and didn't quite make it to the newly negotiated cease fire—if only by hours. It didn't matter then. They were dead. How unfair. How unlucky. And how real.

I knew we would do something onboard in celebration of the war's hopeful end, but none of us knew exactly what was planned. We waited for the captain to make an official announcement from the Bridge at least—a personal statement that the war was ending; perhaps that he was steering the ship due west to Vietnam itself to help in the withdrawal of U.S. troops; we'd pick up as many as we could. Indeed, I'd share my cabin, after all; I'm certain many of us would. But no announcement came. For the Norwegian navigational hierarchy onboard, it was life as usual. No comments, no real emotion. They could care less about America's silly war and America's crazy youth. They cared only about America's wealthy passengers. I remembered when Arne had called them squareheads.

So it was Ted and Anne who seized the opportunity; dramatically announcing a change in that evening's programming. Instead of the originally scheduled fun and games in the Ballroom, we would celebrate with a grand salute to the men and women who served us so well.

All entertainers were expected to partake in this ad hoc extravaganza—quickly thrown together as an evening of patriotic honor and melodramatic sentimentality. Some passengers contributed too—several of the men joining together in a quartet of *Yankee Doodle Dandy.* Ted and Anne performed their tribute to Americana we'd already seen once or twice during weeks past; Roger and Elizabeth adorned the ballroom with endless swags of red, white, and blue fabric.

I stood at the rear of the ballroom that night and fidgeted from one leg to the other. I didn't really want to sit, or even stand in one place, for fear that someone would think that I was somehow a part of that evening's performance. The unprofessional production was embarrassing to me. It seemed silly—amateur, totally insincere. But for some reason I stayed. I felt I should be present.

The finale began when Ted and Anne called all the performers out onto stage one last time. The orchestra quickly segued into the very first chords of *God Bless America.*

The music crescendoed, the lights came up full, and one by one they entered the stage—each performer holding another's hand; swaying gently from right to left along with the music. The overhead lighting slowly faded to a deep red, white, and blue—concentric ribbons of light they were—encircling the dance floor, protecting us all.

Out they came, continually and constantly. Everyone was onstage, it seemed. Even Lar and Archibald, and Percy and the others. And then the crew . . . waiters, and stewardess too . . . and sailors and some officers as well. The stage was suddenly filled with people—filled with everyone. Everyone, but me. Was it spontaneous? Or was I just left out?

One passenger, seated down front, stood and proudly began to sing. Another then joined him, and then their wives. And another too. And before long, everyone in the room was standing, with hands held high. They all sang together, loud and strong—*God Bless America, my home sweet home.*

The outpouring of emotion overcame me just then, and before I could stop it, tears were rolling down my face. I was moved to a sadness and a pride I had never before known. Yes—for the first time in my life, I was proud to be an American. Not Italian-American;

but American so true. And with that, I too walked to the stage.

"Life is moments" Percy had told me just days before in Hong Kong. And that was a moment I will never forget.

I surprised myself that night. I had always been somewhat indifferent to fickle patriotism and the insincerity of politics. Yet there I was—standing with the masses singing *God Bless America* in my loudest and proudest voice, with tears streaming down my face. Was I changing, or just discovering? I didn't really know.

Immediately afterward, I joined the others at the midnight buffet. I rarely, if ever, visited the midnight buffet. But that night was different. Like everyone else onboard, I was overcome with energy and deep emotion—sleep would have to wait.

Arne came by to say hello; he was just about finished clearing his tables.

"What kind of camera do you have?" Arne asked somewhat discreetly as he quickly looked to be sure the Chief Steward would not see us together. "Is it thirty-five millimeters?"

"Yes. It's a Nikkormat."

"He splurged in Hong Kong—didn't you know?" Percy shouted out.

"Oh, shut up" I quickly said at him. "How would you like it if I told everyone about all the crap *you* brought back?"

"Don't you dare, you little twit" Percy snapped back. We all laughed, Arne included.

"Do you have a zoom lens?" Arne asked. He wanted to know if he could borrow the lens for our upcoming visit to Bangkok. It seemed Arne was passionate about Thai architecture; the zoom would document his explorations far more accurately.

Later that night, Arne walked me to my cabin. By this time in the voyage, we had both become a bit more daring and were less concerned about being caught. And once inside my cabin, we relaxed even further; we sat and talked for hours. It seemed Arne and I were both eager to be able to spend some more time together, something we were unable to do since that one night on deck, under the stars.

The more I knew of Arne, the more I liked him. And indeed there were many things to like. But most of all, Arne was kind, and through his kindness he showed me—his new friend—deep respect. I yearned for that caring and respect, and eagerly savored his friendship.

But being with Arne that night alone in my cabin—in such a close and intimate space—was surprisingly awkward. It was the antithesis of a dark and deserted deck—with the safety of miles of open sea around us, and an endless sky above.

Since that night much earlier in the voyage, I knew I wanted to spend more time with Arne; to get to know him better. And I felt that he wanted the same. In a strange way, I wished we already had a history; that I had already known him far longer than I did, so that we would already be best friends, and wouldn't have to take our friendship step-by-step as we were still compelled to do—with all these preliminaries still stifling our intimacy.

That night, I held little back from Arne about my life and about my dreams. I wanted him to know everything about me—except for one thing, perhaps. I trusted Arne. And for the first time in my life, I really wasn't frightened about the truth. I wanted him to understand me, so that we could get on with our friendship, and enjoy life together. Arne wouldn't judge me. He just wasn't that way.

Yet no matter how relaxed I tried to be that night, awkwardness remained, and it appeared we were destined to follow the script after all, as most new friends do. So we continued, and we talked until we each grew sleepy.

I first stuck my head out into the hallway to be sure no one was there—then Arne slipped out just as quietly as he came. I was exhilarated by our time together—one on one. It was safe then—after he'd gone. I could not be happier. I looked towards the new day to follow—quickly, eagerly. I simply couldn't wait for another day with Arne Christiansen.

The knock on my cabin door, however muffled it was, startled me just as it had prior to that savage sea storm off Acapulco several weeks before. A feeling of disgust deep down in the pit of my stomach made me shudder as I imagined it happening all over again. I switched on my bedside lamp and staggered to the door, already half asleep.

"What are you doing here? You're crazy" I whispered as he quickly and quietly slipped inside my cabin. Our shadows were exaggerated by my bedside lamp as we moved further into the room. Arne appeared nervous. I wondered if there was anything wrong.

He walked to the side chair, and quickly sat down. And as he did, I realized I had done it once again. I was wearing nothing but my underpants.

"I just wanted to talk some more, if that's okay" he whispered. "You were already asleep?"

"No not really" I said. "Just almost."

"I guess I shouldn't stay then." Arne stood up. "I'd better let you sleep."

"No. No." I answered quickly. "It's okay. You're crazy, but it's okay. Sit down. Is everything all right? You seem nervous."

"Yes, yes" he said. I'm fine." He was quiet a moment. "I forgot the camera lens."

I realized then that he had indeed forgotten to take the lens with him. I reached for my pants.

"No" he said as he grabbed my hand, stopping me from getting dressed. "Look, it's late I can't really stay. The night watchman may catch me here on his rounds." Arne motioned with his hand towards an imaginary sailor somewhere onboard.

"Why don't you get back into bed? I'll stay here just a minute, then I'm off. I'll remember to take the lens with me this time."

And so I did. I got back into bed, and Arne sat again, next to me on the side chair. All of this made me smile. It was fun; exciting. Arne acted like a little boy—a bit shy, and a bit embarrassed by it all. We were like kids, back in school, spending the night over each other's houses.

He asked me what my plans were when we arrived at Bangkok; I told him about the full day tour I was scheduled to escort. He didn't really seem interested though. He didn't seem to be listening. His eyes seemed to wander about the room in search of something. And before I even finished, he got up and moved to the edge of my bed.

"Steven" he said quietly as he settled down next to me. "It's really pretty late. I think I had better go, and let you sleep."

He paused then a moment, and just as suddenly continued in a voice as soft and as calm as the pure lull of the sea.

"I like you very much" he said. "I want to thank you for our talks—and for your friendship." His presence so near to me was instantly exciting. I was shocked and elated by the physical reaction. I felt comforted by Arne's warmth. And I was tempted to touch him as one would embrace an endearing little boy.

"Can I hug you?" he asked. I was at first taken aback by Arne's openness; I hesitated.

"Just a quick hug" he said. "Then I have to go."

"Of course" I said softly. A shiver of excitement—now a fond familiar memory—shook my body before the words even left my lips.

Arne then reached over and took me in his arms. He held me close and I openly accepted his embrace. Indeed, Arne was my friend.

Our shadows, still grotesquely plastered against my cabin wall—the giants that they were—seemed to watch our every move; they knew our every thought. It felt good to touch Arne like that. I didn't want him to go.

Arne stood then, and without saying a word, stepped into the bathroom, quietly closing the door behind him. This is crazy, I thought. What's he doing? I seriously wondered if Arne was okay.

Finally, after a moment or two of complete silence, the bathroom door broke open, flooding the cabin in brilliant white light. Arne walked towards me—his naked body, crisply silhouetted against the blinding fluorescence. His movements were slow and deliberate, as if in a dream.

He slipped into my bed, and held me gently, yet powerfully strong; lovingly, he pressed his body against my own.

I was with Arne after all, and I knew it was okay.

The Cruise News was our bible. It was how we knew where to go onboard, and when. It offered other important information as well—such as time changes, local immigration instructions, or tour departure times and procedures. Let there be no doubt that *The Cruise News* was required reading for us all as we made our way around the world.

Ted Jones and assistant Hal Carter often tried, although most oftentimes unsuccessfully, to relate the theme of a particular issue of *The Cruise News* to *Sagafjord*'s specific geographic and or navigational location. To get us into the mood for our arrival at Bangkok, for example, Ted scheduled a special screening of the movie musical classic *The King and I* in the Theatre. *The King and I*—together with, and strategically placed between, Archibald's historical lecture on ancient Siam and present-day Thailand, and Maggie's shopping talk—was our only preparation for stepping ashore. Passengers interested in a more substantial background and research were compelled to visit the Ibsen Library on Veranda Deck forward, starboard side—just aft of the Garden Lounge; where, not so surprisingly, there were ample volumes available to satisfy even the most academically starved.

At 5:00 A.M., *Sagafjord* dropped anchor off of the U.S. Naval Base at Sattahip, Thailand—our port of access for Bangkok. All passengers going ashore that day, including those on tour, had to leave the ship by 7:00 A.M. by tender, for the three-hour bus ride north to the city itself. It was hot, and extremely humid, and I knew right at the outset that we would be in for a very difficult day. One passenger, Mrs. Rosalie Segalisi from Forest Hills Queens—a widow who had saved her entire adult life for just such a trip—actually pulled me aside well into our journey that morning, and angrily wanted to know why they built the city so far away from the ship? She thought the whole idea was totally inconsiderate.

Our tour that day first visited the Royal Palace with its superb display of grand Thai architecture. I wished Arne was with us, with or without his newly borrowed camera lens. I knew he would have enjoyed the vast photographic opportunities there. But with the city at least three hours from the ship—together with the intense service schedule allowing the crew little if any time off in such ports-of-call—few of them, including Arne, would be able to see any of what we were seeing that morning.

We stayed at the Palace for well over an hour—always, it seemed, unshaded; unable to hide from the fiery rays of the late morning sun. And passenger Ruth Aimer could take it no longer. As we made our way through the impossible maize of lush palace gardens, she collapsed—falling in a heap onto the beautifully shined marble floor.

She was dead—I just knew it. And I desperately tried to re-member Percy's instructions—stay with the group, he said; the agent would care for the body.

Emar, our local tour guide, immediately rushed to Mrs. Aimer's aid; the group huddled around as if anxiously awaiting the very next play. Thankfully, Mrs. Aimer quickly regained consciousness. We gave her salt tablets to chew on; Emar said they would help her retain moisture—certainly a near impossible task in the intense heat we were experiencing. But Emar was right. They worked. Percy's infamous instructions for death enroute were not needed after all.

We found a small ledge, just slightly shaded, and sat Mrs. Aimer there. It helped. And soon, she was feeling better; up and about with the rest of us.

During lunch at the Erawan Hotel in downtown Bangkok, I glanced over at Mrs. Aimer several times. I was concerned. So was Emar. She seemed fine though—apparently enjoying herself; a bit more animated in her conversations with fellow passengers.

Nonetheless, that very close call really frightened me. I dreaded the afternoon, and what might be in store. For most of it, we would be out of doors, in even hotter temperatures, visiting Wat Phra

Keo where, Emar told us, was enthroned the most sacred Emerald Buddha of them all; continuing on then to the famous Temple of the Reclining Buddha. And after that, we were to attend a special performance of the Thai Classical Dance Theatre presented specifically in our honor. The passengers were already tired, and drained from the intense heat as well. Would we make it, I wondered. I just wanted the tour to end; to be back onboard the ship, safe—and air-conditioned.

Nearly five hours later, we boarded the motor coach for our return to Sattahip. Clearly, I was relieved. I think all of us were glad to have visited Bangkok for that one day, and survived. But we were quite anxious too, to reboard *Sagafjord* and again sail on.

Clifford was quite emphatic about how much he hated cruising. His powerful words were unexpected that day, especially coming from someone as level-headed and sophisticated as Clifford Deetlefs.

It was true after all that Percy and Per and Ornulf really weren't too fond of their lives onboard ship either. But I attributed their unhappiness to the fact that that's all they really did; the ship was their lives—"at sea" eleven months out of the year; forced to spend nearly all of that time with dreary and mostly narrow-minded passengers whose sole conversations were oftentimes about themselves. Indeed, holiday time created a major dilemma—where to go? Not many of the staff had homes ashore—and if they did, those properties were let annually, unavailable for even the owners themselves to visit for a four or five week respite from the sea. Homeless, they all were—they hated the sea, and yet hated being ashore as well. Perhaps that's why many actually chose to holiday in some other exotic place—the Azores, the Canaries, The Caymans, the Costa del Sol. Perhaps shipboard life did indeed become routine if that's all one did—month after month, year after year after year.

But with Clifford—well, there was a quite different story. Clifford wasn't a permanent cruise-staffer. He traveled quite infrequently—choosing to spend most of his time in his postage-stamp sized studio apartment on New York's West 15th Street; working daily at the NAL offices at 29 Broadway in lower Manhattan. I would have thought Clifford would have welcomed the opportunity to get away. How could he not enjoy leaving New York City, at least once a year—especially in winter? How could anyone not really enjoy traveling the world by sea?

Nonetheless, it was clear that Clifford hated the ship, hated being onboard the ship, and had no tolerance or patience whatsoever for contact with the passengers in any way. No doubt the memories of his very early years onboard as a deck steward were too bold to erase. That's how he started, I was told; as a deck steward. In fact, Clifford was the only crew member in NAL history who successfully advanced to a cruise staff position, not to mention moving on to work in the company's headquarters ashore. So Clifford knew well shipboard life from both sides. He understood the lure, and he clearly felt the blisters. He despised the "small town" mentality onboard—and the cutting, incestuous gossip which seemed all too contemptible, often times quite vicious.

"People know everything you do onboard" he warned me one day, his voice unable to betray his bitterness. "Don't fool yourself into thinking you can ever keep anything a secret" he told me. "It just won't happen."

Yet for some reason, Clifford chose to share with me some very personal stories about his life in New York—stories about his daily gym routine and his volleyball league which played intramurally each Thursday evening—and he told me too about his homosexual lover Bruce, a dentist who lived in Philadelphia.

So contrary to my first impressions, Clifford too was gay. It didn't surprise or shock me really. It now seemed commonplace; almost, in a way, expected. Perhaps that's why I didn't notice.

Clifford and Bruce had been together for just over four years, and Clifford hated being away from him.

"If you live in Greenwich Village" I asked him, "and your friend Bruce . . ."

"My *lover*" Clifford corrected me, with a bit of a devilish smile;

in essence, forcing me to actually say the word.

"Your lover" I repeated, openly returning Clifford's smile. "So if your lover lives in Philadelphia, when do you get to see each other?"

"On weekends you twit" he snapped back. "It's only ninety minutes away. Believe me" he continued, "you have no idea how much I look forward to Friday afternoons when I pack my bags and board that train to Philly. I take George with me, my little white cat, and off we go—to the city of 'brotherly love' if you know what I mean."

Clifford's eyes sparkled with an inner contentment as he spoke of Bruce and his life ashore.

"You've got to meet George when you're back" he then said as an afterthought. "You'll love him."

"George?" I snapped back quickly. "What about Bruce?"

Clifford laughed at the irony.

"Oh yeah—Bruce too. I'd like you to meet Bruce. Come to Philadelphia for a weekend sometime. You'll meet them both."

It was over afternoon tea that day that Clifford first spoke about his difficulties in obtaining a green card from the United States Immigration Authority. Naturally, it Clifford's dream was to become a resident alien of the United States. It was only because of Robert Brooks and his continued support of Clifford's working in NAL's New York office that he could stay in the country at all. Apparently, it was Robert Brooks who, because of his top-level position with Norwegian America Line, annually arranged for the renewal of Clifford's working papers. Clifford then was totally dependent on his job with NAL in order to remain in America. Needless to say, he was in constant fear of losing it.

Clifford's voice softened as he spoke. He became despondent—visually frustrated—at having his future clearly placed in someone else's hands.

And there were problems—errors he had been making on the job—sloppiness perhaps, or just stupid mistakes. For whatever the reasons, Robert Brooks had received open complaints about

Clifford's work from travel agents, and from passengers too. Clifford's intense concern for the very basic security of his own future had made him careless at his job—he was afraid, and he was angry. He didn't know what to do, or where to turn. There was near panic in his voice.

"I can tell you one thing" he said emphatically. "I am not going back to South Africa. I just won't do it."

"Who says you'll have to go back?" I asked. "It'll all work out."

Our waiter Franz, assigned to afternoon tea service that day, brought us a special tray of miniature sandwiches and Norwegian butter cookies.

"What's so bad about going back to South Africa anyway?" I asked him. "Don't you have family there? Don't you want to see any of them again?"

Clifford smiled, and looked directly at me. "Yes. And not really" he answered. His smile began to fade. "They—the family, that is—don't really approve of me or who I am, if you know what I mean. They're not too happy having a fag as a son and a brother." He paused, and looked around for a moment, apparently to see if anyone else listened. "They've basically disowned me" he continued. "And I them, because of it. I haven't spoken with any of them in fact—my parents or even my brothers and sister—since I first left home over ten years ago.

"But it's not just that" he continued. "I have to admit that Bruce and I have been having some problems lately too. It's all really fucked up. I don't want to get into it just now, but it hasn't been fun."

Clifford fell silent for a moment; Franz refilled our sparkling white tea cups with a hotter, steamier brew.

"I feel I need—I want—to be with Bruce as much as possible to try and work it all out" Clifford continued. "But then again, who knows? Maybe its better that I'm away from him once in a while like this. Actually, I had no choice on this particular one. I was told I had to come on this trip, by New York—by Brooks. And since they're already pretty pissed off at me at the office, I just kept my mouth shut, and came—onboard, that is. Never questioned it."

Clifford looked around then with a sadness and a desperation I had never before seen in anyone. He couldn't bear to face his pain. And I couldn't bear to witness it.

"I don't know what I'm going to do, kid. I'm real frightened they're going to fire me. And I'm telling you, I'm not going back."

Sagafjord's B-Deck was a world of its own. Just below the passenger quarters on A-Deck—my deck—B-Deck housed all the ship's crew's recreational and sleeping accommodations. It was to where they were all banished, it seemed, when their daily duties were completed.

Captain Brookstad, as no doubt you've already understood, was indeed quite strict enforcing the rules, and most of those on-board ship dutifully followed procedure. Yet as time wore on and the voyage progressed, I began to realize that there were always exceptions to those rules, and many of them—the rules, not the exceptions—were often broken.

I, too, became a bit bolder with my own personal and private activities. I began to see that by taking chances periodically, I would, without a doubt, open myself up to people and to opportunities which might not have been presented to me—perhaps would never have even been possible—if I had simply lived by the book, and played by the captain's rules. Indeed, what a risk it was for me to have Arne in my cabin just a few nights before. And yet how unexpectedly rewarding that was. Most likely it would never have happened if I had simply gone along with Captain Brookstad and his rule book. "Never be seen" Percy had told me earlier on in the voyage. That was the lesson, and I was fast learning it well.

B-Deck ran the entire length of the ship, fore to aft. The men were housed in very cramped cabins—sometimes four to a room—in the forward to mid-ship section; women were assigned to the aft section only—not so crowded as the men though, with only two in each cabin. As most crew members onboard were male, less actual space was required for the ladies, and so, in a sense, they benefited.

Physically separating the two groups, men and women, were the crew's public areas consisting of the garishly lit cafeteria—the "fishball mall" as it was actually referred to by the ship's crewmembers; the crew lounge which also housed the offices of the crew purser and his assistant; and the crew Bar which sold nothing but cigarettes and soft drinks. Liquor was strictly forbidden in crew quarters. Prior drinking "incidents" were the cause—not really from the dining room waiters or deck stewards or the cabin stewardesses, but rather from the "men down below"—"The Black Gang" as they were known—the engineers, the motormen, and the like—who rarely got to see the light of day. They always seemed to be covered in black grease . . . head-to-foot; thus their nickname.

"Give a Norwegian like that a beer or an Aquivit" Percy once said "and that'll be the end." Look who was talking. Nevertheless, there it was; another rule—no alcohol on crew deck.

The men, of course, were forbidden in the women's cabin area, and vice versa—mixing together was only allowed in the crew cafeteria, or the bar. Nonetheless, parties were held often on B-Deck; the crew trying to make the best of their situation. Men with the men; women with women. That's just the way it was. Yes, there were exceptions . . . Dick and Gro, after all had the captain's blessing to share one cabin . . . his, a passenger cabin at that; one or two others—some of them married like Ornulf and Astrid—had "an understanding" as well. But that's as far as it went. Gender segregation was the norm. For a Nordic people so well known for their open sexual understanding and permissiveness, I thought it quite ironic.

My first adventure on B-Deck was somewhere mid-cruise, during a time which most veteran world cruise travelers call "Hate Week"—a time when, perhaps because of the great and unnatural confines of shipboard life, and the forced intense intimacy onboard, nothing is good and nothing is right. The food in the dining room was inedible; the entertainment—lousy; the waiters arrogant; *other* passengers obnoxious; the movies dated—oh God, not another one of those dreadful cocktail parties!—the seas continually rough; the ship's photographer smug (this was actually true, but who really cared at this point?) . . . and on and on it went. Not only did the passengers feel the effects of "Hate Week," but the staff and crew were unable to escape its dreaded grasp as well.

And what a week it was! No doubt it would pass; at least that's what I was told.

I too succumbed to "Hate Week's" hate. I became a bit more depressed, tired of the food and the service; I was repulsed by the formulistic pomposity of the passengers, and the shallow arrogance of the staff. The entire social atmosphere onboard seemed pitiful and tragic. Fake. I could not believe we were only halfway through the cruise. How would we ever survive the rest?

It became so overwhelming at one point, that Percy and I—fully disgusted by the overly rich food night after night—abandoned the dining room completely, and took our dinners together, in either his or my cabin; we'd raid the nearest pantry for a plate of Scandinavian cold meats, a snowy wheel of aged camembert, and a crisp bottle of Beaujolais Nouveau. A hunk of crusty bread was all else we needed. The last thing either of us wanted was yet another serving of beluga caviar, or another hefty slice of blood-red prime rib.

"Hate Week" was also a time when I became just a little bit arrogant about my employment onboard. Suddenly, for some odd reason, I really didn't care whether or not I got into trouble. What were they going to do, after all? Put me off the ship at Bombay? Big deal, I thought. I'll just hop a plane back home. I felt dishonestly confident. The reason for those feelings?—I wasn't exactly sure.

Slowly, and not so silently, I began to desire and demand more freedom in my life—both onboard ship and ashore. If I wanted to talk with Ingemar on deck, or Arne in the dining room—or anyone else for that matter—I would. It was not a terrible thing after all. No one would be hurt. And even if the captain, or even the New York office, did get wind of it and immediately send me home, it wouldn't be the end of the world—although it would certainly have been the end of the world cruise, at least for me.

All in all, I was determined to do just what I wanted to do. So when Arne called one night to say that Erik Jensen—barman from the North Cape Bar—was throwing a birthday party for himself in his B-Deck cabin, I eagerly accepted the invitation.

I had never been to B-Deck, so I had no way of knowing where I was to go. Arne had to lead the way. So we met at my cabin just past 10:30 P.M. Thank God for Arne. I would never have found it otherwise.

Off we went—silently sneaking through the green watertight doorway I had passed so many times before, clearly marked in red *No Admittance—Crew Only*—down the very narrow metal stairway to B-Deck; the heels of our shoes clanging out our true destination with each and every step.

The disparity in comfort was at first quite striking—from passenger accommodation to crew quarters in just one flight of stairs. No luxury here, for sure. An active world though, nonetheless. Like ferrets whose real existence is deep within underground tunnels; only revealing themselves to our world at specific moments and times. Here were the young men I had seen and met all throughout the voyage. Now however, for the first time, I was seeing where they lived and where they slept—where they made their own real lives.

The hallways were crowded with men in faded jeans and tee shirts and clogs on their feet; socially prominent they walked as if on a grand Parisian promenade. Some moved about with just a towel around their waists as they returned to their cabins after a long hot shower—their chests and legs still reddened by the ship's steaming water blasting hard against their skin. It seemed strange to see them like this—those who would never dream of appearing in public without their shipboard uniforms; without their professional image; to see them in any capacity other than dutifully fulfilling their roles as expert waiters, and deck stewards, and barmen and sailors too. Here, they were relaxed—at home. Here, they seemed different. They were real. Each had a distinct character and personality which, up until then, was strictly hidden—an individuality inevitably lost when, up above, they all dressed and acted alike.

Several of them smiled at me as I, or they, walked past. Perhaps they wondered what the hell I was doing down deep within their realm. But their smiles relaxed me, and privately fed my ego. I quickly felt comfortable, and welcomed

We walked further forward, Arne and I, through a maze of brightly lit corridors. Industrial fluorescents glared sharply against the uncarpeted linoleum flooring and shiny beige walls. "How antiseptic" I thought. "Like a hospital. How practical too, and easy to clean." Perhaps, but quite unattractive and visually cold it was.

Up ahead, there were four or five Asian men in loosely fitted pants and shirts, all sitting together well out in the hallway, talking quite loudly in their native tongue. "This . . ." Arne said as he nodded hello "is Chinatown. These guys run the laundry."

"There's a Chinese laundry onboard?"

"Of course. Who do you think cleans the towels, and the bed sheets, and the table cloths, and the passengers' clothing? Yours too. All of them live here together, just outside the laundry room." Arne looked at me for a moment and again smiled his broad Danish smile. "You should be down here at dinner time" he continued. "The smell is unbelievable."

"They cook in the laundry room too?"

"Some of the best Chinese food you'll ever have—even better than what we had at Hong Kong. You don't think they'd settle for fish balls like the rest of us, do you?" Arne waved to them as we passed. They grinned and nodded back to Arne—never a noticeable gap in their conversation. Perhaps they thought I was a new crewmember, I wondered. They thought I belonged. Sometimes, it's good not to know.

"It's best to be friends with them; to stay on their good side" Arne said as we continued forward. "That way they'll invite you for dinner once in a while, and not murder you in the middle of the night." Arne laughed as he grabbed hold of my arm.

"Does Brookstad know they cook in their rooms?" I asked.

"Oh, who really cares what the master squarehead thinks? But yes, I'm sure he knows. He needs his shirts starched too, if you know what I mean. He's even been known to call down and order up some sweet and sour himself."

"Kind of like shipboard take-out" I said. Arne looked a bit puzzled and I realized he didn't understand what I meant. Do they have take-out Chinese food in Roskilde?

The crew lounge was fairly deserted as we walked passed and I saw the space for the very first time. A young man stood by a portable cassette player listening to Carole King's latest album—

> *Music is playing inside of my head over and over and*
> *over again . . .*

Her textured voice echoed throughout the room. Colored lights of red and blue and green lazily glowed overhead; one young man sat quietly in the crew purser's office busily doing paperwork at his desk. Two girls, cabin stewardesses, no doubt, sat in a corner smoking unfiltered Camels, talking feverishly in what must have been heated Norwegian.

"Not too busy tonight" I commented.

"It rarely is. No one really likes to come here."

"Why not?"

"Would you?" Arne looked at me as though I were nuts.

I laughed at his honesty. We both knew the answer.

"Once in a while, the crew purser sponsors a disco night" Arne continued. "That's really the only time this room gets busy. Most everyone comes out to that. Although there's only so much you can do with taped rock and roll, and soda and potato chips."

I could see that a cabin door was open just ahead of us at the end of the corridor—loud music and crisp light pulsed from within. A couple of crewman whose faces I knew but whose names I did not, stood in the hallway with drinks in their hands.

"Come in" Arne said. "Make yourself at home, as you Americans say."

As I squeezed through the narrow doorway, I saw Erik first—a handsome Dane with straight blond hair and an illuminating smile. He too appeared somewhat different out of his usual barman's uniform. With an Acapulco tee-shirt and tight fitting jeans, Erik cast an entirely different image of youthful exuberance. He noticed me too as soon as I entered the cabin; quickly, he greeted me at the door.

"Happy birthday Erik" I said as I attempted to shake his hand. He pushed aside my outstretched hand and took me in a strong welcoming embrace.

"So great to see you; I'm glad you could make it. I'm glad you came."

"Everyone" Arne called out. "This is my friend from the Tour Office—for those of you who don't already know." He pointed around the room as he then introduced each guest.

"That's Jan, Steinar, Erik of course you know, Torleif, Peter, that's Peter too, and Otto, and Dieter. He's German, but we invited him anyway." They all laughed as Arne gave Dieter a playful smack on the head.

Danes, I was beginning to see, had an amazing spirit. They loved life—culturally unable to avoid seizing every opportunity. It was quite apparent from this one night alone, from Erik's birthday gathering. The party was pure celebration. Everyone was up, everyone was happy—happy to be there, happy to be with each other, and happy to be who they were.

Erik himself had an enviable glow about him. It was clear how much fun he was having, and how much he loved his friends. His pleasure at having them all there together with him, sharing his special night, was quite intoxicating.

Out of respect for me I guess, they all spoke English, even though Danish would certainly have made them more comfortable. I was impressed by their consideration. I was overwhelmed by their kindness, and their friendliness.

Erik's cabin was small, with two bunks on either side of an unusually narrow central space. A minuscule porthole, just above the water line, was at the far end of the room; its steel plate in place most of the time to protect it from the heavy seas. The two sailors who were so prompt to install and then remove my porthole cover during our pre-Acapulco storm were far more laxed in caring for their comrades farther down below. In fact, once the covers were secured, they rarely came off at all—until perhaps there was a convenient time to remove them, or until someone just called the crew purser to complain. Erik's cabin, then was most often in darkness; the pride and the comfort of having an outside cabin at all, was somewhat diminished by its inevitable lack of natural light.

Four narrow closets were just inside the doorway, and that was the extent of the storage areas. There was a small sink just under the porthole. All bath facilities were communal, I was told, and down the hallway to the right. There, you would find several toilet stalls, more sinks for washing or shaving, and a large tiled area where the men showered openly, together.

The cabin's walls were covered with posters of all kinds, no doubt to add some color, and to create a more livable atmosphere. Various souvenirs from around the world were scattered about as well, clearly defining an experienced traveler—a carved wooden mask from New Guinea, several molas from the Panamanian San Blas Islands, sheeted wood bark from Acapulco on which were brightly painted images of tropical birds and flowers of all colors; and—no doubt from Haiti—a mahogany statue of a man surrounded by a large barrel which, when slipped up or down, revealed an extremely large erected penis.

Four alarm clocks sat atop the narrow shelf above the sink.

"That's to make sure we get up on time" Arne said. "If the first one doesn't do it, the second, third, or fourth one will."

Arne's comment made me understand that Erik's cabin was Arne's as well. They were cabin mates. Arne and Erik . . . and two of the others there with us, no doubt.

Most guests at the party stood, as there was really no place to sit other than on the two lower bunk beds. And that's were I remained, wedged in next to Dieter; safely scrunched down between Arne and one of the Peters.

For me, Erik's party was a dynamic shot in the arm. Something I desperately needed at that time in the voyage. In a way, it became my own personal antidote to "Hate Week." I was energized by the infusion of youthful personality. I felt empowered, I felt renewed.

For the first time on the voyage, I truly felt as if I belonged; as if I was one with them. My new friends—Arne and Erik, and all the others too—made me feel welcomed, and at home; they made me feel as if we had been friends for years. These young men accepted me without really even knowing me. They didn't seem to care what my faults or problems were or might be. It was all unimportant to them. I was welcomed—included openly into their world and into their lives. It was a feeling I had longed for my entire lifetime. And it was finally there.

I admired them for their fraternity; I wished I could be as open, and as loving. But I wasn't. With all the changes I had been going through, I was still a bit guarded and genuinely distrustful when I met new people. I would never invite a stranger to my home, or to my cabin, without first really knowing and trusting him. Perhaps that's what I had been missing the entire cruise—my entire life. Taking that risk. These people and their friendships had been available to me ever since we sailed from New York, yet I—not them—created the barrier which prevented our communion. I was the one who simply would not let them in.

Indeed, I envied many things about these men—their strong friendships with each other most of all—the camaraderie; I hoped that that night in Erik and Arne's cabin was only the first of many more, when we could all be together.

I envied too their communal living conditions which seemed to demand a balance of intimacy. It afforded these men a close, almost incestuous bond; a covenant of masculinity; a familiarity which clearly did not exist one deck above.

Indeed, how ironic it was to think about all those people up above—the passengers and the cruise staff and the entertainment staff too. How privileged they all felt—with their very special social classes, their designer clothes, and their all too pretentious parties and excessively dear accommodations. Little did they know or realize just what, in fact, they were missing.

Yes, on B-Deck, it was simply the bonding of men I so craved—

the pure honest friendship which I was experiencing right there, in that tightly cramped crew cabin. It was really all that mattered. In faded jeans and tee shirts and sneakers and clogs, we together shared a warmth and an understanding that those above only dreamed about—and perhaps, as Percy had said, searched their entire lives to find.

A vast realm of newly found friendship had opened up for me just one deck below. And the world, at least as I knew it, would never be the same.

We pulled alongside at Singapore early Monday morning, the 19th of February. I knew little of that great Malaysian city and it's history, so I could only look forward to our stay because everyone else onboard seemed to look forward to our stay.

"You must go to Raffles Hotel" Percy encouraged over breakfast. "We're meeting Ted and Anne there later on for drinks. "

Archibald said that it was at Raffles Hotel where the very first Singapore Sling was poured. I tried to act interested, although I really wasn't quite sure what a Singapore Sling was. But if Ted and Anne were heading off to Raffles, it must be chic; it must be glamorous. It certainly must be the place to be.

But before I could run off to Raffles for a Sling, I had to work; and I was assigned to escort Tour 34, entitled simply *Singapore*. We visited the Botanical Gardens that morning to see its colony of small monkeys freakishly running about; and the Haw Paw Villa—with an unusual series of grottoes and grotesquely bizarre sculptures depicting scenes from Chinese mythology. We then toured the city's various cultural districts too—Malay, Chinese, and European—before finally stopping off at Raffles Hotel for a quick tour-group refreshment.

At the beginning of the voyage, I was quite thankful to Lar for assigning me to all the introductory tours. It gave me a good overview, after all—certainly what any world-travel novice would need. Nonetheless, as the cruise progressed, these tours became routine. In a way, they all seemed the same. My once youthful enthusiasm—the eager excitement of visiting a new place for the very first time—began to fade. Traveling from one botanical gardens to the next, and then on to the next, was becoming redundant. One shopping district seemed not unlike the next, or the one before. On and on, the synonymous images continued around the world. I hungered to see some of the more unusual sights, visit far more interesting places than just those within a twenty mile radius of the docked or anchored *Sagafjord*.

Yet with all the hints I put out about wanting to take on more adventurous adventures, my requests appeared to fall on deaf ears. I wasn't experienced enough, Lar felt, to escort the more complicated excursions. There was no question about that, at least in his mind; yet I would never be experienced enough unless he in fact gave me that opportunity.

Lar would laugh. "Of course they're all the same" he said to me one day. "What we really do is leave one port, sail in a circle over night, and return the next day. All they do is change the sign." Lar's words weren't very far from the truth. It was all different, yet always the same.

Raffles Hotel was nothing very special, at least in my view. Ordinary, in fact. Sure, it was nicely decorated with an interesting blend of the European and Malaysian styles, but it seemed all too obvious; just what one would expect.

I could not understand what all the fuss was about. Perhaps it was the hotel's history, or one's very creative imagination which brought about such celebrated repute. Or perhaps it could simply be the city's specific location on most world itineraries—the fact that Singapore is in fact the first port of call immediately following that dreaded mid-cruise period called "Hate Week." It was the desperate relief of finally getting off the ship and dining ashore. It was a respite . . . a refreshing watering-hole. Any place would do—but Raffles it was. The perfect example of being in the right place and the right time.

Ted and Anne were already well positioned just off the bar when we arrived. This in itself, was quite unusual—Ted and Anne were always fashionably late; a grand entrance seemed their usual calling card. Yet there they were that day, sipping their Slings, giddy like children—opening and closing their hands to simulate a wave of greeting as only a grand Italian would.

L ar invited the entire tour office staff ashore for dinner that night—Per and Ornulf declined the invitation so that they—and their wives—could enjoy some private time ashore. So off the rest of us went—Percy, Archibald, Philip Pound, and me—to a very local restaurant for a typical Malaysian meal.

After the usual shipboard gossip was out of the way, our conversation centered around our after dinner activities— to "soak up the very unique Singapore night life" they all said. And naturally, I was included in their plans. At first I was not too enthusiastic. Flash images of our evening ashore together at Honolulu bolted across my mind.

"Wait till you see Bugis Street" Lar said to me. "When the shops close up and the lights come on, everyone comes out into the streets—in more ways than one."

"Sounds like a bit of a drag to me" Philip said with his crude Australian giggle.

"You *are* funny, aren't you?" Percy answered, then turned to me. "Now don't you freak out on us like you did the last time" he said. "At least we're telling you up front. It's fun. Just relax, and have a good time."

"I don't like that kind of thing" I said to Percy and the others. "You know that. I don't like men dressing up like women."

"Oh shut up" Percy said. "Just come along. And don't get your knickers in a twist."

"P-e-r-c-y" I complained more firmly this time. "I told you—I really don't like that kind of thing."

"So what am I hearing from you?" he asked. "You're telling us you don't like the idea of men being with men?"

I was silenced. Where was he going with this, I wondered?

"You could have fooled us." Philip quickly jumped in, and continued his annoying giggle. I'm certain I reddened like the beets on Archibald's plate. I was intensely embarrassed and angry too to be confronted like this, in front of everyone. Archibald and Lar remained quiet; Philip clearly savored the moment.

"Just what do you mean by that?" I snapped back. And suddenly, my reaction was to laugh. In a flash, it all seemed funny. Indeed, how ridiculous all of this was.

"Oh calm down" Percy then said. "Stop getting all worked up. It's all in fun. Just enjoy it. Start enjoying life, for God's sake."

It was clear that Percy was trying to ease the atmosphere a bit, and I was pleased about that. I clearly wanted the subject changed.

But just what did Philip mean by his comment? Did he in fact know about the nights I spent with Arne, or even my night with Vincent? Did he, and everyone else for that matter, know that I did indeed have feelings—sexual and otherwise—toward other men?

And did they then even know about my visiting B-Deck, and perhaps some of my other hidden feelings and thoughts?

I was certain that homosexuals could sense those kinds of things. I just knew it. And this only confirmed it. Maybe I sensed it too. And if they did know after all, I didn't want to have to face them. I was embarrassed, and angry. My thoughts, certainly my sexual activities, were a part of my own very personal life and were of no one else's concern. I chose to keep my private life private. I still believed that the less others knew about me, the less opportunity they had of judging me or criticizing me. It was, I still felt, my best chance of being liked, and staying liked.

Ironically, with all we had been through together, and with how much I felt I had changed throughout these past months, I still found myself gnawingly intimidated by these men. Their personalities were indeed powerful. My uncomfortableness during such personal conversations still urged me to escape—something I did quite well. Yet I believed that if I ran this time—scared and cowardly, with my proverbial tail held tight between my legs—they would never let me live it down. So I surrendered once again. I joined them for that walk on Bugis Street that night. Nervous yet daring; it seemed the simplest way out.

The street that night was ablaze with people of all kinds, in all states of dress and undress, in all styles, all orientations. A transsexual denizen it was, it was true—some were quite beautiful and surprisingly quite feminine; I certainly would never have known the truth if it were not shared beforehand.

The lavish gowns were many; the exaggerated wigs too. Those who indulged seemed energized by the presentation—wallowing in a passion of ecstatic enjoyment. It was harmless, just as Percy had said. And in an odd sort of way, it did in fact make me smile.

Nonetheless, I stayed close to Archibald and Percy. At least at first. But quickly I relaxed, realizing it was indeed safe to be out on my own. No one was going to threaten me. They really weren't interested in me at all. Nor did they seem to be too interested in getting to know each other. It seemed more a parade—a show. An open exhibition of one's own truth and inner pride. So I surrendered again, yet this time in the midst of the spectacle, and I soon found myself laughing openly with the others, enjoying myself as I never dreamed I would.

Within the crowd of avid observers were some of *Sagafjord's* crew members—mostly dining room waiters off from duty and out for a good time; many with their cameras in hand. They certainly would not believe any this back in Oslo or Germany.

Claus Haber, another of the ship's wine stewards, joined our group after seeing Percy waving his arms frantically. It was clear that Claus had been drinking, quite heavily too. He was ashore alone, wondering aimlessly amidst the scene. Consciously or not, he was perhaps looking for the familiarity, and safety, of others he knew.

Claus, clearly heterosexual and quite openly aggressive in his drunken stupor that night, seemed unaware that the beautiful Malaysian women parading before us were actually men. He lusted after many, even began conversations with a few. Clearly, Claus was aroused, and wanted to get laid.

"Let's have some fun with him" Percy whispered, and then began a conversation with a beautiful young woman in a strapless blue gown with a chestnut mane of shoulder-length hair.

Claus was the one to first catch her eye. It was clear she was his type as well. But it was Percy who egged her on, letting her know that Claus was indeed interested in a little more than just a harmless look.

The woman responded as if on cue. Claus blushed with embarrassment, although I was uncertain if his feelings came from his obvious sexual arousal or from his lingering alcoholic fix. In either case, he hugged this buxom beauty as only a true young, handsome, heterosexual Germanic male could.

The conversation wandered teasingly between the two, as did Claus' adventurous hands. Percy coached from the sidelines; the woman wiggling and squirming about seductively on Claus' lap. He touched her breasts then, grinning wildly, throwing his head back with pleasured approval.

His hungry hands continued to explore until finally reaching their intended destination. Suddenly, he yelled something in guttural German. He jumped up excitedly, throwing the very surprised young woman up into the air, struggling to her feet, clutching for her balance.

The laughter from our group was intense. Even I, too, had to laugh. It was funny after all—the stunned looked on Claus' face when he felt the quite healthy bulge in his young woman's crotch, and his continued ranting and raving in unintelligible German.

The woman ran off—somewhat disheartened, clearly debased. Claus did eventually calm down. He even seemed to forgive us all for making him the butt of our joke. That is if, of course, he could remember any of it by next morning.

Unlike with the rest of us, Archibald's "Hate Week" symptoms never fully disappeared and his depression deepened as the sea days continued. He no longer visited the office each day as he usually did to pass the time; he rarely came to the Dining Room for meals. He seemed to withdraw to his cabin, and was only seen at lecture time or when his presence at social functions was absolutely required.

I knew that Archibald had not heard from Matthew for quite some time. Matthew's last letter, in fact, was rather vague, and lacked the warmth—the sensuality—of his previous correspondence. Archibald believed that Matthew was drifting away. He desperately feared that he was losing the boy.

"Matthew's been troubled lately" he told me one afternoon in a futile attempt to justify the young man's behavior. "It's the father/rape issue resurfacing. I just know it. He's filled with rage, and I don't know what to do."

"Is he getting help?" I asked.

"Getting help?" he repeated incredulously. "The boy sees his therapist five times a week!"

"Maybe that's the problem." I wasn't quite sure what I was getting at.

"I don't think so. I've always believed that everyone should examine his life; delve deeply into his soul—his innermost thoughts and feelings. It's how we learn. You know—the unexplored life is really not worth living."

"And it might just fuck us up even more" I said to him. "I could just imagine some crazy therapist overly-dwelling on certain incidents in a patient's life—perhaps an incident which might not really be a problem until the therapist places the seed of its importance into his patient's mind."

"Just what are you saying?" Archibald pleaded, hoping to God I might have the solution.

"Look" I continued. "If a therapist thinks something is a problem or some particular incident in a patient's life is the source of a problem, he might certainly know what he's talking about. Maybe it *is* the problem. And maybe not. But how the therapist actually deals with the incident could possibly complicate things all the more. Like Matthew's rape, for example. He didn't even know about the rape until his mother told him. Before that, it wasn't a problem, was it? And how do we know it really happened in the first place?"

Archibald thought for a moment. He seemed to weigh what I was saying quite seriously, but didn't respond directly. And then he shook his head.

"It's the anger" Archibald confided in me. "He doesn't know how to deal with the anger. I don't know how to deal with it either. He's just so . . . angry."

"At you?"

"At me. At his father, his mother. At everyone, it seems. He's probably even angry with you and he's never even met you. Matthew is angry at the world."

"I'm not sure you can change that."

"I'm not sure I can either." Archibald paused again in a pensive mood of hopelessness. I could see that he was terribly hurt, and very very troubled. I did want to help him, perhaps just as intensely as he wanted to help young Matthew. And like Archibald with Matthew, I just didn't know what to do.

"I never told you this" he continued, "but the last time Matthew came to visit me in New York, just before sailing on this cruise in fact, we were both invited to my friend Tim Merton's apartment for a quiet dinner. Matthew looked very handsome that night." Archibald smiled as he recalled his handsome young man.

"He's a big guy, you know—six feet tall, with very dark brown wavy hair, and strong facial features. I remember he wore a crimson pullover that night; his horn-rimmed glasses only magnified his sweet—very boyishly innocent—blue eyes.

"I was tensed that night, as you can well imagine. Tim was the first of my friends to meet Matthew; and Matthew, for obvious reasons, was not too open to meeting anyone new.

Now you have to understand that Tim's apartment is rather uncomfortable and not welcoming, to say the least . . . small and cramped; you know, with the type of artwork everybody hates but no one can really fault...

We moved about awkwardly at first, beginning the evening with the usual small talk. But after we each had had a martini, and a glass or two of the exceptionally delicious Yugoslavian wine I brought, we relaxed a bit, and our conversation flowed more freely. Perhaps the wine was responsible. Perhaps the wine was the culprit. Who really knows?

"During dinner, Matthew seemed to display some erratic behavior—almost schizophrenic at times, if you ask me. He became loud and boisterous, almost out of control. One moment, he was the bright young man from Lawrence Kansas I fell in love with—brilliantly intellectual with his unique style of conversation and manner, boasting a pleasant smile and sense of humor as if everything in his life was perfect—just perfect. And at other times he would snap, suddenly jumping into violent fits of rage. He screamed at me quite often that night, and believe me, those screams were real. The screams of a hurt young man."

Tears welled up in Archibald's eyes. It was clear that Matthew wasn't the only person hurt.

"When dinner ended, we withdrew to Tim's living room area for a brandy. And that's where it all happened. All of a sudden, Matthew stood up and shouted at me 'the only thing you want to do is fuck me—you just want to rape me, just like my father.'

"I don't know why—I guess out of feeling hurt, or feeling embarrassed—I angrily shouted back 'Yeah, you probably have that dream about everybody, don't you? But this time you may be right. I *am* your father.'"

"Naturally, this sent Matthew into a maniacal rage. He violently tore his sweater off his back, and flung it at me across the room. There was a great deal of yelling at this point; I cannot recall what was being said. I do know that Matthew and I were both very angry, and Tim no doubt was shocked, and very frightened.

"That anger soon turned to violence when Matthew stormed across the apartment and pushed me down, slamming me with great force into Tim's side chair—my glasses flew off my head and crashed to the floor. Tim rushed to my aid, grabbing on to Matthew and calling out to him to stop.

"Suddenly, just as quickly as it all began, Matthew was silenced. As soon as Tim touched him, he was stilled. They stood quietly for a moment, Tim embracing Matthew as he relaxed his head low on Tim's shoulder. And Matthew would not let go. He wept for nearly five minutes, holding on to a stanger who, at least for the moment, appeared to care for him deeply. Matthew held on for dear life that night. He held on for love."

By this point in his story, Archibald was overcome with great emotion and wept openly for the first time.

"I love him" he whispered. "I want to help him. And I just

don't know what to do."

"Look Archibald. Clearly he's a very troubled young man" I said. "And you've got to be sure *you* are not hurt—emotionally and physically—while you're trying to help him."

I thought about Matthew for quite sometime after that conversation. As the days passed—as Archibald shared more and more about this mysterious young man—his words gave life to the faceless Matthew in my mind. I felt tremendous compassion for him. To me, Matthew appeared as a little boy lost. A boy deeply scared, who desperately needed guidance. And it appeared he simply could not make it alone. It was obvious Matthew was reaching out for love and for companionship. He'd been troubled all his lifetime. And he didn't know where to turn.

Even though we had never met, I felt—in an odd sort of way—that I knew him. I felt that if I could perhaps talk with Matthew—perhaps become his friend—he would begin to trust people a bit more; to love, and perhaps even allow others to love him. Perhaps I could do what Archibald so wanted to do. I would not be Matthew's father, after all. I would simply be his friend.

I knew I had to be mad—fantasizing about a power I knew I did not have. But for some reason, I felt intimately close to Matthew, or at least to the image of the Matthew I created in my mind. I wanted to help him, and somehow thought I could. For some reason, I actually believed I could.

And it simply didn't stop there, where no doubt it should have stopped. In truth, I soon found myself sexually attracted to Matthew as well—passionately drawn to the young man I had so vividly created in my mind solely from the stories and great emotions Archibald had shared. These were feelings never before felt. I was excited by an imaginary figure like a character in a book. How crazy that was. Yet how safe too. I was uncomfortable with these feelings; I was confused by their meaning.

And in a way, I also felt towards Matthew the desperate yet caring feelings of a parent . . . perhaps not unlike what Archibald was feeling. How ridiculous, I thought. Me, still a teenager myself, having fatherlike feelings for a man my own age. Fatherly, yet passionate as well. Incestuous attractions to a young man I didn't even know. What was this about, I wondered? Could it be that Matthew made every man he met—either in person, or purely in imagination—want to care for him?

Over the next few days, Archibald and I spoke often of Matthew. It was clear to me the boy was filled with fear of everything and everyone—fear of life itself, and the people who, he felt, only wanted to fuck him; to hurt him just as he believed his father had. I wanted to ask Archibald for Matthew's address—perhaps a letter from me would extend a contemporary's hand of friendship, and offer Matthew an opportunity to not feel so alone; perhaps let him know that someone else cared. I didn't dare though. It was a fantasy after all—and one, I knew, must stay just that.

At night, after settling deep within the safety of A-54, I thought of Matthew and I wondered why I would ever want to get involved with anyone as troubled and as volatile. Indeed, I had gone through some confused and emotional times of my own—dealing with my own personal feelings of love and sexual identity and intimate friendships too.

But what I seemed to be going through appeared to be on a much simpler scale—far less complex. Perhaps because I felt I had been able to deal with my own fears and desires somewhat adequately, I might be of some help and comfort to Matthew. I would be a peer with whom he could talk—someone who would understand him and his fears, without being a threat. Someone who wouldn't fuck him.

In a strange way, I felt I could relate to Matthew far better than Archibald could, or even Percy or any of the others. How typical of me. To desire a relationship with an idea, a person I didn't even know. How safe that was; how protected.

One afternoon, Archibald mentioned that Matthew's only friend in Boston was Hillary Buckingham, a successful 72-year-old author and dear friend of Archibald Hannon's for over a quarter century. It was Archibald who first introduced Matthew—the then budding young writer, to Hillary—the more mature and far more experienced literary artist.

But what I found most interesting about this information was that Hillary Buckingham was disabled—a cripple, as Archibald called it—stricken at a very early age with paralysis of the legs. A disability of any sort was something Matthew could grasp; something he could relate to, to hold on to. In a way, it was an obvious symbol of Matthew's own life. To him, Hillary Buckingham was a heroine. "She's strong" he once told Archibald. "She will not let anyone treat her as a victim."

Her highly acclaimed authorship aside, I fully believed that Matthew admired Hillary Buckingham for that great strength alone. Nearly a psychic cripple himself, Matthew openly identified himself with a physical cripple. He didn't want anyone to treat him as a victim. Least of all himself.

"Hillary won't even allow the word 'cripple' to be used in her presence" Archibald told me. "She becomes outraged." Perhaps, I thought, that was the problem. Perhaps if Hillary Buckingham was able to say the "C" word, and admit to herself just once that she was indeed disabled, then, and only then, would she be able to move on. And Matthew then could move on as well.

The vast Indian continent lay ahead. And as the days passed, Archibald perked up just a bit. Thoughts and conversations of the troubled young Matthew were temporarily put aside. Archibald bounced about the ship as he had much earlier on in the voyage, with the wide-eyed excitement of a child on his first visit to the fair. He seemed to take on a bit of an attitude with the passengers —a cockiness of sorts. Sort of an "I-know-something-you-don't-know" boastfulness which I found just a bit obnoxious. I wondered if his change of mood was due to the anticipation of again setting foot on that great land—the subject of his one and only published book.

Nonetheless, it was good to see him jovial again. It had been so long since he was like that, and through all his intense brooding and his moods of great despair the last few days, I had forgotten just how much fun Archibald Hannon could be.

With "Hate Week" and its miseries a far memory, the cruise continued on with a fresh vision, a new inner life. It was as if we were all revitalized during our Singapore visit. Certainly Claus was. Perhaps it was the water; or Bugis Street. Perhaps the Singapore Sling. Whatever it was, we were family once again.

Even the atmosphere in the Tour Office seemed renewed and refreshed. A revitalized energy had come over us all—except for Percy. His drinking was becoming more and more evident as the cruise advanced, and interestingly enough, a pattern to his alcoholism began to emerge. Percy seemed to drink only when everything was going well. In a crisis, or when there was a job to be done, Percy was there and Percy was sober. But when we were all feeling good and doing well, and just wanting to have a bit of a good time and enjoy each other's company, Percy would inevitably spoil it all by showing up with the horrid smell of gin on his breath. Apparently, he couldn't really enjoy himself without the numbing aid of a stiff gin and tonic.

The next morning, the tour office was pulsing with anxious passengers eager to confirm their excursions in India and Africa. Tours often sold out far in advance, and so waiting lists then would be their only possibility. How disappointing to spend one's life saving for a glamorous world cruise, only to find the tour of your dreams completely sold out.

Archibald stopped by to offer assistance, and to answer any historical or cultural questions. And thankfully, he stayed with us all morning.

Later that afternoon, the audience for Archibald's talk on Sri Lanka was somewhat smaller than usual. The seas were picking up again and its effects were already evident.

Yet the sea's movement was unable to stop some passengers. Those not at all interested in learning about Sri Lankan history stood shakily outside the theatre entrance where Maggie sat uncomfortably behind a table covered with various kinds of fabric. Distributing costume materials for the upcoming *Black and White Ball* was her purpose, and passengers—although mostly women—crowded about her like ants on a crumb of bread. Fabric and crepe paper flew in all directions as they reached and grabbed for the material of their dreams—some black here, more white there—fancy-dress ideas were tossed about as nonchalantly as the fabrics themselves. Fortunately for us all, men were expected to wear only one thing that night—a black tuxedo. Maggie's table then was a women's world all its own, and Maggie was its queen.

We came alongside at Colombo quite early in the morning. I was assigned to escort Tour 38—*The Kandy Train*—scheduled to depart from the Queen Elizabeth Quay at 7:30 A.M.

We traveled inland along the seventy-mile route to the magnificent city of Kandy—the holiest of Buddhist shrine-cities. The modern air-conditioned railcars—quite unusual in these areas I was told—had large picture windows through which spectacular views could be seen of the lush green vegetation and the overly fertile valleys, rice paddies, coconut and banana plantations, and strategically-perched hillside towns. Our passenger group was quite large that day—*The Kandy Train* being *the* tour to take on Sri Lanka. So once off the train, it was difficult for us to keep everyone together. "They wonder like goats" Percy said as we first tried to get them to board the awaiting motor coaches.

Like with most of the introductory tours, the Botanical Gardens—yet again—was our first scheduled visit. And as usual, it was beautiful and it set the tone for the rest of the day. From there, we visited the Temple of the Tooth, where the actual tooth of Buddha stands proud—or so they say. And then off to shop at a roadside market—definitely not on the scheduled itinerary—operated, we soon learned, by our guide's older brother. By this time in the voyage, I was beginning to believe that every guide in the world had a brother who owned a roadside shop specifically designed to give the best possible prices for *Sagafjord's* passengers. It happened so often, in almost every port-of-call. And if you wanted to keep your local guide happy—and I can't express to you how important an investment that really was—any tour escort worth his weight would inevitably surrender to his guide's tantalizing request for a brief unscheduled stop at his brother's roadside shop.

Most of these visits were harmless enough, and this one was no exception. The passengers usually enjoyed the opportunity to get out of the bus and stretch their legs, or to use the bathroom, or even purchase whatever miscellaneous souvenirs they just absolutely had to have.

I was surprised though to receive an envelope from the guide at the end of our visit. In it, I found 150 American dollars—my "cut" from that afternoon's shopping spree. Just a thank you, he said. Indeed, I was beginning to like this very much.

Just adjacent to the market was a cliff which overlooked a rapidly rushing river 200 feet below. Several elephants were bathing—their massive tubular trunks raised high, spouting clear cold water up and over their backs as they snorted and moved about playfully. This scene alone was worth the stop. Cameras clicked frantically in an effort to catch the gushing water just as it squirted high above the elephants' heads, and splashed down again quite sloppily on to their backs—a spectacular display. The water, spraying high in all directions, reminded me of New York City fireboats as they traditionally salute a new ship's maiden arrival. While we watched, several Sri Lankan gentlemen approached us with an elephant all their own.

"Anyone would like a ride" one of the gentleman asked in heavily accented English. Laughter was the only response—just a look at our elderly passengers made it obvious that they were not of the age who would attempt such a thing.

"How about you?" the man said to me as he held out his arm. "Would you like a ride?"

Clearly, there was no way I was going to get on top of that thing—its massive body quite unsteady on its feet; its hairy, smelly skin definitely off-putting.

"Very cheap my friend " the man said to me through his nearly toothless smile.

"Sorry" I said, trying to reach quickly for a believable excuse. "I have no more money." I lied, of course, and turned away.

A little voice then came from deep within our crowd of passengers—they had gathered near the elephant, most of them taking photos. The voice belonged to Millicent Morgan, an elderly passenger with whom I had hardly conversed the entire voyage. She walked forward, slowly through the crowd, quite determined, as she busily searched her travel bag.

"I have some extra change" she proudly said. "Here, let me treat the young man. He's been so kind to us on all these tours."

The others agreed encouragingly; some applauded. And even before she could pay the elephant's owner, he had the animal kneeling down before me in anticipation of the great mount.

My legs could just barely span the vastness of its back. The coarse black hair was so sharp and prickly that it poked like spikes through my white cotton pants. As the animal began to stand, I anxiously grabbed on to the rope which was loosely tied around its neck. I held on for dear life.

"Take it easy" I cried as several passengers laughed uncontrollably. "Go slow. And don't fall down that ravine!"

The creature finally settled itself upright into a full standing position. I only hoped he was comfortable with riders. I clearly wouldn't want to have been his first.

But as the elephant took its first step, and moved closer and closer to the edge of the cliff, I realized that I had no option but to trust the aging pachyderm. It was all in his hands, after all. There was nothing I could do. I'm sure he didn't want to tumble down either.

That elephant ride was an experience I will never forget. In a way, it symbolized our visit to Kandy. And it was continuously remembered—if not memorialized—in stories told by passengers onboard ship for days and weeks thereafter. Forget about Buddha's tooth. It was my elephant ride at Kandy that was truly the sight to see.

On the return trip to Colombo, we were served a specially prepared boxed luncheon . . . a sandwich made with a meat of unknown origin, some candy from Kandy, and a large slice of locally grown pineapple. In our ravenous state, it was gone in minute. All of it was delicious—anything would have been at that point. The morning tour was indeed quite strenuous—and much longer than originally scheduled—with little if any refreshment available along the way. So by 3:00 P.M., we were all quite hungry, and just a bit grouchy too.

It was about an hour after sailing that evening when I first began to feel uneasy. A bit achy, some stomach cramps; just plan listless. As the night wore on the symptoms grew with steady intensity until the cramps prevented me from standing fully erect. I began an endless series of runs to the bathroom. It was like water. Nothing coming out but water, bursting with a frightening force.

I called Percy, just barely making it to the telephone. I needed help; I needed to hear from someone else that I was indeed all right.

Thankfully, Percy was there, in his cabin. But hearing that he felt fine almost made it all the worse. Clearly, I wanted company in my misery.

"You ate something bad, that's all" he said. "You didn't eat the pineapple, did you?" He laughed. "Welcome to the glamorous world of travel."

"Thanks" I answered. "But if this is what the world feels like, I want out."

"You're not dying, you silly twit."

"How do you know that?" I just barely got out the words between two more intense cramps. "I may not be dying, but I certainly *feel* like I'm dying."

"Oh shut up" Percy replied sharply. "Call the doctor if you'd like. He'll give you something to stop your runs."

Dr. Raold Dalle, accompanied by Sister Karre, was soon knocking at my cabin door. Norwegian nurses were called "sister" I learned. I got nervous at first. I thought she was a nun. Actually, the way I felt, I didn't care what they were called, or whether she was a nun or not. I was just so happy the doctor and his nurse had come to my aid.

"You too, I see" Dr. Dalle joked. "Quite a few of the passengers who went ashore at Colombo are sick—the same."

Indeed, I was pleased to hear this. I wasn't the only one. I finally had some company.

"Could I have something to stop the cramps, and the diarrhea?" I pleaded with him. Sister Karre looked on with a smile.

"Absolutely not" the doctor said as he stood and repacked his medical bag. "You've eaten something you should not have eaten and the body is reacting to that. It's telling you something. Yes, I could give you something to plug you up, but that would be defeating the purpose, now wouldn't it? The body is trying to purge itself of the foreign matter within your system. We must let that happen naturally."

It wasn't something I really wanted to hear. I just wanted him to make it all stop; to make me feel better, that's all. Anything he would have given me to ease the pain and the discomfort I would have taken, no questions asked.

"You Americans are all alike" he continued with a smile, and shook his head as though scolding a small child. "Instantly, you want something to make you feel better. You never let nature take its course. Just take aspirin for your aches, and drink lots of water. We can't let you get dehydrated now, can we?"

"I guess not" I mumbled. Sister Karre smiled caringly, and helped me back into bed. As Dr. Dalle closed my cabin door, he called back "don't be concerned." And they were gone.

I slept for nearly twelve hours.

The effects of the illness continued for three more days. Arne visited each night, and sometimes he even stayed, only to flee silently as the first sign of morning's light gently peeked through my porthole.

Arne was there to care for me—to cool my fevers, and to hold me close. Just his presence made me feel better. He cheered me up; he made me laugh. Most of all, Arne made me feel safe.

Sagafjord sailed majestically into Bombay harbor at 5:
00 P.M., the 26th of February. With great fanfare, the
Police Brass Band blared out their usual cruise ship welcome as
we gently touched our berth at Ballard Pier.

I noticed Swedish American Line's *Gripsholm* laying at
anchor just off to our starboard side. Her white hull glistened
as if new; the sleepy rays of the late afternoon sun shot pin spots
across her bow. She was with us at Hong Kong; and now here at
Bombay—she was accompanying us around the world. That made
me smile.

As we tied our lines, *Gripsholm* graciously dipped her flags
to us in honorable salute. I dreamed of boarding her then; I
fantasized about what life would be like onboard. Was Swedish
better than Norwegian I wondered? It really didn't matter. She
simply looked beautiful lying silently at anchor, with the entire
Indian continent as a grand cyclorama. I thought of the young
Swedes onboard—crew members, for sure—and suddenly had the
urge to be there . . . to meet them.

There was so much I wanted to do. Each day, each
moment there was something new for me, something unknown,
unexpected; mysterious, yet thrillingly adventurous. More and
more, it was clear—there was an entire world for me to see and to
experience. And this was only the beginning.

I was assigned to escort several tours throughout our five-day
visit. Tour 45 was called *Bombay City*—that's right, just change the
signs! And of course we visited the botanical gardens; only here in
Bombay, it was the Hanging Gardens on Malabar Hill.

The vastness of Bombay city was clearly evident during our
morning bus ride, as was the widespread poverty unlike any I had
ever seen or could even imagine. Intense squalor was everywhere;
aggressive begging was a constant sight. Indian mothers wrapped in
colorful silks with brasslike adornments—with an army of raggedy
children by their sides—approached us at every opportunity. With
outstretched hands, they hoped and pleaded for a coin or object

of any value just for the taking.

The children seemed abused—certainly neglected—but their abuse seemed to come from life itself. They were intensely dirty and appeared hungry—starved, perhaps—not only for food and water, but for attention; for basic human comfort.

One woman—her head loosely draped in a pale blue cloth—carried her young child slung wildly on her hip. Silently and without a word, she begged for any thing we could spare. The child, unusually quiet, had a dirt-smeared face, and a make-shift plaster cast on her right arm. Her expression was one of undeniable suffering; not the face of a child beaming with a great expectation of life. I gave the mother some rupees, and off they both went to the next available tourist innocently waiting along the way. I was horrified later to learn that some Indian mothers purposely break their children's arms or legs in order to invoke greater sympathy from tourists, in the hopes of increasing that day's take. I hated to think that the child I had just seen, was perhaps one of those victims.

That evening, I accompanied sixty-two passengers to *The Music and the Dances of India*—a special celebration presenting classical Indian dancing accompanied by a local sitar orchestra. The entertainment followed a lavish Indian buffet which included a variety of regional dishes served beautifully on highly polished silver platters.

But just before we left the ship that evening, something truly remarkable happened. I stood next to my motor coach doorway collecting tour tickets and helping those elderly passengers hobble up the narrowed steps. I watched them moving along, one at a time, boarding the buses like sheep in a pen. And there in the queue was Arne—tour ticket in hand, a big smile on his face.

"What the hell are you doing here?" I asked him excitedly. "Are you crazy?"

Arne laughed as he proudly waved his hand in my face.

"I have a ticket" he said as he thrust it high into the air for me to see.

"I'm seeing the dances of India. Is this my bus?"

Arne's laugh was incredibly infectious. I loved him when he was like that.

"One of my passengers at table twenty-four bought the ticket, but she's not feeling well" he explained. "Since I have the night off, she offered it to me—its open-sitting you know. So I thought I'd come along and surprise you."

Surprise me he did; and I couldn't have been more thrilled. Even so, understanding full well the formalities onboard, I quietly asked Lar whether or not it was okay if Arne came along. I didn't want him—or me—to get into any trouble.

"I could care less" Lar said. "As long as he's got a ticket. Just tell him to have a good time."

Arne and I spent the remainder of that night together safely and comfortably in A-54.

And the next day, we were ashore early, eager to experience what we considered to be typical Bombay life. We each brought our cameras along—Arne passionately making use of my 80-200 zoom.

For us, Bombay was a shopper's delight. And so by mid-morning, we had bought a host of brightly colored Indian carpets and hand-carved wooden screens, wooden statues and wall hangings too. Lunch was tenuous though—remembering well my Kandy experience. Just the smell of curry—which seemed to be absolutely everywhere—made me unbearably sick to my stomach.

At the end of the day, my cabin could easily have been called *my* brother's roadside shop—I simply didn't have the room for all that we had bought. No doubt Bruni heard the anxious commotion as I hopelessly tried to make room for it all; a futile attempt to find a place for everything. Thankfully, she came to the rescue.

Bruni offered a vacant passenger cabin farther aft on A-Deck as my very own storage closet. But when Percy got word of the availability of cabin A-68, some of his antiques and collectibles were brought there as well, and Lar's too. And soon, it became the place where all of our purchases were kept for the remainder of the voyage, for storage and for safekeeping—solidly and safely packed away until arriving in New York, and the 12th of April.

It was the next morning that Lar and Archibald and I, accompanied by fifty-nine of *Sagafjord*'s more spry passengers, departed by air for the two-day excursion to the cities of Delhi and Agra—a tour which became for me the highlight of the voyage.

That Air India flight was my baptism into air travel—my maiden flight, if you will. A young Indian stewardess stood atop the jetway in typical sari—pale pink it was—her forehead bejeweled with a single glittering ruby, and her jet black hair, center parted of course, was tied behind her head in a tightly woven single braid. Her hands were clasped together against her chest as if in prayer. What the hell was she praying for, I wondered as I stepped from the jetway and onboard the aircraft.

The flight was smooth and, for me, quite exciting. I sat together with Lar towards the rear of the plane; he joked and laughed obsessively the whole time, while he devoured the rather skimpy breakfast of hard rolls and strong black coffee.

Local sightseeing began almost immediately after our touchdown at New Delhi's International Airport—the usual "must-see" sights of both the old and new sectors of the city—and yes, the Botanical Gardens too.

Both the Red Fort and the Raj Ghat where Mahatma Gandi was cremated were remarkable if only for their unique architecture and keen historical importance.

The landscape surrounding us was soon becoming familiar—as if I had known it all sometime before. Archibald Hannon's *The Emperor's Throne* was the reason for my keen appreciation of the Indian continent thus far, and its dramatic history and culture. Because of his book, I believed I had a far deeper understanding of where I was and what it all meant. His book brought the history and culture of India vividly to life. And here it all was, just before me.

That night, Lar and I hosted an informal dinner for our passengers at the Oberoi Intercontinental Hotel—the beautiful facility in central New Delhi where we spent the night. Since most of us were exhausted from our early morning flight and the five hour sightseeing excursion which immediately followed, the evening ended quite early. No one lingered in the dining room; everyone soon left for his room. We had an early pick-up the next morning.

But before I could escape to the comforts of my bed, I first had to settle the evening's account with the maitre d' hotel on duty.

I slowly walked across the lobby, fully enjoying the busy atmosphere. Although quite tired from a very long day of touring, I found I was hesitant to retire just yet—a bit disappointed that my one and only evening in Delhi would end so early, so uneventful. Yes, I needed to sleep. But deep inside, I wanted to explore.

The attraction seemed to come from nowhere. We looked at each other with a casual glance at first; each of us then quickly turned away. He continued to walk past the elevator bank—then he stopped and fidgeted a bit, casually looking back in my direction. Again I looked, and glanced back—then turned away again just as quickly, his face reddening in sterile embarrassment.

He was handsome. And suddenly, there was another flashing glance. He stood near the massive archway which soared above his head—holding his gaze for just one lingering moment—his face illuminating into a subtle yet welcoming smile. I knew what it meant. Indeed, I'd come a long way since New York.

We greeted each other somewhat timidly; quickly, silently, we moved to the bar.

He was from Bombay, in New Delhi on business—some kind of government position he held, I wasn't really certain; I didn't really care. I liked his easiness, his openness. I desired his strength, his unforgiving power. We sat for just a few minutes of awkward conversation; his silence though said more than his words. It was clear that neither of us really wanted to talk.

He undressed me slowly in the darkness of his room. The raw notion of being together with this handsome stranger, totally naked—a young man who I would probably never see again—was powerfully exciting to me. We made love quickly yet passionately—we both had to rise early the following day. We had little time to waste.

I left his room without even knowing his name. Just a chance encounter, or so it seemed. Or perhaps is was just an opportunity for the two of us to feel the warmth and the touch of another human being for an evening of passionate faceless love. Was it an act as empty as it may appear? Perhaps so. But it did serve its purpose—a purpose for us both.

What can be said about the Taj Mahal which hasn't already been said? A truly remarkable work of art and architecture; a magnificent example of the power and strength of the human spirit and its endless abilities. An amazing symbol of love.

I stood before the monument that day in awe of its size and its beauty—its white marble gleaming in the morning sun as if the entire structure was lit from within.

Built as a mausoleum for the wife of the great Shah Jahan, the Taj Mahal stands today as an ageless tribute to his young queen. A similar black marble structure, fully designed but never built, was to be the Shah's own tomb—the site of which was to be in direct line of sight of the present Taj Mahal.

Their grand romance came alive for me that morning, so powerful was their love. And that image will always be etched in my mind.

The sun was piercingly hot. The breeze brisk off the Indian Ocean. Archibald, Percy and I sat together on Verandah Deck aft taking some much-needed sun. We had sailed from Bombay just two days before—and were swiftly steaming toward the Seychelle Islands and the great African continent beyond.

"What's that writing on your shorts?" I asked Archibald as I positioned a fresh towel strategically over my deck chair.

"It says 'Buffalo High'" he answered. "Why? What's wrong with my shorts?"

"My God" I said to him incredulously. "You sure make clothes last a long time, don't you?"

"What's that supposed to mean?" he snapped back, as Percy and I both began to laugh.

I finally settled into my deck chair after carefully adjusting its angle directly in line with the sun.

"You know" I said to them both. "Speaking of high school—I had a really strange dream the other night about my high school gym class."

Archibald and Percy both seemed completely disinterested; nonetheless, I continued. My words seemed more for me to speak, than for either of them to hear.

"First, I have to tell you that when I was in school, I really hated gym."

"Oh, now *that's* surprising" Percy said with a huge does of sarcasm."

"What?" I snapped back. "Just what do you mean by that?"

"Oh, nothing. Nothing at all" Percy answered. "Just continue..." And I did.

"So, I really hated gym; really hated it. But I had no choice; four full years of gym were a graduation requirement."

Percy sat quietly with a large straw hat atop his head. "Never let the sun hit your face" he often said. "It's devastating."

"By the time I finished junior year, I already had enough credits for graduation—don't ask me how that happened, it just did. So for my senior year, I just signed up for classes I liked; classes that interested me—like Russian history, and Painting & Sketching, and Medieval life. But gym was still a requirement. So I had to take it as well—although I cut class as often as I could. I was never real good at throwing or catching a baseball, or gymnastics, or trying to toss huge bouncing balls into baskets three times my height."

"I'm shocked" Percy added. "Truly shocked." Archibald smiled and looked on from his chair.

"Anyway, the other night I dreamed I was at home. There was a knock at the door, and standing there was Ernie Fawser, my high school gym teacher—tall and blond, and as solid a man as ever. Needless to say, I was quite surprised to see him—we were never really friendly—for obvious reasons. I was never the jock type he admired so much.

"Well—Mr. Fawser brought devastating news. It seemed that he was looking over his files, and realized that I had cut gym class quite often during my senior year. Far more often than was allowed. And by so doing, I never really completed the requirement for that term. Unfortunately, then, I never really graduated from high school—and therefore everything I have achieved in my life since then was invalid."

Percy laughed out loud.

"When I woke up, I was in a cold sweat. I thought it was real. I thought it was true—that none of what I'm doing now was real, and that I had to start all over again."

"That's what guilt does to you" Percy said. "Never ever feel guilty for anything you do."

While Percy spoke, Archibald was silent; he stared at me oddly.

"What are you looking at?" I asked. I hated when he stared at me. It was creepy.

"I'm just looking at the hair on your arm. It's golden, like the sun."

"So? I'm Italian."

"I wish my hair was golden, instead of this old man's gray" he said with a sigh. Although, if you really want to know, I'm really pleased its not red. I hate red-headed people. Did you know that the circumference of just one red hair is thicker than any other?"

I didn't know what the hell he was talking about. But it didn't seem to matter. Archibald just continued, as he always did, regardless of another's comprehension or interest.

"Anyway, those days are gone I guess—of fantasizing about the color of one's hair. The gray keeps coming now—day after day. There's nothing I can do about it."

Oh God, I thought. Here he goes again—on and on about being an aging homosexual with no hope for the future.

"I have good hands though, don't you think?" Archibald moved his arms forward, hands extended for me and Percy to see. "They've often said I have good hands."

"Who's they? And yes" I said to him. "They're very nice hands. Just don't touch me with them."

Archibald looked at me intently. "You really don't like me, do you?" he said. "If you did, you wouldn't be so cruel."

"Oh come on Archibald" I shot back defensively. I actually felt a bit sorry for somehow hurting him. "You should calm down and not expect so much from people."

Percy shifted his deck chair even more away from the sun.

"One can never expect too much from friendship" Archibald said.

"Oh I don't know" I answered. "Besides, you always seem to invalidate my friendship because you obviously want it to be more than it is."

"That's because you have so many others—friends, that is."

"Jealous?"

"Yes. I love you Steven. Doesn't that make you feel secure?"

"No. Not at all. In fact . . ."

"The thing about you that annoys me" Archibald interrupted, "is that you've never really considered that another human being might just be the answer to your problems. Unlike me. I realize that I'm nothing without someone else—without Matthew."

"Look at it this way" Percy jumped in as he reached under his deck chair for his icy drink. "You may be losing a lover Archibald, but you're gaining a gin and tonic. Call that waiter over please . . . Chin Chin everyone."

Percy sipped with specific purpose, savoring each and every taste.

"Now for me" Percy continued as he smacked his British lips together. "I'm getting just as tired of people as I am of lovers." He returned his drink to the deck—placing the glass, quite neurotically, directly over the glistening moisture ring it had just left behind.

"In fact, I *loathe* people" he said commandedly. "The older I get, the more I despise being around them." He paused for a moment, then continued. "When I'm at Smith Street, or at Valbonne, or anywhere else for that matter, I never invite people over for dinner. For sex, yes—but never for dinner."

"You're a lunatic, Percy" Archibald said as he tossed his head back and closed his eyes to the sun. "You know that, don't you?"

"Not at all" Percy continued. "Not at all. I never have sex

with people I know—I think it's vulgar. Maybe I loathe people so much because there really aren't many I trust. It's true, you know. Sometimes I wish I had more friends—real friends. Sometimes I even fantasize about throwing a grand party. At Valbonne."

"Maybe you should throw a party then" I added.

"Oh, I could never actually do it—most of the people I'd want to invite are dead."

"I don't know what's wrong with you guys" I interjected as I shook my head. "You think being with other people—being in love let's say—is the only thing that matters. That sex and love is all that life's about."

"Did you say you love me?" Archibald asked, quite sarcastically.

"No I most definitely did not" I shot back. "You know me better than that."

"Besides" Percy said between sips. "It's not how much someone loves you, it's how much he likes you that really counts."

"How true" Archibald confessed. "How true." He closed his eyes again, and surrendered willingly to the sun's warmth. "Anyway, I don't want to discuss love with either of you because it's hopeless" he said. "It's too complex."

"Hey, I'm more complex than you think" I said teasingly, with a smile.

"You're right" Archibald responded. "And you're far more intelligent than I think you are too."

"More importantly" I said, "I'm beginning—just beginning mind you—to think I'm even more complex than *I* think I am."

The heat of the sun forced sweat beads to roll down my chest; I grabbed a towel to wipe them away.

"And another thing" I said after a moment. "I'm just as romantic and as loving as the next Italian-American guy. Only you just don't get to see that side of me, Mr. Hannon." I laughed just a bit and waited for his response.

"There's nothing wrong with Italian sentimentality, unless it be Jewish." He sat up just then, and spoke directly at me. "You see, I accepted more definition in life than I ever cared to. That's my problem. My life hasn't been wonderfully successful—like yours still has the probability to be. I don't think I have to prove that to either of you; it's obvious. But I decided I'm going to start to treat myself royally from now on—if no one else will. I'm realizing more and more that I'll never really be happy with Matthew. He constantly withdraws from true intimacy."

"Oh?" I interrupted. "And you don't?"

"Whoever said that sex was intimate?" Percy added with a laugh.

"And I also fear he may be taking drugs or something. I've had that fear for a long long time."

"Every young person is into drugs these days" Percy said.

"Not everyone" I answered quickly.

"Name one we know who isn't."

"Me."

"Well, you don't count" Percy snapped back.

"Well then—Marshall Smith." For some strange reason, the bridge pro's name was the first and only one to come into my head.

"Well, he's well over thirty, isn't he? So he doesn't count either. Besides, I don't think we should include anyone onboard ship. We're already fucked-up. We're a whole different kettle of fish balls. We need to consider only those ashore. That's where life is real, after all. That's where it really matters."

"No. No. That's bullshit. We need to consider everyone" I said sarcastically. "We need to consider anyone living."

"What about Bill Evans?" Archibald asked. "You know Bill Evans, Percy. Don't you? Professor at Columbia?"

"Sure, your friend from New York—he's definitely over thirty though, I dare say. But you obviously don't know him very well Archie. I heard—through my own very private sources—that he not only uses drugs, but he's been known to sell drugs to some of his more attractive and very male students."

"I can't believe it." Archibald said, aghast. "Certainly quite a come down for someone who wrote his master's thesis on Joseph

Conrad."

I listened intently to their conversation, thoroughly amused by their sharp quips, and witty opinionated banter. I withdrew for a moment, and became their audience—it was best to watch these two from a distance.

Ingemar came by just then, offering another towel to each of us. Percy ordered another round of drinks.

"Iced tea for the boys" Percy said to Ingemar. "And the ususal for Percy. A *tall* one this time."

"That *was* a tall one" Ingemar said as he laughed.

"Taller then. Just a bit taller."

"It's a pity you gave up on Bill Evans" Percy continued. "He certainly would have been a good lover for you. Perhaps you could have set him straight . . . regarding drugs, that is. I know he cheated on you that one time. But you could have used him later on in life because of that. He's an influential man at Columbia, is he not? Couldn't he help get your next book published?"

"You can't just use people like that" I said to Percy, interrupting his sermon.

"Not selfish people, anyway" Archibald added. "And selfish he was—and is. Bill always annoyed me, you know. He only cared about who he was fucking next. He had no concern for me, or my feelings."

"Yes, yes, we know Archie . . . a stiff prick has no conscience" Percy said in mocking display.

"Yes, that's true. It certainly doesn't. At least his didn't. I despised him for that. I'll never talk with him again, especially now that I know he's nothing but a common drug dealer. He'll never get an autographed copy of my next book, that's for sure; and he'll definitely not appear in the acknowledgements."

Percy rolled his eyes, curling his lips in clear disapproval.

"What do you want—revenge for his poor treatment of you?"

"Yes" Archibald said emphatically. "That's indeed what I want."

"Well, that's childish."

"Perhaps. But it's marvelous. Look, I'm sitting here drawing reality back in through my naval. The trouble is, just what does Vishnu do after he stops dreaming the world?"

"Just what the hell are you talking about?" Percy said as he and I laughed in total confusion.

"It's the dog's philosophy gentlemen. If you can't eat it or fuck it, piss on it. That's the way I'm living my life from here on out."

I looked at my watch. It was time to go. The office was to open in fifteen minutes.

"Come on Percy" I said. "Let's go piss on it then."

"But what about my gin and tonic?"

It rained for the next three days. Ironically, I felt secure when it stormed at sea. The ship, usually so exposed to everything and anything, seemed comfortably safe when it was embraced by the grayness of clouds; protected by the surrealistically-steamy mist which hovered just above the blue tropical seas. I felt a serenity not unlike I felt at home, when, as a child, my mom would close the living room drapes at the very first hint of the approaching darkness—sealing them tightly shut. Night—the devil's time after all. And with those drapes closed, I no longer felt exposed; no longer vulnerable. If no one could see in, no one could see me. So onboard ship, with a storm around us, I felt protected and safe.

Yet along with that feeling of safety and security came the end-lessness of long days during which passengers were confined deep within the ship. None ventured out onto the open decks during those times; rather they tried to occupy their days with the daily shipboard events, or those of their own making. Many simply chose the cinema—it was always the easy way out.

The quality of the movies shown onboard had, by this time in the voyage, deteriorated greatly—no doubt because of our already exhausted supply. Ted Jones was therefore forced to repeat those same films which had so freshly dominated the early portion of our cruise—those which two months ago seemed to be "first run," were now old and tired. In addition, we were condemned to watch the classics over and over again—*Camille, North By Northwest*, Bela

Lagosi's *Dracula, Gone With The Wind,* and the old MGM musicals
too . . . *Bandwagon* and *Singing in the Rain*—films, believe it or
not, which I had never seen and perhaps never would have seen
on my own, ashore. Out of sheer desperation, however, I viewed
them all; as often as I could. And quickly, I became a new young
fan of these old and sometimes obvious storylines and vividly rich
characterizations. "They don't write dialogue like that anymore"
Archibald said to me. And indeed, it was true. "The children of
the night; what sweet music they make."

With most of the voyage by then well behind us, the evenings
onboard turned merely routine.

The same old ladies, still "dressed to the nines," sat near the
dance floor from cocktail hour onward—some patiently, and
sometimes impatiently—anxiously waiting for the question to
be asked. Their painted faces couldn't disguise their hope for that
one special stranger to sweep them off their feet. Would they ever
understand that if it hadn't happened by that time in the voyage,
it most likely would not happen at all? They had certainly met, or
at least seen by then, all the eligible men traveling onboard, young
or old; no one else was scheduled to board ship for the remainder
of the voyage.

And so, their very special stranger would inevitably turn out to
be Marshall Smith, or Hal Carter, or any one of John Marratisch's
dancing boys. Nonetheless, their spirits soared—the ladies still sat,
and still hoped. Night after night. Alone. Waiting.

Each night, as I walked through the Ballroom, I was saddened
by the sight. Not unlike Archibald, they all seemed to feel that
love and companionship were all that really mattered. Their lives,
they felt, would not really be complete without someone to share
their remaining years.

As Marshall pushed Mrs. Acker around the dance floor one
more time, a sort of desperation came over me. I watched as   Assistant Cruise Director Hal Carter sat with Mrs. Furlager; and
dancing boy Jim Palace with Susie Snow. Their masquerading sadness seemed to overtake the room. Socially euphoric the women

acted, as if their lives were perfection—at least for the moment; moving quickly to the music while held firmly within the arms of their fantasy men. But I knew, as they all undoubtedly did too, that at the end of the evening, they would simply move on to their cabins as sheep to a pen—inevitably alone and ultimately unsatisfied. No one special would get to see Mrs. Acker's new scarlet gown; no one special would see Mrs. Furlager's shimmering pearl necklace. Ultimately, they dressed for themselves, no matter what pretense they claimed, in a desperate masquerade of life's emotions and wants and dreams.

I wanted no part of their charade. I wanted no part of their future for mine. Indeed, if this was the formula for growing old wealthy and successful, then I would make sure that in my later years I would never succumb to such misguiding and mishandling.

It became clearer to me then that I alone must be the true strength in my life—the solid foundation on which a future could be built. I could not become dependent upon others for success, or happiness—as all these ladies had become dependent on their husbands. I knew that if I could indeed be the sole source of my own life's success and satisfaction, then I would be clearly in control. And only then, I believed, could I be happy and secure.

If only Mrs. Acker had learned that lesson. And Mrs. Furlager, and all the rest too. It was clear that they allowed themselves to become far too dependent on others. No doubt each of them thought that life would always be as it once was, when they were happy, sharing a common bond—a common life, with their husbands. And now, since all that was gone, they seemed lost.

I'm sure none of these women had asked that her spouse be taken away; none had asked for the intense loneliness which resulted from widowhood, or the obvious sense of lost self-confidence and endless feelings of fear and abandonment which no doubt followed. Nonetheless, it was the card they were dealt. And one must play their hand accordingly, or simply beg out.

As I undressed for bed that night, I was bombarded with constant and confusing thoughts about Archibald and Percy, and the other singles onboard—men or women who, at least through my own interpretation, had created—positioned—themselves to be the sole center of their lives. None had chosen a lifetime partner with whom to share their world. And yet, even *they* seemed unhappy.

Archibald longed for the pains of a doomed love; and Percy too searched—perhaps subconsciously—for a very special stranger to lure him away from his shipboard charade; off to a far better and more satisfying life. Yes even Percy—his outward resistance aside—longed for such a relationship. Percy... who had wealth, and houses in London and the south of France too, and many friends who all seemed to adore him. Even all that, simply did not matter.

Maybe they were right. Maybe it was, after all, only about love, and companionship, as they both claimed. Maybe *I* was the one who was wrong.

Arne arrived at my cabin just after midnight; the buffet service had ended, and he was free until morning. It had become our routine. Each night, I would leave my cabin door unlocked in anticipation of his arrival—sometimes long after I had slipped into my bed and drifted off to sleep. Just the thought of Arne's arrival made me rest easier. The comfort he brought me was light to a new day. He was the sun I hoped would never set.

The friendship Arne and I developed became enrichingly strong, powerfully intimate. Whether we spent hours in heated moments of naked conversation, or in playful and sometimes highly adventurous lovemaking—or simply sleeping together, quietly and safely, holding each other as close as my single bed—and our hearts—would allow; it didn't seem to matter. Being together was what mattered. It was clear that we both loved each other, and revered each other's company. We trusted each other. And that was our love.

In after dark; out by morning's first light—those were the rules. They had to be. It was life onboard. Our life. I admired Arne's tenacity in maintaining the routine. I knew it could not have been easy for him. And I loved him all the more for it. Like the soothing rains embracing the ship, Arne made me fell safe. He made me feel special; he made me feel loved.

I awakened that night just as Arne closed the cabin door. He tried hard to be as quiet as he could, softly walking about the room as a cat in the night—as an archeologist tiptoes through an unknown tomb, conscious to preserve the artifacts around him. It didn't matter though how quiet he tried to be. I was invariably aroused by Arne's presence. I felt him near, whether asleep or not; my entire body smiled.

Arne always preserved the cabin in total darkness as he silently undressed and showered quickly. Most nights, I would drift off again, dreamily and light as he prepared for bed—and then he was there, with me, warmly snuggled against my chest, his still damp hair just brushing against my neck. Sweet, strong, powerfully my friend.

But the silence of his touch was not to be that night. Something was different. Perhaps Arne sensed that I had been troubled by my thoughts the last days; perhaps he himself was unsettled. I sensed he wasn't ready for sleep. His heart pounded powerfully against me, yet it was unlike the pounding our usual passion brings. He seemed nervous, and I didn't know why.

"I'm worried about you" Arne whispered softly. "You've been acting different lately. I hope you're not getting caught up in all this."

I wasn't sure where Arne's words were leading, or really what they meant. He knew me well—my feelings, my concerns; they couldn't help but betray my silence, even in sleep.

"I don't just mean the life onboard ship" he continued. "The gay life." He paused a moment, pulled me a bit closer to him, and then continued again.

"All this may be fun for now, but do you really want to end up like all the others—like that bridge instructor, or that assistant cruise director—or even worse, those dancing boys? Do you really want to become an aging homosexual, living onboard a ship the rest of your life? . . . wandering the globe because you cannot create a satisfying life of your own? . . . Because by then, it's too late. You're older, and not as attractive, and no one really wants you? Please, my friend" he continued, "don't let that happen to you."

His words frightened me. They came from nowhere with a

seemingly dangerous purpose. Why was he saying these words to me, I wondered. Just when everything seemed to be going so well for us.

What was our relationship after all, if it wasn't a homosexual relationship? I had traveled many miles to reach that point in my life. I had finally come to the realization that it was indeed just that—a homosexual relationship. I loved another man; and he loved me. I wanted it. And I welcomed it. And I was angered by his belittling it; appearing to sever its life before it could even grow or thrive.

"What are you talking about?" I said to him somewhat heatedly. "You're here—you're in my bed, naked, holding me close to you. Just what are you talking about?"

"Yes, that's so. And I'm very glad I'm here. I'm happy to be here with you, tonight and every night. I wouldn't want to be anywhere else. But this cannot go on forever . . .

"You know I like to be with women too" Arne continued. "When I'm older and feel the need to settle down, I want to marry—perhaps my Lizzie back in Copenhagen—and raise a family. I love children, and I'd want them to be a part of my life."

This was a side of Arne I didn't want to know, certainly didn't want to talk about. It was as if his words of marriage and children betrayed our friendship and our love. Suddenly, there was another Arne in my bed—still a man filled with love and respect; but his love and desire did not include me.

"Come on, Arne, how can you do that?" I said to him. "How can you have both?" I was confused and a bit dazed by his focus.

"You *can* have both. Just allow yourself to love, and accept life as it is. Don't try to make it anything its not."

I could hear Percy's words just then—life is moments. How more and more right he was.

"Here, like we are now" he continued. "It's beautiful, right? We like each other very much, and want to spend our time together. But after this cruise is over, who knows what the future will offer? We don't know yet what that will be." Arne was vague, somewhat purposely, I thought.

"Wait a second" I said to him as I pulled away and propped myself up a bit. "If you go home and eventually marry, won't your wife, and perhaps your son or your daughter, find out about your desire to be with men as well? They're going to eventually find out, you know." I spoke to him almost as a child asks questions of his teacher.

"Yes. They probably will. But most likely it's because I'll tell them. In Denmark, you see, it's not such a problem as it is in the States. We Danes are far less judgmental than you Americans. Certainly more open. Being together with another man could be something I may do on a Friday night—perhaps visit a sauna in Copenhagen for an hour or two—but then I would get back in my car and return home, to my wife and to my son or daughter, as you say. That will be what really matters.

"I don't want to spend my life alone" he continued. "Believe me. I'll be sharing my life—all aspects of my life—with my family—with those I love, and those who love me. And I know that I must never underestimate them for what I may fear they will or will not accept of me.

"So you—you must respect yourself" Arne continued. Care for yourself, and think about your future."

Arne held me close again, and gently brushed my hair off my forehead as a father lovingly touches his son.

"Don't worry, it's okay" he whispered. "Just let it be what it is." He paused a moment, and kissed me softly on my lips. I was instantly aroused by his warmth and intimacy. The unwelcomed stimulation angered me though; it seemed unfitting to be sexually excited by the man who just destroyed my newly found calm.

"It's dreams" he continued. "It's all about your dreams, and about making them happen. And we should never, ever, sacrifice those dreams for the passions of the moment."

And with his words we slept, with me nestled warmly in Arne's arms—uncomfortably afraid, yet beautifully safe.

Clifford was already at the breakfast table by the time I arrived the next morning. That, in itself, was unusual—

Clifford often preferred to stay to himself most of the time; he rarely took meals with the rest of the staff. A loner if ever there was one.

"I can't wait to get off this thing" he said between spoons-full of steaming Irish oats and sips of cold milk. "I'm leaving the ship at Mombasa; I just found out. Brooks wants me back in New York to start putting together the tours for the next one—the Med. Thank God" he said happily. "And not soon enough."

"That's great" I said, hoping to encourage Clifford just a bit. "Great for you, at least. But we'll miss you, you know."

"*You* may; I doubt the others will."

Clifford looked away as though not wanting to hear my words; not wanted to think about their impact. Something was troubling him; his uneasiness could not be hidden.

"Is everything else okay?" I asked him after a long pause.

"Not really. I spoke with Bruce last night too, ship-to-shore. He's being a real prick. Do you know what a real prick is?"

"Ah—yes" I said with a quick laugh. "I think I do know what a real prick is."

"He really doesn't want me traveling anymore. He's glad I'm coming home, but he knows I'll inevitably be leaving again . . . sometime. That's what my life is. Coming and going. He just doesn't understand that I have to do this once in a while—it's my job. I don't think he understands—or wants to understand—that if I left this job, or if I got fired, I'd lose my visa, and then you know what would happen. And you also know that I won't let that happen.

"I really don't know what to do" Clifford continued with an even deeper sadness in his voice. "Bruce is beginning to make me crazy. I really feel pressured—between a rock and a hard place."

Clifford became more and more agitated as he spoke. It came and went with him as quickly as a sea breeze.

"It seems I'm damned if I do and damned if I don't." He paused a moment as he slurped down the last of his milk, leaving not one sallow drop in his glass. "Besides" he continued, "if you really want the truth . . . I have a feeling Bruce is seeing someone else."

That was it, I thought. That was the real issue. Clifford feared he was losing Bruce—his lover slipping away from him from a distance of some five thousand miles, yet right before his eyes; and he felt it was inevitable, he knew he couldn't do anything about it.

Clifford was torn between loyalty for his lover, and commitment to his work. Clearly, if he lost one, he'd no doubt lose the other. And if he did his job well, and traveled when required, he'd most certainly lose Bruce—a man who apparently couldn't wait for Clifford's return, yet couldn't control his roving urges, couldn't keep his pants tightly zipped, until that return. A man who apparently felt right at home in The City of Brotherly Love.

"Come on my young friend" Clifford said to me. "Its time to go to work."

That very personal conversation with Clifford that morning, together with my own uneasy thoughts and concerns about *my* future—and Arne's odd encouragement to move on to more substantive things in life—opened up new ground for me. I began to see how really ill-equipped I was to judge anyone else's life or anyone else's relationship, mainly because I never really had one of my own. How, then, could I even begin to understand what one feels and how one acts when an inseparable and emotional bond exists between two individuals? Clifford and Bruce; or Archibald and Matthew; or Ted and Anne, Roland and Elizabeth, and even Arne and Liz. They all had someone special in their lives. Whether or not the relationship was good or healthy, that really didn't seem to matter. And who gets to judge whether a relationship is good or healthy after all?

They all held close something I did not have; a personal knowledge—the power of experience. I understood little of its essence. I couldn't. Speculation might always exist with me. But knowing—actually understanding—could only come after one experiences for himself. Never by proxy. Not by living vicariously through someone else.

In an odd sort of way, I found myself envying Clifford, and I laughed at the irony. I coveted his eroding relationship with a wacky and blatantly disingenuous dentist named Bruce, living somewhere off in a darkened Pennsylvania city—envying the intense problems that now plagued Clifford's life, and ripped apart his soul.

Yes, that perhaps was the answer. Clifford's intense love for another human being was what I most envied, no matter how much pain it caused. It was the feeling I longed for, even if that feeling brought heartbreak. It must be far better to feel, I thought, than not.

And it was also the passion. Indeed, I craved the passion. Why hadn't that yet touched me, I wondered. Or perhaps it had, and I just didn't know it. Maybe I hadn't *let* the passion happen?

"Just let it be" Arne told me. Just let it happen."

If I was truly able to see my life clearly, I would have realized it *was* happening.

Arne was what was happening.

When would I be able to fully admit that I did indeed love Arne more than any other, and that the romanticism I longed for and fantasized about was nothing more than what I felt when I was with him? When would I stop bouncing through life like a deflated ball tossed out of a playground; always searching—always looking for something else, something better, something new—something I was programmed to believe was love from television movies or the vast silver screen? When would I understand that love did not have to fit the sole guise of those faceless author's and screenwriter's visions; that it could—and most certainly did—take upon itself its own form and its own life. If I could simply cease hoping in eager anticipation for something better, for something more to come along—I could then appreciate what I had; what was before me. If I could just go with it; commit to it fully...

Life is indeed moments—and moments pass quickly. And before you know it, they're gone.

I was frightened. But finally, and at last, I felt I was beginning to feel.

The end was coming.
We still had the Seychelles and all of Africa ahead

of us, but that would pass quickly. And then, what remained was the endless emptiness of the Atlantic—and home.

I was haunted daily by the decisions before me. Would I stay onboard ship for the next series of cruises—a thirty-day Mediterranean and then a forty-five-day voyage to the Norwegian Fjords and the Baltic? Would Robert Brooks even want me to stay? Should I permanently disembark at New York on April 12th and return, like a good little boy, to my home and to college as my original plan specified?

And what about Arne? How did Arne fit in to my life, if at all?

I knew these decisions would be difficult enough to make in themselves. And then Archibald complicated my choices even further.

He suggested I leave the ship as originally planned, but not return home at all. Rather I should continue my studies in Europe—at a university in France or Switzerland, where I would be able to perfect my then quite feeble knowledge of the French language. What an incredible idea, I thought. To actually live among these great European people, whose lives and whose culture so fascinated me. It was tempting, the epic and romantic fantasy of it all. But I never really believed it. I never believed I could. I was not Archibald Hannon, after all.

I avoided making decisions, especially when compelled by some outside force; and especially when they meant so much. My options seemed so simple just several months ago. Then, I had so little to lose. Then, I held the protection of the world before me. The future seemed as unfocused as the horizon up ahead—always there, yet impossible to reach.

But suddenly, that horizon was there, before me; and the decisions I would make would effect a lifetime.

Indeed, the pressure was time itself. And I simply could not give in. Was I not ready to decide, or just unable?

I felt forced to apparently—randomly—choose between just the options at hand; only those I could see—with no real focus, no clear objective. To make a decision solely because the voyage was ending; not because it was right. But what if there were indeed more options to chose from, and they were simply unknown?

Perhaps I was fooling myself. Perhaps there was no choice at all. Did I really believe I could just simply return home and be content; happily settle into a far quieter life than the one I was living; simply pick up where I had left off—with college courses in static classrooms which seemed so second rate, so unimportant? Would I really ever be able to read history the same way I once had—the way a student should?

And why would I want to *read* it? I had seen it, after all; I had lived it.

Yes, I had actually stood before the great Taj Mahal; actually walked the cavernous streets of Hong Kong; actually bowed before the Giant Buddha at Kamakura—tying my own little wish to that remarkably stalwart tree. How could I ever again sit in an antiseptic classroom with students who had never enjoyed such experience?—never set foot outside a stifling suburban town; students who were unable to comprehend just where I had been, and what I had become.

Suddenly it was clear that *Sagafjord*, and the world itself, had made my past academics seem trite; a practice solely for those who were unable to do what I was indeed doing. I knew I could not go back.

But did I really want to stay?

Like Champagne Hour earlier in the cruise, Ladies' Night was a popular event onboard, at least with the ladies. Cruise Director Ted Jones had scheduled the event just prior to our arrival at Victoria on the Seychelle Islands—a sort of *Asian* Ladies' Night if you will, as ladies were requested to wear their locally purchased fashions—saris, kimonos, or whatever else struck their fancy.

Naturally, dance cards were all aflutter at dinner that evening. The eligible women hunted like hawks, hungrily flittering from table to table in search of their next dancing prey.

"I've got a Cha Cha open" I heard Mrs. Ledbetter say as she

aggressively accosted Philip on the stairway landing, even before he could sit down to dinner.

Yes, many of the ladies hovered near our dining area that night. After all, that's where most of the danceable men dined—all of us, of course, from the tour and social staffs. It didn't matter in the least that most of them were homosexual.

Percy and I hid away as much as we could that evening. He even had a plan; ingenious too. We would write fictitious names on our dance cards. It would then appear, at least to the ladies anyway, that our ten dances were already assigned and accounted for.

Percy and I both agreed, though, that we should be seen dancing at least one time during the evening. So we listed that very first dance on each of our cards with a real passenger's name—someone we liked of course. We made sure, Percy and I, that as many passengers as possible, and staff members too, were witness to our moving about the dance floor, diligently doing our terpsichorean duty.

But when that first dance ended however, we each slipped out of the Ballroom silently and discreetly—Percy from the forward entrance, I from the aft—and met together at his cabin where we talked and ate pate and brie, and listened to music on Percy's new stereo.

It worked—for those first lucky ladies, and for us as well. One dance was certainly better than ten. And the evening was over before we knew it.

The Seychelle Islands were shrouded in fog as *Sagafjord* approached our anchorage. The rains continued in heavy downpours, making the island appear as if secretly hidden by a scrim. The winds spun us around our anchor drop; each time I looked, our ship faced in yet another direction. The tender ride ashore, I knew, would not be a pleasant one.

We anchored quite a distance off shore—with the seas as rough as they were, we could not take the chance of lying too close. The sailors and deck crew, brightly dressed in slick yellow mackintoshes with collapsible hoods, quickly unfastened the tenders from their davits and lowered them to the churning sea below. The tour staff met at the A-deck gangway to board launch No. 1 and be the first to step ashore.

This was *Sagafjord*'s inaugural visit to Victoria—her maiden arrival; no one onboard then, with all our travel and touring experience combined, had ever before been ashore at the Seychelle Islands. So tying up at the landing place that day was uncertain and difficult. The extensive rains had caused massive flooding and the pier area was already significantly submerged. Our local tour agent had placed long wooden planks strategically in to position; these became our gangway ashore. There were no available railings, and the planks shifted and buckled precariously as each of us walked their length to the muddy area ahead. Just to our right, the tour vehicles awaited—windshield wipers dancing; aging diesel engines coughing out smoke.

"Truly first class, don't you think?" Percy commented sarcastically, as we stepped ashore.

"N-A-L." Per shouted from behind. "Never Again Line."

The first passengers came along with the next launch. We were all amazed at the exceptional turnout; we expected massive cancellations due to the uncomfortable weather conditions. Surprisingly, though, the passengers seemed more eager than we were to spend the afternoon ashore on this rain-soaked paradise.

My personal instinct would have been to stay onboard in my cabin, dark and safe, with book in hand, listening to the rain pounding hard against my porthole. But no. And appreciatively so. Thanks to the indefatigable forcefulness of our little old ladies, we all got to visit the Seychelle Islands after all.

Perhaps it was our passengers' true and honest desire to experience that rarely visited land, uniquely isolated off the eastern coast of Africa; or perhaps it was because they had purchased their tour tickets so long ago, and would simply not allow a passing tropical rainstorm of any intensity to dampen their day. There were no refunds, after all.

So off we went, finally, after loading a rain-soaked busload of elderly Americans; cameras in hand, souvenir funds at the ready.

All in all, I was grateful. For even in a storm of such power and intensity, the Seychelle Islands were incredibly beautiful.

I was grateful too for the lesson our passengers taught me that day—not to take the easy way out; and to allow myself to experience whatever was offered; whatever was there before me.

Chapter Six

"Afraid Of The Dark"

Africa.

The port of Mombasa—ablaze with activity. One hardly knew where first to look.

Two government-run tugs gently edged us into place near the aging coastal steamer *Uganda*; she lay quietly still next to several rusted freighters and container vessels heavily laden with goods, and trash, and open decay. There hardly seemed room for us at all.

Our pier was deserted. The shrieking noises of a restless port city were all that greeted us. I had the feeling we were interfering in a world not for visitors. Voyeurs we were; welcome we were not.

My tour assignment was No. 54 *Tsavo National Park and Mzima Springs*—a two-day overnight safari to view the wildlife at Kenya's largest game sanctuary.

We drove through the city in air-conditioned motor coaches (somewhat unusual for that part of the world, I was told), then out to the land to the north. And it was there that this magnificent world first opened up for me—grandly, like the pages of a child's storybook.

The vastness of the space around us, with the jagged hills quite vivid in the distance, made me realize just how much I had missed land—its lush greenery, its rolling hills and soaring mountains; the incredibly beautiful wildflowers and other natural flora innocently bursting into bloom along the roadways.

Everywhere I looked there was a new experience to consume

and digest—the children in gray and blue elementary school uniforms walking along the roadside, carrying their books atop their heads; the local farmers, intensely busy with their burdening field tasks; the thriving trees gently leaning away from the constant coastal breezes. All these images helped to give the scene a calmness, a stability. The longevity of the lives I witnessed that morning, and their customs, were clear; their future, insured.

The opportunity to view game in their own natural habitat is an experience not to be missed. With its great awe and beauty aside, it allows one to experience the grand simplicity of life, and to profoundly understand the unnecessary complications we so eagerly create in our own hectic world.

I saw firsthand the interaction of species, some of which I had never even known existed—sharing together the resources of the land they understood and instinctively respected; the land on which they depended for their own basic survival. Each of those species had his own instinctive role. Mutual regard was obvious, and envious.

The peacefulness of this world—its profound simplicity—was indelibly etched in my mind. It fostered thoughts of what our world could be like if we just respected each other as simply and as beautifully as did these creatures of the land. They had no choice. We did. Why couldn't we learn from them? Where was *our* peace and calm coexistence?

We spent that night at the Kilaguni Safari Lodge—a popular tourist resort built deep within the reaches of the game park itself. Passengers and escorting staff members were assigned individual huts, each with its own private bath.

The glassless windows were quite expansive for such a small room; they overlooked the vast watering hole for which the Lodge was internationally famous. The furnishings in the hut were as simple as one would expect; the white gauze netting—canopied and grandly draped over the bed—conjured up images of Hollywood's own depictions of romantic explorations on Africa or the Amazon. Could Katherine Hepburn in flowing white cotton and large picture hat be resting comfortably in the next hut?

But as I was learning—everything had its reason; and this netting certainly had a purpose.

Before bedding down, I carefully adjusted the fabric just as I had seen in epic movies of great exploration and adventure; it was a part of the fantasy, after all. Within it, I felt safe and secure as I dozed into sleep—the sounds of the African night, alive and naturally calming, were my lullaby.

And then it was dawn. And the sounds of the night were then loudly silent; the sun already warming the very top of Kilimanjaro which stood tall just outside my window. Phantom birds called out to the morning in their own special language—rough, and tender; soothingly real.

I opened my eyes to a canopy of insects—a menagerie which clung to the fabric like a living quilt. Spiders and mosquitoes, some of which were the size of my fist, were firmly affixed to the netting. Where the hell did they come from, I wondered? Were they really trying to eat me?

I shook the net with violent intent. They scattered in a matter of seconds, some more quickly than others—each to his own daytime hiding place of damp darkness and blind security. It seemed safe then to part the netting, and cautiously step down to the wood flooring below. You can be sure I checked my shoes that morning . . . and my overnight bag as well.

The sun's expanse generously illuminated my windowsill—suddenly full, gently warming the Kilaguni watering hole already laden with vibrant herds of zebra, elephant, and giraffe. Flocks of birds, species of which I had not before seen, flew overhead—some even swooped down, periodically landing atop the water for an early morning drink or a poke at a surfacing fish. The sun's luminescence slapped hard against their bodies as they drank and washed and playfully shook the cool water away. They seemed endlessly happy.

If this was Africa, I never wanted to leave.

Back onboard ship, the shocking paradox of the beauty of the African continent and the absurdity of *Sagaf-*

jord's shipboard life became clear. That evening's show featured Ted and Anne in their newly choreographed rumba medley, a musical segment featuring the Jan Walesky Orchestra with Carmela—The Chilean Nightingale, and a new performer who had just joined the ship.

"Mr. Entertainment" as he was billed, was Carmela's husband, Julio; he embarked at Mombasa earlier in the day. We were told Julio and Carmela would remain with us for the remainder of the voyage.

"Mr. Entertainment" looked quite pitiful as he walked on to the stage that night. His aging suit was encrusted with musical instruments of all kinds—cymbals atop his top hat, taps below his shoes. His costume looked worn and ragged—clearly consistent with his overall image and appearance as a man. He didn't even feel it necessary to shave for this event—his NAL shipboard debut. Was it simply stupidity, or just laziness? Or just a theatrical bit? Nonetheless, the music began and "Mr. Entertainment" went into action.

He played the harmonica, the kazoo, the spoons and the cymbals too, all while tap dancing to his own rendition of *The Yellow Rose of Texas.* Each of his numbers were the same—his talent was not unlike one would see on a New York City street corner or in a seedy subway station—only there, however, the performer's hat would have been turned upside down, lying on the floor before him, awaiting the clang of coins of any kind and denomination.

It wasn't until his finale, when the music abruptly segued into a rousing *Dixie* (yes, that's right . . . Mr. Chilian Nightengale performing *Dixie*), that he pulled out all the stops. Two miniature American flags shot out from each side of his top hat and his bow tie began to flash on and off—the little light bulbs just barely visible from the rear of the Ballroom where I stood. He held his cymbals high with arms outstretched, and kicked the highest kicks he could—knees bent, naturally—and this is how he theatrically "brought it home."

Welcome to *Sagafjord* "Mr. Entertainment." We were certainly in for a long voyage home.

The theatrical arts have always been of interest to me. Ever since my earliest days at St. Thomas Elementary, when I was asked to portray Christopher Columbus in a mid-October pageant, my heart would pound and the adrenaline would flow each and every time I had the opportunity to set foot on a stage, or present myself before a large group of people—even, I guess, when escorting a land excursion and standing at the front of a motor coach, addressing fifty-or-so tour-hungry passengers with admirable authority and confidence.

Yes, life on the stage seemed an exciting one to me. So it was an interest I actively pursued by joining the Thespian Society while at high school and participating in their seasonal productions— *Little Mary Sunshine* (I played a Mountie), *The Sound of Music* (a Nazi storm-trooper), and *West Side Story* (finally, a Jet.). I enjoyed the camaraderie and the teamwork; and the energy with which everyone joined together for some oftentimes long and difficult hours of rehearsal and set construction, all to get the show up and open on time. Not unlike working onboard ship, it made me feel as if I belonged. The theatrical community seemed to be a family. And I wanted so much to be a part of that family.

So I was quite thrilled when Anne Dickson re-lit that flame of theatrical interest when she asked if I would take a part in a special variety show she and Ted were preparing for the westbound voyage from Dakar to St. Thomas. I was to be teamed together with Philip Pound, Hal Carter, and a dancing boy or two, in her own very special rendition of *The Varsity Drag*. How could I refuse? Someone needed to give "Mr. Entertainment" a run for his money. Why shouldn't it be me?

Rehearsals were to begin in a week, just after sailing from Cape Town. And so the onboard gym became my after-work haunt. Indeed, if I was to be making my performing debut onboard *Sagafjord*, I needed to get into shape.

Sagafjord sailed south, then, to the vibrant cities of Durban and Cape Town. Numerous tours set out from both metropoli, and passengers, staff, and crew alike were quite eager to get ashore and experience as much as possible during our rather brief stays.

A second overnight safari excursion took me and sixty-two passengers to Hluhluwe Game Reserve, just north of Durban and deep within Zulu territory. By then, being the experienced old hand at game viewing, I was far better equipped to handle the demands of the trip. The rare white rhino, or square-lipped rhino, as it is sometimes called, made one of its very infrequent appearances as we drove throughout the spacious park to the Zululand Safari Lodge. Just that experience alone, of seeing those endangered animals in their own natural habitat, made the entire tour worthwhile.

Conversely, Cape Town was a modern and extremely sophisticated city, beautifully set against towering Table Mountain. I was enchanted by the city's beautiful landscapes and surroundings—from the picturesque and precariously winding drive south along the majestic Atlantic coastline, to the breathtaking Cape of Good Hope to view the actual spot where the Atlantic Ocean and the Indian Ocean meet; to the pastoral scenic drive just north of the city, deep within the Drakenstein Mountain Range, to witness the spectacular valley views and to enjoy a lavish outdoor barbecue luncheon at the popular High Noon Farm in the heart of South African wine country.

Indeed, South Africa was a complete surprise. I had heard so many dreadful things about this country during my early school years—the hatred of its people against people, apartheid, and all the rest. It frightened me when I first stepped ashore. But it wasn't like that. Yes, I encountered public restaurants and restrooms with separate doorways for "whites" and for "colored." But the city and the surrounding areas had a serenity about it all—a certain beauty, an understanding. Everyone had his role. There seemed an accepted calm. It wasn't anything like what I had been told, or created in my head. But then again, I wasn't "colored"—I got to walk through the favored door. How could I ever really know?

Percy was off escorting the five-day overland tour which had left the ship at Durban and would return to Cape Town by the famous garden route inland. With him was passenger Florence Cardwell, an affluent elderly woman who traveled with NAL many times before. Most often she traveled alone, but on our particular voyage she was joined by her secretary Joan Johnson.

Ms. Johnson was a younger black woman, the only African-American passenger on the ship, in fact—always charming, invariably fun-loving, with a sparkling laugh and an intoxicating sense of humor. Joan was intensely well liked by the entire staff and crew. She was always friendly, always anxious to make us laugh. It was refreshing to have someone like Joan Johnson with us. As Philip once said, she brought a bit of "color" to the very drab and mundane world in which we all lived.

Joan Johnson and Mrs. Cardwell sat together in the Dining Room sharing their rectangular table for six with Mr. and Mrs. Aaron Steinheim of New York, and the traveling spinster sisters Ruth and Mildred Kane of Shreveport Louisiana. There was talk that Mr. Steinheim was not at all pleased about having to share his dinner table with a black woman—rumors circulated that he had demanded she be removed. Nasty comments were made, I was told, and harsh and sarcastic words periodically passed between them. But Florence Cardwell, being the strong, powerful, dominant woman that she was, seemed to have kept it all under control. Until, of course, she left the ship for those long five days ashore, leaving Joan and Mr. Steinheim, and the Kane sisters too, to dine together alone for the very first time.

It all happened so fast; the details rather sketchy. The commotion was all I was able to hear, and the loud voices too—the very loud and shouting voices.

Dinner service had nearly ended, and those seated at Mrs. Cardwell's table were deciding whether or not to order coffees and dessert. Discussions were heated during dinner, I was told, and the atmosphere quite tense. Joan, as sweet as she appeared, was quite aware of Mr. Steinheim's bigotry, as were the others. So the scene was volatile from the get-go, and inevitably set for what followed.

An argument began, over what—no one could recall. All they remembered was that the quarrel apparently culminated when Mr. Steinheim, perhaps after a bit too much wine, called his much younger table mate a black bitch.

Ms. Johnson remained calm, and at first seemed to overlook Steinheim's crude statement. Needless to say, however, the Kane sisters were both stilled and frightened. Old world southerners though they were, they were still quite appalled with Mr. Steinheim's behavior.

Joan simply continued on in conversation as if nothing had happened—finishing up the last of her dinner, essentially dismissing Mr. Steinheim from that moment on.

As their plates were being cleared, Joan ordered a cup of coffee, as did her table mates. Joan chatted as usual with the sisters Kane about what they had done ashore earlier that day. To them both, Joan seemed remarkably gracious to ignore a very awkward situation, and what could have been a potentially volatile scene. Mr. Steinheim, on the other hand, smiled broadly; satisfied, and no doubt proud—the smile of a man who feels he's played the game, and actually emerged the victor.

When the coffee finally arrived, however, Joan simply grabbed the cup and threw the hot coffee in Mr. Steinheim's face. She then took hold of her dinner knife with aggressive determination.

"You call me a black bitch again Mr. Steinheim, and you'll be real sorry, do you understand me? *Do* you?" she demanded.

Mildred Kane's scream was heard across the room, and the maitre d'hotel and several of the waiters too rushed to the scene in an effort to come between Steinheim and Johnson, and to calm the others down.

The Steinheims immediately complained to the captain of Joan Johnson's despicable behavior, and demanded that something be done. She, he announced to anyone who would listen, had humiliated him and threatened his life, and he demanded she be put off the ship.

And Captain Brookstad agreed. Ms. Johnson had to go. The relationship between Johnson and Steinheim was too volatile, he determined. And Joan Johnson, at least in the captain's mind, was the culprit. In a sweeping and impulsive decree, Brookstad had Joan Johnson confined to her cabin, with an armed sailor guarding her door. Everyone anxiously awaited Percy's tour to return, to see what Florence Cardwell would do.

Mrs. Cardwell made it quite clear to Captain Brookstad that she did not agree with his interpretation of the incident, and that Mr. Steinheim was indeed the instigator and had been all along. His attitude, she told the captain, had not altered from their very first day onboard.

But Brookstad would not budge. He stood firm with his decision, just as he always did. He never could back down. It wasn't manly; it wasn't Norwegian. What would one expect of a square-head, after all? Joan Johnson would have to leave the ship at once.

Yet Florence Cardwell was just as strong. And as a repeat passenger, she held an even greater power than did Captain Brookstad—the power of money.

"If Ms. Johnson is not good enough for this ship and for Norwegian American Line" she strongly stated to Brookstad loud enough for all around her to hear, "then this ship and this company is not good enough for me."

And with that, they both withdrew to their cabins, packed their bags, and disembarked that very afternoon at Cape Town.

An unfortunate incident it was for us all. We lost Joan whom we all adored. We lost the energy she brought to our insular world. But most of all, Norwegian America Line watched and stood by while a very loyal and long-time client walked down our gangway for the very last time, never to return again.

"I think I've missed you more days than I've known you"

Archibald read from a letter he had composed to young Matthew. We sat together at afternoon tea one day, enjoying a chocolate-almond biscotti. Archibald wanted to share his words with me before sending them off to Boston. I guess he wanted my comments.

"I long for the time when you might again come for a visit, and share with me my little monk cell on 22nd Street."

Why, I thought, was Archibald so persistent with the young Matthew? Why was he putting so much pressure on the boy? And why was he so eager to lose. Besides, I thought after listening to his words, no one talks like that anymore. Matthew is sure to run.

"I must send it off quickly" he said. "Matthew desperately needs the love and the support that only I can offer him. I yearn to guide him. I'm right for him" he continued. "He just doesn't know it yet."

"Maybe he's not ready for guidance—yours, or anyone else's right now" I said to him, thinking as I would if I were Matthew. In my opinion, the last thing Matthew needed was more pressure, especially from someone who he clearly interpreted to be his much-hated father.

"Maybe you're freaking him out by pursuing him so obsessively, with such strong and romantic words. Remember, he hasn't written to you for quite some time—not since that one and only letter you received at Honolulu. That was many weeks ago. And even then, you said his letter was somewhat abrupt and unfeeling. Maybe that says something. He hasn't communicated with you at all since then . . . not even a postcard."

I wasn't trying to hurt the man. I just wanted him to see the reality of what I believed was there before him. I wanted him to re-think his letter, before he perhaps made a fool of himself.

"So what does that mean?" Archibald snapped back defensively, then continued again after a long pause. "People send you letters and postcards for a while. Then they stop. Then they stop remembering." Archibald seemed dazed, almost in a dream. "Then when you die, they really stop remembering. That's why it's better to be buried, and not cremated. Then at least they will have a grave to visit once in a while."

"Well that's certainly a cheerful thought. " I said to him as I took another biscotti from my plate.

"Perhaps. But it's reality." Archibald stared for a moment, and then continued. "Matthew loves me, I just know it. Only he doesn't know it. He needs me. I'm the only man who can sort out his life for him."

"Archibald . . . no one can sort out his life *but* him. And what if he doesn't want his life sorted out anyway?" I asked. "What if he just wants to be left alone?"

"Look. I'm not like his father. I'm not going to rape him or abandon him."

"Don't tell *me* that" I said to Archibald as I bit into another biscuit. "Tell Matthew. He's the one who needs to hear it."

Archibald looked at me as though I revealed to him the secret of the ancient pyramids at Giza. I waited for a profound statement to follow, but Archibald just starred. Apparently, it wasn't my words which fascinated Archibald so. As was typical with this man, he was already off, somewhere else.

"I can't believe you put that whole cookie in your mouth without breaking it" he said to me with a look of incredulity on his face. I shouldn't have been disappointed or surprised. Archibald always had a way of jumping from one idea to another, with no relationship whatsoever between them.

"Look" I said to him after I chewed and swallowed, following it all with a sip of steaming hot tea. "This conversation is not about my eating habits, or that biscotti. It's about you and Matthew. Stop getting off the subject. Face it. Is it too uncomfortable for you to face the fact that perhaps he doesn't really want you?"

Archibald looked as if I just smacked him across the face.

"Just what is your relationship with Matthew really about?" I asked him.

"As I've told you over and over, he needs me. He just isn't aware of it yet. He seems to withdraw from intimacy of any kind right now. When he's with another person—his friends, students—it's almost as if he's tricking all the time. He just goes from one to the next. There's no connection. No love. He doesn't relate to anyone, even to those his own age."

He took a sip of tea, then thought a moment.

"I can change that" he continued. "I know I can. I can make him appreciate the love of another human being."

"Are you sure? He's young" I said, quite aware of how pretentious that statement might seem coming from someone who himself was not even twenty years old. "Perhaps he needs to take some time for himself right now, to think about his life; to think about what he really needs and what he really wants. Perhaps settling down with someone is the last thing on his mind."

"Are you kidding?" Archibald responded quickly. "It's just the opposite. I've got to get to him as soon as possible. He's dealing with these issues now. Besides, his attention span is limited—he doesn't even stay for the second act of a play."

"Don't worry about me" Archibald continued. "I know what I'm doing. I know it doesn't really sound like it . . . but I really don't like to go to bed with anyone whose heart really isn't in it. I'm no fool. Just because I'm nobody, doesn't mean I put myself down."

I smiled at hearing Archibald's words. It made me feel as if he still, at least, maintained his sense of humor.

But through our smiles I still saw indelible sorrow and pain. Archibald's desperate obsession with the young man Matthew continued to sadden me. In his eyes, I saw clearly the inevitable plight of an aging homosexual in his doomed search for lost youth—a forgotten beauty he perhaps once knew well; a beauty he no doubt had available to him through frequent encounters with eager younger men.

I watched Archibald sip his tea that afternoon, his vulnerability stripped naked. He was going to be hurt. It was clear. I knew it, and maybe he did too. And I wondered if whether he was indeed Matthew's father figure, or whether Matthew, in some strange way, was his.

The Cape of Good Hope was a turning point for us all. We began to sail north then, back into the Atlantic and well into the final leg of our journey. And with that directional change, the atmosphere onboard became resolute. The friendships and the relationships—the familial community which had grown from all that we had experienced together throughout the voyage—would soon be coming to an end.

We had settled well into our insular maritime lives; we were indeed experts at this unrealistic world we had created. It was the challenges of soon stepping ashore, however, which suddenly seemed traumatic and uncomfortable. In less than twenty-one days it would end, and we would all be home. In less than three weeks time, the fantasy too will have ended, and we would be compelled into the reality our own lives once again.

I spent more and more time on deck those days, admiring the sea and its ceaseless beauty; it's tranquil yet overpowering lure—hoping to hold on to those images and memories forever. I was its captive, it seemed; I had no choice but to respect its strength. I was a part of that sea, and was saddened by the thought of leaving.

There was a unity in my vision of the sea and where it led. A beauty and serenity beyond compare. There were times when I was unable to recognize exactly where the sea ended and where the sky began. It was all one, after all. I finally felt a part of it; it, a part of me.

As the days passed, the thought of returning to college seemed more and more distasteful. I felt confident that it was only personal experience which mattered,—not living vicariously through text-books or other's interpretations of their, or other's, experience.

Arne and I never spoke of the future much anymore; a sure sign, perhaps of there not being one to share. Nonetheless, we continued along with the friendship we built. Sharing my cabin—and my bed—was all we had. And I guess it was all that mattered.

Still, with the safety of the end in sight, I found myself daringly in love with Arne. I fantasized often of a romantic future together—perhaps in Denmark—or just an endless reoccurrence of the relationship we then knew, knowing full well in my heart that it could and would never be.

Although the details were sketchy, I often dreamed of Arne too;

my friend—the one with whom I might possibly share my life.

But dreams were just that. Reality was what mattered. Either I was going to leave the ship at New York, or I was going to stay onboard. Whatever I decided though, the outcome would not change. Arne would be signing off permanently at Copenhagen soon after the upcoming eastbound transatlantic crossing. Our separation was inevitable, no matter what I wished or dreamed; no matter what decision I made. It was a dreaded pain I welcomed, for it protected me from knowing that Arne didn't really dream as gloriously as I.

It soon became evident too that my frank and honest opinions about Archibald's relationship with the young Matthew were not what Archibald really wanted to hear. Our words soon betrayed us. Perhaps unfeelingly, I held the mirror up a bit too often for a man of Archibald's sensitivity. So quickly, our relationship soured.

Subconsciously, I believed Archibald knew I was right, but he would never admit that to himself, or to me. He knew his and Matthew's relationship was doomed from their very first night of intimacy, out on a windy sports field somewhere off in Kansas. But they weren't in Kansas anymore. Archibald simply couldn't—or wouldn't—acknowledge the truth, for it was the truth he feared which aged him—and, at least in his mind, made him obsolete.

Yet even though Archibald flat out rejected my naive insights about his relationship with the young Matthew, they did indeed succeed at one thing; they helped to divert his attention. Unfortunately, though, that attention subtly shifted toward me. And in an odd way, I became the symbol of his pain; and the solution for his love.

With our intimate discussions by then long behind us, Archibald finally began to realize that I, too, was an intelligent young man—bright enough, at least, to capture his intellectual awareness. Perhaps not as bright as the young Matthew. But that didn't seem to matter—the degree of intelligence seemed less an issue than the proximity of the body. And I was there; Matthew was not. And that, in itself, made me even more desirable.

There was no doubt that Archibald began to misinterpret my interest in maintaining our friendship, with romantic intention. And this concerned me greatly. Once again, just as I felt nearly three months before, I could no longer relax when in his presence. I became all too conscious of where we would meet, and where our discussions together were headed.

Our talks became threatening to me in a way they never had before. He attempted to delve more and more deeply into my own emotional needs and fears. And I tried my best to avoid such intimacy whenever I could. Indeed, I thrived on such intellectual stimulation, yet during those days with Archibald, I could only hold such discussions at a distance. I was consciously aware that I was manipulating my words so as to set them in the third person, rather than making the feelings my own. I felt I had no choice. I clearly understood his agenda. I believed Archibald was getting too close.

One day, during his daily office visit, Archibald silently leaned over to me and whispered "I love you." Immediately, I withdrew.

Later that same evening, while at dinner, Archibald sat silent and pensive, staring directly at me; eyes blatantly infected with lascivious desire.

In my honest fervor to aid a friend, I apparently had created a horny monster, eager to devour the bright young man who, only recently, gave him the hope of a life renewed.

A few days later, Archibald asked if I would help him photocopy various documents he had compiled on the lives of George Sand and Frederick Chopin for an upcoming book he was researching. He was hopeless when it came to operating any type of machinery, so Archibald's request for technical assistance did not seem unusual to me, or indeed out of the ordinary.

"We won't be long" he told me. "It should only take thirty minutes or so."

I had already made plans for later that evening—Arne was hosting a party for a friend down below, in celebration of his third year with Norwegian America Line. I'd have plenty of time I thought; the party wasn't to begin until 10:30 P.M. So Archibald and I agreed to meet in the Tour Office just after dinner.

And dinner that evening was no more comfortable than it had been the previous nights, although Archibald's mood seemed far more divergent. He sat quietly, wallowing even deeper within his own obtuse world. He was not hungry and didn't want to discuss it. He had nothing to say, and didn't want to discuss it. The usual shrieks of laughter from our table seemed to cut right through him like an impaling shaft; he seemed totally oblivious to our presence.

Archibald told me his notes were in his cabin; we had to stop there first. So I decided to walk with him, get the notes, and then quickly head to the office for the copying. It just seemed easier that way, rather than meet him at the Tour Office; what if he was late? What if he didn't show?

We walked the deck in silence. And even after we arrived at his cabin, he still said nothing. He just stood there, alone to the world.

The awkwardness was unbearable. Again, I asked what was bothering him. Again, he refused to say. He was perfect at this. He traveled well within his own privately drawn borders of passivity. I was growing increasingly impatient with his moods; I could put up with it no longer.

"Well, let's get to copying then" I said impatiently as I picked up the notebooks and started for the cabin door.

When Archibald witnessed my complete disinterest in his deepening depression, he perked up just slightly, finally admitting that it was all about Matthew—still about Matthew. I wondered if it were true. I wondered if this wasn't just some grand plot to trick me into compassion—or passion—one more time.

He had always wanted love, Archibald admitted to me softly, and Matthew was his last chance. Then he fell quiet. He sat on the edge of his bed and blankly stared forward—his head slightly lowered, glasses askew and off to one side.

I was very uncomfortable. I was torn by what to say. If I encouraged Archibald at all in his relationship with Matthew, he would flatly say that I was right all along— that it would never work out, that Matthew doesn't want to have a relationship with an aging man. If I told him to forget about Matthew and to move on with his life, he would get angry and call me insensitive. And worst of all, he may become even more encouraged to pursue a relationship with me. I was doomed in the trap I had set for myself. And what the hell was I doing in his cabin anyway?

Archibald asked for my hand in a pitiful solicitation of comfort. Not wanting to encourage his already misunderstood affection, yet at the same time understanding the man's great anguish, I reached out—as a gesture of, I'm not really sure what. But that's what I did. It was all I could do. He grabbed my hand. I stood there for a moment in painful silence—Archibald sitting awkwardly on the side of his bed; me, standing next to him, as distant as I could reasonably be.

Nothing further was said. We maintained silence together—a vigil for someone we didn't even know.

Suddenly, Archibald looked up at me, and grinned, a grin of winning satisfaction. I realized then he enjoyed this brooding of his; it was a way for him to get attention. I began to wonder if there really was any copying to be done at all—if this was all just another ruse for further attention. It was a clever ploy to hold my hand, to touch me, to keep me in his cabin as long as possible.

By that point I had been with Archibald for well over an hour; I realized the time we had wasted. I suddenly became angry that he would trick me so. I was saddened too that our friendship had so degraded.

I told him that I was late for another appointment, and left his cabin without a word, leaving Archibald sitting alone on his bed.

The next morning, I found the following note slipped silently under my cabin door:

"Dear Steven,

    I'm really pissed off at you. Let me tell you why:

    A. I asked you, yesterday afternoon, to help

me do some xeroxing; i.e. to reserve the evening after dinner in order to help me.

B. For involved reasons, I fell into a mood of black despair toward the end of dinner and as you know, withdrew to my cabin.

C. Quite correctly, in the direction of a committed and loyal friend, you then came to my cabin to find out what was wrong. Quite incorrectly however, you didn't even bother to sit down; you stood, because you had made a date and didn't want to overstay your time. When I asked for a hand as a gesture of solidarity, you gave me a finger! Instead of sitting down and discussing what provoked my mood, instead of dispelling the mood by giving true warmth and friendship (by which time you could have said "Now get your ass in gear and let's do that xeroxing."); instead of this, you fidgeted and fussed, and finally told me what you might have been honest enough to tell me at the outset—that you had made a date and "were already twenty minutes late." Could you not have made the date for the following evening? Even if I hadn't succumbed to such black despair, would you have been fidgeting and looking at your watch the whole time of xeroxing? And what if it had run overtime, past your 10:30 P.M. rendezvous? When sex takes precedence over friendship, then the friendship cannot be that important to you. Can I look forward to a lasagna dinner in New York with you, and an evening of conversation, only to be turned out after an hour and a half because hot pants commit you elsewhere? I have never, for my part, deferred friendship in such a manner. To sum up: love or friendship, both require a certain seriousness of purpose.

Forgive me for saying so, but I don't really

think that, to date, you have made what I would call serious friendships, which can be relied upon in crisis or in turmoil as well as in good times. Until now, you have committed your life to one thing: to doing more or less exactly as you please—the pleasure principle. It doesn't bode well for your future, unless you begin to take yourself seriously.

You've drawn back from me several times during this voyage when you felt that maybe I would make you look at a mirror image you'd rather not see. You drew back again last night; I didn't like the colors you showed. Of course, it's your option to avoid this particular 'passage' of your life. But you know it will crop up in the future with renewed intensity. To rely on the good-looks and the Harold-teen personality which have neatly gotten you thus far is to repudiate your own considerable native intelligence. But maybe it's not a question of intelligence; maybe what you are repudiating is your own feelings, which is even worse.

I think you need my friendship more than I need yours. If you reject it, you're the loser. If you want me to be your mentor, then please treat me with some consideration, which means: sit down when you come to see an imaginative man in a state of depression; give him the minimal 'ego strokes' that he would give you in similar circumstances. In other words, give something of yourself, and break a pattern—which, if you examine it, has really been rather selfish vis-a-vis other people. If you want to discuss all this, I'm willing.

A."

Archibald's letter astounded me. What *was* all this nonsense? What was he expecting? I never said I would spend the evening with him; I only said I would assist with his copying.

Perhaps he *was* depressed—or so it appeared—but I interpreted it more as an act, a performance performed solely to gain the sympathy of his captive audience—me.

It was very uncomfortable to be alone in Archibald's cabin that evening, hearing him say words like "I've always wanted love;" "I've never had it—and I will never have it;" and "let me have your hand." It was creepy.

In fact, I didn't believe one word. He wanted to suck me deep into his whirlpool of black despair, as he called it, and I simply would not allow it. I liked Archibald very much, and my friendship with him was just as important to me as it appeared to be to Archibald. But if such a friendship was going to create more and more convoluted and emotionally complex dilemma in my life, then Archibald Hannon was wrong. I certainly did not need his friendship more than he needed mine.

"Dear Archibald,

I was most interested by your note, but I must say I sort of expected it. First of all, let me say something about your comment with regard to selfishness. Actually, I find your letter a bit selfish in itself. You had asked me to xerox thirty minutes worth of material the other evening after dinner. I agreed to help you, naturally. If we began after dinner at 9:00 P.M. or even 9:15 P.M., I don't think that making an appointment for 10:30 P.M. was unreasonable. I did not agree to spend the entire evening with you—I just agreed to help you with some xeroxing. If you needed or wanted something more from me, perhaps you should have asked. Maybe it was a bit selfish and possibly presumptuous on your part to just assume I would stay with you the entire evening.

I said to you that evening when you were in such 'black despair' as you say, that if it was a legitimate depression you were feeling perhaps, I could help, or at least try to help. But by writing that note to me, and suggesting to me what I should have done, or how I should have reacted in such a circumstance shows me that it was not a legitimate depression at all, but rather I believe you just wanted to see how I would respond.

Archibald, I cherish our friendship very much. But I can't see a relationship continuing on this basis. You, yourself, said that friendship is consideration and caring for each other. I must accept you the way you are, but you must also accept me the way I am, for myself, as well. I stayed with you more than an hour that night trying to get you out of your 'black despair,' which is a lot more time I would have given someone else. And by the way, don't you feel writing a letter is a pretty stupid way

for friends to communicate—especially when they
are living across the hallway for one another?

S."

We arrived at "0/0" Monday March 26th, 9:05 P.M. Crossing
the equator is one thing, and many travelers have done
just that. But few experience "0/0"—traversing the exact point
where zero longitude meets zero latitude.

When *Sagafjord* reached this precise position, just off the
western coast of the African continent, enroute from Walvis Bay
and Lobito to Dakar Senegal, Captain Brookstad commanded
that the ship navigate in an absolute circle as a grand salute—our
foamy wake creating a nautical mandala completely sealed, totally
unbroken.

A special celebration was planned that evening in the Ballroom
so all passengers together could share such an unusual benchmark.
The ceremony was complete when Ted Jones chose two couples
and instructed them to shake hands crosswise, while the Waleskys
played the Norwegian National Anthem.

"Dear Steven,

If you feel that writing letters is a pretty stupid way for friends to communicate, especially when they are living across the hallway from one another, then why complicate the stupidity by writing me a letter in return? Why not just pick up the phone and call me, and say, 'Archibald, let's meet and talk to clarify this misunderstanding'? I made it very clear in my note that I was perfectly willing to have a community dialogue. Since you declined that dialogue, I am obliged to reply by another note. I felt, and I still feel, that the fault was yours; it seems to me that you should have taken the proper action to close the gap. For the record, I did not ask you for thirty minutes of xeroxing time; there was no specified time limit implied. Nor was I at all aware that you had a previous appointment; nobody told me that fact, least of all you.

If you believe that it was not a legitimate depression, but that I 'just wanted to see how you would respond,' then you are accusing me of being positively Machiavellian—a nasty emotional manipulator. I categorically reject such a judgment of me. It was indeed a legitimate depression, and my suggestion as to how you should have reacted was an afterthought and not a forethought. Yes, friendship (like love) is indeed consideration and caring. If, by your watch, you stayed with me 'over an hour' then I can only marvel that you never once sat down during all that time. I repeat my original contention: you stood; you fidgeted; and you only told me under duress that you had a rendezvous. Why? I suggest that you felt a little guilty because the fact of the rendezvous placed a very definite limit on the time which you felt you could accord me.

If you cannot see a relationship continuing on this basis, then neither can I. Accepting a friend the way he is does not mean that critical judgment should be suspended. When I saw you withdrawing from amorous intimacy with others, I pointed out to you what you were doing, and I only asked you to consider why. It is now evident to me that you do the same thing in friendship, too. You withdraw from any real intimacy; and again, I ask why? The truth, I think, is that you do not want real intimacy in love or in friendship, because such intimacy would apparently make demands on you; you prefer everything to be open-ended and easy. If it's not open-ended and easy, then it becomes a threat to you. That, I think, is the key to your secret; though it is by no means clear to me just why you withdraw: that's an even deeper secret still, and one which you are obviously very much afraid of facing.

If you choose to be friends with me, I assure you that I would want—for your own deepest sake—I would want you to have the courage to face that innermost self. Unless you do, your life will be an evasion. Surely you don't want to evade your deepest being. Steven, don't rationalize; don't disappoint the confidence I have in you. If you like me very much, then I like you even more. If you want my love—which for me means my utter personal commitment to you through thick and thin—then call me and say 'Let's talk.' Do it today; this afternoon. Choose your deepest self; choose me as a friend, make an absolute choice. I don't want to lose you; and I don't want you to lose me.

A."

I arrived at the Tour Office just past eight the next morning to find Lar and Percy sitting at opposite ends of the room in tragic silence. I knew something was wrong.

"We have bad news" Lar said quietly. Percy remained still.

"Clifford has taken his own life."

Clifford had been in New York only days. Apparently, he seemed troubled ever since his return.

One night, during his weekly handball game at the 23rd Street YMCA, he abruptly stopped playing and told his friends that he had to leave; he had forgotten something at home, he said—there was something he needed to do.

Clifford went home and carefully pulled the sheets from his bed. He cut them into narrow strips, evenly and cleanly as only Clifford would do. The braiding was simple. Knowing Clifford, I would have thought he enjoyed that part.

He then opened his bathroom skylight and hung himself down the main shaft. He left no note behind, or any suggestion that that was indeed his intention.

"We just got the word from the New York office" Lar said. "Brooks called the ship. I had no idea . . ."

"What else did Brooks say?" I asked anxiously.

"Nothing much. There wasn't much he could say" Lar answered. "Robert was pretty straightforward —no emotion really. His only real concern was that the pre-booking for the next cruise would not be compromised."

"My God" Percy finally said. "Brooks didn't even give the boy the dignity of being shocked by his suicide."

Thoughts of Clifford's death began to haunt me from that moment. I remembered our times together onboard ship; his sharing with me the deep unhappiness he felt with his life; about Bruce. I remembered Clifford's obsessive fear of having to return to his native South Africa if, for any reason, he lost his position at NAL. "I won't go back" he said to me. I guess he won't after all.

Needless to say, I was shocked and heartbroken at the news of Clifford's death. I was saddened by what must have been Clifford's intense unhappiness. It was so final, I thought; far far from complete.

And I was angry with him for actually going through with it. Why didn't he ask for help? Why couldn't he talk to me? Maybe I could have stopped him. Maybe I should have been able to see through Clifford's unhappiness; maybe I should have been more sensitive to his needs and his feelings. Yes, maybe I could have prevented it all.

The days at sea which followed seemed long and lonely. My moods were dampened by intense grief and emotional pain, no doubt the cause of constant fatigue and lingering headaches.

One afternoon, I decided to take a nap—an unusual occurrence in itself. What was supposed to have been a one-hour rest, became three. And during that sleep, I had a dream.

I found myself in a large structure, a mansion of sorts—so large, it was difficult to see the surrounding walls which apparently enclosed it. Its space seemed endless. I was unable to recognize the place, and yet felt quite comfortable within its confines—I felt as if I had been there once before; as if I knew it well.

The area was filled with people walking and milling about, none of whom I recognized. There was constant movement, yet little sound. And then I saw Clifford and we hugged each other in greeting.

Facts inevitably get confused in dreams, and mine was no exception. In my mind, I had mistakenly understood that it was Clifford's brother who had died, and I warmly offered Clifford my condolences.

Clifford laughed out loud. He held me with both arms, and lovingly shook me just a bit, gently, so that I might see the truth.

"My God" he said as he continued to laugh. "You didn't get it either, did you?" He shook his head. "No one really got it. It wasn't my brother who died, it was me. I'm the one who died. I'm also the one who put the article in the newspaper about my death.

"But you see, it wasn't a real death—it was the end of an old life and the beginning of a new one. And do you know what, my young friend? I'm happy. Just look at me. For the first time" he said, "I'm really happy. "I don't have to worry anymore."

Clifford's exuberance comforted me and eased my pain. I realized he was okay.

We then came together in an embrace of love and understanding—an embrace which soon aroused us both. But we were not to give in to our passion; although we tried—running from room to room, looking for a quiet, more private place to be. But none was found.

When I finally awoke, I was drenched in sweat. My sleep was extremely deep; the dream intensely real. Was it just my imagination which created this scenario, or was it indeed Clifford somehow communicating? Perhaps he was telling me "it's all right; it happened. I'm fine; I'm happy in my new life. So get on with your own." The message was quite obvious, at least to me.

But whatever the truth—whether he truly came to me or not—I thanked Clifford for giving me that peace of mind, and for leaving me with his lovingly warm and eternal smile.

D akar Senegal had come and gone. Its Islamic influence was beautiful and enchanting. Yet with all it's glory, the events of those last days stifled my enjoyment and appreciation of where I was, and what I was seeing.

Ted and Anne's *1001 Nights Ball* was a smashing success among the passengers and staff alike. Arabic dress this time was the code for the evening, and most everyone complied in displaying their kaftans, djellabahs, burnooses, or gandoras from cocktail hour on up to late night games in the Club Polaris.

The Ballroom was decked out with drapes and fabrics of all kinds and colors to create the feeling of a fantastical Casbah, and the Walesky Orchestra added to the flavor of the evening by constantly performing various renditions of the *Sheik of Arabee*—with pixielike Carmen dressed as a Harem girl wearing sheer pantaloons, a tight-fitting vest, and a bejeweled fez with sweeping silk scarf dropping down and back across her shoulders.

Our final oceanic crossing had begun, westward, from Dakar to Charlotte Amalie, St. Thomas in the United States Virgin Islands.

Tour office responsibilities had by then all but ended, except for the final accounts and settlements and the end-of-cruise reports for the NAL executive offices in New York and Oslo. Once completed, our days and our nights were our own, and for the remainder of the voyage we were, in all actuality, passengers enjoying the few days at sea we had left. With the world finally behind us, we savored that time to relax, and to focus on our own individual lives.

Archibald and I had not actually spoken since that eventful evening in his cabin. Although quite thought-provoking were his letters, I was angered by his pompous criticism of me and my life. I vowed to stand my ground. The last thing I wanted was turmoil—something on which Archibald obviously thrived.

With our voyage virtually over, I very much needed the support of my friendships onboard—including his. Yet I was simply unwilling to accept Archibald's critical comments and suggestions on what he felt I should do, or what I should be. I had my own life to live, my own future to consider. I needed and wanted this quiet time at sea for myself, to weigh my options and to plot my own course; a time far released from any kind of work-related stress or personal interference.

Nonetheless, on a ship of *Sagafjord's* size, it was difficult to avoid anyone. It is inevitable that you'd come cross each other while walking past the Purser's Office, or perhaps out on deck where most of the staff by then congregated, trying to take as much sun as possible before returning home.

Most staff members ignored the silent feud between Archibald and me—except for Percy, who, at times, would try to calm the reticence, and get us, as he put it, to "stop the childish nonsense."

With Archibald self-banished to his cabin, Percy and I became good and constant companions—ironic, I thought. Just three months before, I had held such disgust for these two men—Percy and Archibald. And yet now, each of them—individually and together—had turned out to be the most important influences of my life.

Percy and I began taking all our lunches together on deck. We preferred it that way, since most passengers still opted for the more formal Dining Room service. By lunching in the Veranda Cafe, Percy and I would be left alone, and not interrupted by the their endless questions:

"How much am I able to bring back into the United States duty free?"

"When should I have my baggage put out?"

"What time will we be disembarking in New York—I have to let my driver know . . ."

As Percy would say over and over again—"I loathe people!"

"A burger again?" I asked him as he carried his very full tray to our favorite table for two, quietly tucked away in the corner just near the Ballroom entrance, starboard side aft. "Is that all you eat these days, hamburgers?"

"Naturally, you silly twit. One often tires of Dom Perignon and caviar."

He sat down abruptly, knocking over the rose-filled bud vase.

"And you?" he asked. "What's that on your plate?"

"An Arugula salad. Would you like some?"

"Heavens no! It's too bitter."

"Yeah, so's life" I answered him sarcastically.

"Yes, and I already have enough bitterness in my life. I don't need any more of it on my luncheon plate."

"Well, try this bitterness" I said to him as I placed just a bit of the arugula next to his burger. "You'll like it."

Together we talked about Clifford and his suicide, and how it affected us both—personally and professionally. Now that a few more days had passed, and the original shock had subsided, Percy seemed far more casual and open about the subject. And after my dream, I was able to discuss the tragedy without the burden of crippling sadness.

"Suicide is quite the thing within grand society, you know—with *old* money in particular. I've known four before Clifford, of course. All of them were very affluent—quite P-O-S-H you know." Percy spoke with pride, as though it was considered chic in his world to be that close to suicide.

"Who were they?" I asked him.

"Well, there was . . ." he said, pausing for a moment, not able to remember a single one; his half-eaten burger lingering halfway between his plate and his lips.

"My God" he continued, "I seem to be losing track of my suicides."

"Did you know Kaye Fitzsimmons?" I asked him.

"Who?"

"Kaye Fitzsimmons. At least I think that was her name. Ted told me she had been an entertainer onboard a few years back. She committed suicide too—jumped over the side."

"Oooo, how romantic! I like her already." Percy giggled as he bit into his burger.

We spoke about Archibald—but only just a bit. We spoke about the success of the cruise, and about me and my future.

"I'm not sure what I want to do now that the voyage is over, Percy. We'll be home in a few days . . . I received a cable from Robert Brooks this morning offering me the Spring Mediterranean Cruise—it leaves just after the westbound transatlantic from Oslo—sometime in late April I think."

Percy listened as I spoke, and for the first time since first meeting him, I began to believe he was genuinely interested in what I had to say. He seemed unusually concerned. I felt good about that. I liked his attention.

"I'd love to do it—I'd love to do them all" I said. "I've never been to the Mediterranean, to Italy. And yet at the same time Percy, I feel I don't want to do anything, right now. In a way. I really don't care if I do the trip or not. I just don't want to deal with it."

"The most horrible thing in life is indifference" he said to me.

"I know. I'm afraid I really do know."

Petre, a young Austrian waiter came to clear our lunch dishes away. We paused in our conversation just a moment until he had gone.

"What about your friend Arne?" Percy asked quietly.

I was stunned by the sharpness of his question. How did Percy know about Arne? And the others—did they know about Arne as well?

"What do you mean?"

Percy smiled and lightly shook his head.

"You know very well what I'm talking about" he said. He smiled lovingly, like a mentor to his ward.

"You know about me and Arne?" I asked.

"We all know about you and Arne. This is a very small ship. There are no secrets onboard. Haven't you gotten that by now? We've known all along, you silly twit. It's no big deal. Actually I think it's wonderful that you've found someone you like and with whom you're comfortable."

"I can't believe it." I shook my head. It was incredulous to me that they all knew. Arne and I tried so hard to keep our relationship quiet.

"So what that I know?"

"Nothing, I guess." I paused a moment and thought of Arne as I smiled. "He's really nice Percy. I like him a lot."

"Yes" Percy said. "I'm sure he is. And attractive too. So what's he going to do after April?"

"He's signing off at Copenhagen, after the eastbound crossing. He's been wanting to open an inn somewhere in Denmark—a town called Aarhus."

"Perfect. I can just see the two of you—greeting guests at the door." Percy laughed a bit as he mimicked how I would act in such a role.

"No. No Percy. I don't think Arne's plans include me. We had a great time together onboard, but he really wants to settle down, to have a family. You know . . ."

"A family? Who is he kidding?" Percy was flabbergasted at the thought.

"Oh come on, Percy. Leave him alone. Arne can do whatever he chooses."

"Indeed he can. There is nothing like a Dane . . ." He began to sing the melody from that Rogers and Hammerstein classic.

"Oh stop it" I said to him as we both laughed. "Arne has his own life. And I guess I have mine."

"Nonsense." And after a moment or two he said "So just convince him he's wrong; that he's making a mistake." I smiled at Percy's persistence. The care he showed for me then was so welcomed.

"I can't. I just can't. I don't know how. Besides, I'm not so sure he is making a mistake. Arne has his own life and his own dreams—at least his dreams are clear. I can't change that, nor would I want to.

"All of this has made me start to think as well" I continued, a bit more upbeat. "I'm not sure if I should leave New York again, especially so soon after such a long trip. Everything I have is there. My roots are there."

"Your roots?" Percy laughed out loud with a cackle loud enough to shatter glass. "You don't even have a tendril! What are you talking about? Roots, dear God. He thinks he's got roots!"

He looked at me, quite seriously.

"Forget all these nonsensical considerations of yours. Do what you want. Do what you feel. This is it. This is all we have. How many times do I have to tell you, for God's sake. Don't let it go by without making the most of it. Look at poor Clifford."

"And Hans."

"Yes, and Hans. And look at our friend Archibald who's wasting his life away in his cabin right now brooding and fantasizing about what he thinks his life should be, while he's missing out on what it is."

"It's just that I'm not too sure I know what 'making the most of it' really means."

"You will" Percy said. "Just shut up and listen."

Rehearsals began promptly at 2:00 P.M. later that afternoon. Anne Dickson was there of course, as were her guest performers and the Walesky Orchestra. We were told to wear jeans and sneakers—rehearsal clothes as we called them. It was the only time we were allowed to wear jeans onboard ship, and it felt good to be so at ease with the others.

Anne was clearly in control; this was her world after all. She began by explaining the concept of the musical number she was about to stage, and as she did, she assigned each of us to a particular position on the dance floor. Height was the discriminating factor—she went from left to right, short to tall. I was naturally set furthest stage left—the towering Philip Pound, the furthest to the right. And so we began . . .

Here is the drag,
see how it goes,
Down on the heels,
up on the toes,
That's the way to do the
Varsity Drag . . .

Physically, and with attitude, we mimicked her every move.

"Now turn completely around—then to the right" Anne said as she walked through each movement meticulously with care. "Now, slide back like this—dragging your left leg along with you, holding your hat with your right hand—fingers extended; right arm out like this."

The music played loudly over and over again, and soon the routine was staged. Anne watched us then from out front, correcting our movements with perfection, repeating each section continuously, until we got it right.

Performance night came and went with all the pomp and spectacle of a Broadway Opening Night—or so I imagined. The adrenaline was pumping as we all met at the Dance Studio for the post-show party—a lavish cocktail reception thrown by Ted and Anne in thanks of our participation. We toasted each other, and the success of the show, and joked about waiting for the reviews in the next day's *Cruise News*.

Anne hugged me sweetly, and pulled me aside, away from the others.

"You were really quite good tonight" she said. "Have you had and professional dance experience?"

"Only in school plays" I said. "But no real training or anything.

And ten years of classical piano lessons too, but I guess that doesn't count."

"Well, you're very musical—and talented" she said. "You have a great presence on stage. It's a shame to let it go to waste in the Tour Office. Have you ever thought about the theatre? About bcoming a performer?"

Naturally, I had fantasized about a career in the theatre—as most everyone must some time in his life—but never seriously. It would have been unthinkable for me to have shared any of those real fantasies with Anne Dickson.

"There's always a need for talented male dancers" she continued. "With your natural ability, I'm sure you would do very well."

I laughed at first, not really knowing what to say. "I'm flattered" I said sheepishly. "But don't you think I'm a bit too old to start dance lessons?" I asked.

"Normally I'd agree with you" Anne said "but not with your natural ability and stage presence as I saw tonight. I think you'd do just fine."

The party was ending; most were making plans to meet in the Club Polaris for a nightcap.

"Well—if you ever think about going into the theater, let me know." Anne kissed me on both cheeks—like the French do, she said—and joined Ted as they both left the room.

Me—a professional dancer. How utterly ridiculous.

But then again . . . Why not? Maybe she saw something in me and my abilities that I was unable to see. If Anne Dickson believed I had talent, who was I after all to discredit her? Why should I simply disregard that option?

Options, I thought. That's just what I needed—more options to confuse my life. My already ambiguous decision-making process was dysfunctional enough as it was. I needed no other.

Later that night, safely in bed, I thought long and hard about where I was going, and what I would do; about my talks with Percy and with Anne. And even about the wonderfully enlightening talks with Archibald from earlier on in the voyage. And I finally understood that it *is* all about options—endless options just waiting to be seized and explored.

There was a release in just that thought alone. Indeed, I was fortunate to have such options before me. I just needed to be sure I chose the right one. Or chose one—at least.

The vast Mid-Atlantic. Somehow I feared I would never see it again.

How I loved the sea. And it was then passing below me faster and faster each day. I didn't want it to stop. I didn't want to leave.

I held my crystal tight in my hand, and dreamed as I had done so many times—so many years—before; of the sea and its wonders, and of sailing the world in a ship not unlike *Sagafjord*.

It had become so much a part of me, the sea had. I wanted us to be together always.

The toss was easy, the splash quite loud. Deafening, yet perfect. I pictured my crystal falling quickly through the waters—down and down—until resting quietly and comfortably on the sea bottom below. There it would be until the end of time. There it would stay, lovingly embraced by the sea I so loved.

My passing friendship with Quartermaster Jan Groendahl had remained just that. His position onboard ship had made our connection more difficult than with other members of the crew. Invariably, whenever I found myself on B-deck for parties and the like, Jan stood watch up on the Bridge. He worked the evening and night shifts most often, so he rarely walked the decks after hours.

But several days outside of St. Thomas, all that changed. I had pulled aside a lone deck chair on Promenade Deck starboard side, staking claim to the area just under lifeboat No. 8. With book in hand, I settled in for the afternoon.

Jan was working additional shifts that week, and—unbeknownst to me—was assigned to No. 8; repainting its interior a brilliant coast guard orange.

Jan was silent as he painted and clearly out of sight. So when I heard a noise at one point, I paid little attention. How could there be anyone inside a lifeboat, at sea, as we sailed ahead full speed? Naturally, I was quite startled when Jan first appeared, just before me—his head over the side—poking up from deep within the lifeboat.

"Hello there" Jan shouted to me. "Hope I'm not making too much noise."

"Jan—I didn't even know you were there. No. You're not disturbing me at all. I'm just reading." The sounds of the winds made it difficult to hear.

"The deck is nearly deserted this afternoon" I continued. "I'm not sure where everyone is. Packing perhaps. It's kind of nice though to know I'm not the only one up here."

"No, you're not. It's me" Jan shouted back. He must have felt the same. Before I knew it, he was straddling down the rope ladder, jumping to the deck with a pounce.

"I can't believe you can climb down those things" I said to him. "With this heavy wind and everything. And with the ship rolling too. Actually, I think you're nuts."

We both laughed. Jan walked over to my deck chair where the wind was more silent. He crouched down lower to better hear my words.

"It's nothing really" he said. "You should see when we climb up to the top of the mast. Were you onboard at Christmas?"

"No, I wasn't. Why?"

"We tie a tree atop the mast" he continued. "With Christmas lights too. It's an old Norwegian tradition."

"Oh, like looking into each other's eyes as you Skoal?"

"What?" Jan asked, totally confused.

"Oh, nothing. Forget it. Sounds wonderful though. Maybe next Christmas I'll get to see it." And for a brief moment, I sincerely wished it were true.

Jan and I spoke briefly, reminiscing about the time off Balboa when he sealed up my porthole with that dreadful steel plate. We laughed about the endlessness of the voyage; he was clearly looking forward to the next—the eastbound transatlantic from New York to Oslo, and home.

"If you have some time before St. Thomas, would help me do

something" Jan asked. "You see, I have a girlfriend—an American. Janet is her name; we met on the Christmas cruise. She's from Top-aka?"

"Top-aka?"

"Ja. It's in Kansas?" Whenever he said "Ja" he seemed to powerfully draw air deep into his lungs—the suction sound loud and obvious, as if almost a gasp.

"Oh, Topeka!" I finally caught on to what Jan was saying. Although Jan's English was fairly good, his pronunciation at times was quite confusing.

"Ja. That's it. To*pee*ka Kansas."

"How great."

"Ja. Mange takk" he said with a smile. "But can you help me then?"

"It depends" I said to him. "What do you need?"

"I'm writing to her, and I'd like to post the letter from Charlotte Amalie. And I think I've gotten all confused with my English words and grammar. Would you have a look?" Jan seemed so excited by his new girlfriend, I couldn't not agree to help.

"Of course" I said emphatically. "When? Where?"

"Well—we can't talk much longer out here. They can see me from the Bridge, you know. Can you come to my cabin tonight after dinner? You've been to B-Deck before. So you should know the way."

I was amazed. Even Jan knew I had visited B-Deck. Clifford was right. The sea had no secrets.

"After dinner then."

"It's crew cabin four-three-two—all the way forward. If you go any more forward, you'd be in St. Thomas."

We laughed. I could only imagine where Jan's cabin was located. I hoped to God the seas would be calm. Being that far forward in heavy seas would certainly make me sick.

I moved along the corridor which by then I knew quite well. The Chinese tailors were there, as always; they waved to me as I passed. I had become familiar. I was no longer alien on B-Deck.

I could be trusted.

The corridor narrowed the further forward I walked; the passage veered to the right, indeed the center line of the ship. There, up ahead, was a lone door— 432; the overhead fluorescent lamp cast harsh shadows downward against the letters. The glare bounced off the linoleum on which I walked.

Jan's cabin was a single, the first I had seen on B-Deck. He told me all navigational crew were assigned single cabins; their hours were too irregular to bunk with the others; and when off duty, they, more than anyone else onboard ship, needed their rest. A welcomed perk, no doubt, on a deck full of quads.

Jan's bunk was on the right as I entered, with a small writing desk to the left. A wash basin stood at the far end of the room, as it had in Arne and Erik's cabin, and I'm sure in all the others too. The main difference, though, was that Jan's cabin had no porthole. No window of light. At the furthest point forward, in the exact center line of the ship, there was no access to the outside. So Jan lived sun-less. No wonder he took such pride in sealing over our portholes. No wonder he saw no reason for our great upset that night.

He offered me a drink; we each took a beer. Ringeness—Norwegian, of course. As long as there no were fish balls, I'd be fine.

Together, we sat at his small writing desk—me on the side chair, Jan on the edge of his bunk. With an aisle of not more than inches between them, there really wasn't anywhere else to be.

Jan retrieved the letter he had written, and began showing me the sections where he was confused. But as he spoke, I couldn't help but notice the photos he had taped to the wall above his desk. Numerous they were, almost a collage. Some were of cities around the world, others showed skiers high on the glaciers of a Norwegian fjord. And others too showed naked couples in various poses—some artistic, others not. I must have stared for a while, because Jan soon noticed where my attention had gone.

"Do you like them?" Jan asked me. I was instantly embarrassed. I didn't know what to say. I realized I shouldn't be sitting in this man's cabin staring at his somewhat erotic photographs. I should be helping him with his grammar and syntax, as he asked.

"Of course I do. They're great. Do you ski?" I asked, hoping to divert his attention a moment, hoping he hadn't noticed that my eyes were clearly drawn to the nudes in the center.

"Yes. I'm a fine skier. I began when I was three."

"I went skiing once when I was eight" I told him. "But not since." There was a moment of unparalleled awkwardness, and then Jan again spoke.

"Was it just the photographs of the skiers that you liked?" I was feeling uncomfortable. I thought perhaps I should leave.

"No—not really. I like them all." I was quiet a moment. Intrigued. "What do you mean?" I asked him.

"What about these?" Jan pointed to the naked couples.

"What about them?"

"Do you like those too?"

"Yes of course." I smiled nervously. "I like those very much." I didn't know what he was getting at. All I knew, though, was that I was instantly and intensely excited; rigidly aroused, yet cautiously embarrassed that Jan would notice.

"And which ones do you like the most? This one, or that one?" Jan pointed to two photographs in particular—the first showed a naked man in full frontal view, the second a woman, openly exposed in similar display.

I couldn't lie. I had to tell him the truth. I would think, after all, it was obvious.

"I like them both, but I prefer this one" I said as I pointed to the male, "if you really want to know."

Just a moment passed before Jan walked to the doorway and switched off the light. I heard the soft sounds, the rustle of his bed sheets, as he settled into his bunk.

It was time. And I wanted nothing more. I stood silently, and moved to Jan's bed.

We kissed then, and Jan was openly willing. Fully exposed within the blindness of the dark, we made love, never saying a word. Totally unexpected it was; wonderfully exciting.

I left his cabin just before dawn. And I never saw Jan Groendahl again.

Chapter Seven

"Sundays Are For Going Home"

With each day we sailed majestically further on toward the setting sun—closer and closer to the final decision I was eventually destined to make.

There was an edginess onboard. The passengers all seemed anxious to disembark; all eager to go home. Psychologically for them, the cruise had already ended—the transatlantic crossing, merely a formality. Their mental baggage had already been packed and diligently set outside their cabin doors.

Our eight-hour visit to Charlotte Amalie on the beautiful island of St. Thomas came and went without much notice, although it was certainly a much-needed rest stop after seven long days at sea.

Not many passengers went ashore that day, except for those still seeking a bargain from duty-free liquor allotments, or those rummaging through end-of-season jewelry opportunities. For the rest of us, other than a quick romp to Morning Star beach for a last blast of Caribbean sunshine, St. Thomas seemed almost anti-climactic.

Arne and I were seeing less and less of each other as the days passed. How and when our separation began, I really couldn't say.

He just didn't spend as many nights with me as he used to, and the invitations to join him on B-Deck seemed far less frequent. I think we both realized the end was near, and neither of us really wanted to say goodbye. His periodic absences made me all too aware of just how much I loved him, and just how much I was going to miss him.

Even if I did decide to stay onboard ship for another voyage or two, I just couldn't imagine what it would be like without Arne Christiansen.

An evening of Norwegian folk dances was presented by the crew toward the end of every Norwegian America Line voyage. It was a tradition dating back to the company's turn-of-the-century beginnings—an activity very much encouraged and supported by the Line. And it was an evening which both passengers and crew members anxiously looked forward to—a warm and friendly sharing of cultures, if you will. The performance re-emphasized just how much of a family we had all become.

Arne was a member of the NAL folk dance troupe since he first signed onboard. I peeked in to the Dance Studio just prior to the performance to wish him well. He looked handsome in this traditional Norwegian costume—brilliant red jacket, with black knickerlike trousers; tall white knee socks and shiny black shoes. He smiled when he first saw me, and waved.

"Break a leg" I shouted to him.

I was proud of Arne that night. And I felt even closer to him then. I wanted to take him in my arms right then and there. I wanted to hold him—and never ever let him go.

The closing events onboard all seemed to happen quickly. In the blink of an eye, it seemed, they were gone. The captain's gala farewell party and dinner were only a prelude to Ted and Anne's solo performance in *Something Old, Something New* which proved to be brief highlights of their own performances throughout the cruise—a sort of terpsichorean re-cap. Indeed, our voyage was over. It was time for us all to move on.

"På gjensyn, but not goodbye"—was the headline in *The Cruise News* which was slipped under my cabin door the night before our arrival at Port Everglades.

We arrived at the pilotage at daybreak, then silently moved to our berth. The beaches glistened and the palms trees swayed, just as they had done nearly three months before. In a way, it was the same as I'd remembered. But I knew it couldn't be.

I stood on Promenade Deck, pensively watching as our passengers filed down the open gangway; their hand baggage, and straw hats, and oriental wood carvings, and awkwardly packaged artwork clumsily in hand—fragmented momentos, they seemed, of memories long gone, never again to be rekindled.

In a way, it was like dropping off a hitchhiker at the side of a highway, without any concern or references made to the many and sometimes personal conversations which took place during the ride.

It was sad. Many of these passengers, already quite aged, would never sail again. Together, we shared these last three months, but our paths would never again cross.

Within hours, we pulled away from the pier and sailed north along Fort Lauderdale's beaches—slowly, out of sight of land, toward home.

The ship was enveloped in fog—so common in a spring-time New York. We drifted slowly through the mist. The silence was eerie. Visibility near zero. I knew not where we were. I stood up on deck, eagerly looking for some clue, something to tell me I was home.

Suddenly, just ahead, the mist began to part, and there stood the massive twin towers of New York's World Trade Center looming above us as a giant gateway to the Hudson's North River and the great city beyond.

To my left, I faintly saw her torch, and then her body—shockingly green as ever. She stood there, just as we had left her ninety-eight days before. I choked a bit with emotion, and the tears suddenly came. I was home.

Sagafjord moved silently ahead to her berth; her ropes were thrown ashore and hastily tied fast. I listened sadly as the ship's engines stopped for the very last time.

I saw my parents waving to me from the pier, standing by their car high atop the open-air parking deck. My mother was crying, and I'm sure quite anxious to hug her wandering son.

Percy soon joined me at the rail. He waved briefly to those I identified as my parents—he greeted them warmly, although they had never met.

"Did you hear about Gretal Heckettson and your young Danish friend?" Percy asked. "The crazy old woman—she did it again. I guess you weren't the only one who liked the boy. She tipped him fifteen thousand dollars—as a downpayment, she said, on his Danish inn."

It was unbelievable. I was thrilled for Arne more than I would have imagined. I loved him. And now he could move on.

"So how does it feel to be home?" Percy then asked.

"I'm not quite sure I know where home is anymore" I said to him. "I thought this ship was home; now I'm not too sure. But since you asked—it will be nice to spend time with my family and my friends. It's funny, I didn't realize how much I missed them until this very moment."

The gangway was quickly swung into position, and the first of the Customs and Immigrations officials stepped onboard, followed by Robert Brooks, and some of the others from the New York office. Vincent was not with them.

"What are you going to tell Brooks?" Percy asked. "Are you signing off, or not?"

I was quiet for a moment. A string of multi-colored flags were being rigged off the mast. The wind took them quickly, blowing far to the south.

I watched a flock of seagulls circle overhead, as if to welcome us home. As they soared further off and out of sight, the ship's public address system began to play the *Norwegian National Anthem*, quickly followed by the *Star Spangled Banner*—a traditional farewell to *Sagafjord*'s passengers as they finally disembarked; a fitting end to each and every voyage.

Tears filled my eyes once again. I could not control the emotion. It was Sunday morning. I knew, at home, a typical Italian dinner awaited my return—the gravy, I'm sure, already simmering hot on our white kitchen stove.

The ship's whistle blew one long frantic blast. I waved to my parents once again. A few other people began arriving then as well—anxious no doubt, to welcome their very own loved ones home.

"I love that sound" I said to Percy as the whistle's fierce intensity slowly faded, dissipating into the damp spring air just as quickly as the heavy white smoke it expelled. And the mundane yet jarring noises of a city coming to life swiftly took its place.

I looked forward, further down Promenade Deck, and saw Archibald, alone, standing by the rail—so fitting the picture he invariably created for himself. He looked my way, and we made eye contact for the first time in many days.

A cool breeze blew gently against my face, not unlike it had so many weeks before as I stood below a paper-strewn tree in beautiful Kamakura. I smiled with the understanding, and satisfaction, of knowing just what that breeze meant.

Once again, *Sagafjord*'s whistle blew—a fast and final farewell.

"Yes Percy" I said. "I do love that sound."

A moment passed.

"I think I'll stay."

THE END

Epilogue

Cruise Director Ted Jones and his partner Anne Dickson were abruptly dismissed by Norwegian American Line management in 1980. Apparently they were too old-fashioned—perhaps a bit too stodgy—for the more contemporary image a new cruising industry demanded. He eventually settled in Florida where, for several years, Ted continued to teach ballroom dancing in a popular condo community.

As the years advanced, Ted's health began to decline, and in late 1996, he died alone in his one-bedroom West Palm Beach condo. His wife Helen, from whom he had been separated for over thirty years, finally arrived to claim his belongings.

§

While working in a popular Chicago art gallery in the early 1980s, Anne Dickson met a successful businessman who quickly became her most loyal patron. Week after week he would return to her studio—with each visit, another painting was sold. It was not long after that his true desires became clear . . . he would only deal with the beautiful Anne Dickson after all. And soon, it became apparent that his unusually obsessive art spree was in fact designed solely to attract Anne's interests; to win her affections. The courtship lasted several years.

Reluctantly—as she was still desperately in love with Ted Jones—Anne finally surrendered to her client's keen interests and agreed to marry her new suitor.

It was said that she wept for six weeks thereafter, overwhelmingly uncertain if she had indeed made the right decision.

Over the years, Anne has adapted well. Today, she shares her husband's great fortune and separates her time between their magnificent Miami Beach condo and the "grand house" in Bar Habor, Maine.

§

At the grand old age of eighty, Archibald Hannon has long retired from the sea. Today, he eagerly maintains his intellectual life in vibrant New York City. Over the years, he's authored numerous plays and dramatic histories, some of which have been fully staged and published throughout the world. He successfully recovered from quadruple heart by-pass surgery two years back; he even frequents a local gym, and is quite proud of his treadmill accomplishments.

Archibald still spends his days in that same "monk-cell" studio apartment on West 22nd Street, tutoring handsome young men of Latin-American heritage. He's paid in various ways.

§

Percy Hayes retired from the sea in the mid 1980s at the perfect age of fifty. Fully enjoying the generous gifts he's received throughout his lifetime and the fruits of his most clever investments in the Cayman Islands, Percy today winters in Melbourne Australia with his young—platonic—companion Michael, and summers on the Greek Island of Mykonos. In transit, he visits his Smith Street townhouse in London's Chelsea and his home in Valbonne, both of which he lets out for quite exorbitant sums.

§

Senior Social Directress Maggie Sinclair shared the same unfortunate fate as Ted Jones and Anne Dickson—abruptly released from her NAL contract. She too was told her "style" was no longer compatible with contemporary cruising. Maggie retired then to her Park Avenue apartment, and continued to enjoy an active New York City life.

In 1992, Maggie learned that her gentleman friend of nearly 55 years had died. She also learned that he left an estate of nearly $9 million, with no apparent heirs. His Will soon revealed, however, that Maggie was bequeathed just $15,000—the balance of his estate, left to the Roman Catholic Church. Maggie was devastated.

In the mid-1990's, Maggie sold her Park Avenue apartment and relocated to a senior citizen facility near Buffalo New York, just miles from her only living relatives. There, Maggie continued to live her philosophy of "this is my ship, and its going to be run the way I God-damned want" . . . she often rose havoc at the home as she reorganized the daily programs, and hosted various musical evenings.

Maggie died in August 2001, peacefully in her sleep, at the incredible age of 97.

§

In 1979, while attempting to navigate an uncharted fjord somewhere in northern Norway, Sagafjord's mast sliced cleanly through a massive electrical cable which spanned the waterway, plunging most of northern Norway into a summertime darkness. Captain Brookstad was at the helm. Within days, he was released of his maritime duties with NAL, and thusly accepted a forced retirement from the sea.

In the spring of 1984, he was discovered on the floor of his Costa del Sol condo, the victim of a massive stroke. Apparently, he been dead for several weeks. His wife, alone in Norway, had simply assumed he was too busy to phone.

§

Still married to his stewardess-wife Ilsa, Ornulf currently owns a successful travel agency in beautiful Bergen Norway, offering customized excursions to all parts of the world. His son, Steinar, will soon take over the reigns.

§

In 1987, while still married to his stewardess-wife Astrid, Per Sanders died suddenly of a brain aneurysm at the age of forty-nine.

§

Soon after Assistant Cruise Director Hal Carter was released of his duties for excessive drinking, he accepted a position as activities director with a local Pompano Beach Florida condominium. He died alone, of AIDS, in November 1987.

§

Former Golf Pro John Maratisch today lives alone in a one - bedroom condo on Florida's Gulf Coast.

§

Marshall Smith continued to teach bridge on numerous cruise ships throughout the 1970s, but abruptly returned home in the summer of 1983 when he became ill with a rare pneumonia. He died of AIDS in 1984.

As were his wishes, his ashes were scattered in the deep Atlantic, just off his Fire Island home.

§

Songstress Gennifer Grey works part-time in a local department store in Hollywood, Florida. She continues to sing at her weekly church services, her guitar still not very far from her side.

§

Lar Vandelis returned to the corporate arena soon after his World Cruise stint on *Sagafjord*. Rarely working "on staff", he preferred to remain a consultant, allowing him ample time to travel at his leisure.

Retired for several years, Lar currently lives a life of self-imposed solitude somwhere in suburban Washington DC.

§

Although having played on the "other team" for most of his adult life, Philip eventually married a Norwegian stewardess all his own, and relocated to Oslo, Norway.

Today he "reps" various American cruise lines throughout the Scandinavian marketplace.

§

Longtime passenger Gretal Heckettson remained a permanent resident onboard *Sagafjord* for the next several years. Without Percy onboard, however, she had few staff members on whom she could rely.

In June 1976, while traversing the great North Sea, she died quietly in her suite. And as true to her final wishes, she was buried at sea, somewhere off the coast of the windswept Orkneys.

§

Shortly after the 1973 Great World Cruise, Bruni Amman and her pastry-chef boyfriend Gerhard abandoned their life at sea, and moved back to the Bavarian region of Germany.

Today, they operate a successful bed and breakfast, just outside of Munich. They have three grown children—Gretl, Christian, and Peter.

§

Ship's photographer Dick Dichosian continued his monoply with NAL for the next ten years, maintaining an on-again/off-again relationship with his Norwegian stewardess Gro. Eventually however, when his mental cash register finally stopped ringing, he retired from the sea and returned to his wife in rural Connecticut.

Dick suffered a massive heart attack in the summer of 1988 and died while enjoying linguine and clams—al dente, of course—in a local Westport ristorante.

§

Cruise reservationist Vincent Pagente continued with Norwegian America Line for the next several years, eventually joining Holland America Line just prior to their relocation from New York's Pier 40 to Seattle in the pristine Pacific Northwest.

He died of AIDS in his Capital Hill home in December 1990. Mark Murphy, his partner of nearly six years, was lovingly at his side.

§

Although Matthew Scott finally settled in Boston, he was unable to hold a job of any stature for very long. He became sexually obsessive throughout the years—constantly moving from man-to-man, from boy-to-boy—in his continual search for a love he believed he never had; desperate for the love he could never really attain.

Matthew died of AIDS in a cold Boston Hospital in August 1992. Archibald Hannon was at his side.

§

Arne Christiansen
            ...any reader with information as to the whereabouts of this fine man, please notify this author immediately.

§

MS *Sagafjord*

Sagafjord was built specifically for Norwegian America Line by Societé des Forges de la Mediterranee, La Seyne, France. She made her Maiden Voyage from Oslo to New York October 2, 1965.

At her launch, *Sagafjord* weighed in at 24,002 tons. She is 550' in length, with a breadth of 80'.

Sagafjord is a motorship, equipped with two Sulzer type diesel engines. She has twin screws, giving her an average cruising speed of 20 knots. It should be noted however that speeds of 22.5 knots were reached during her original sea trails in early 1965.

When on transatlantic voyages earlier in her career, *Sagafjord* accepted 70 passengers in First Class; 720 in Tourist Class. A maximum of 450 passengers were carried in *one class only* when the ship was employed in the worldwide cruise trade.

Sagafjord has flown several flags during her lifetime. In the early 1980s she was sold (along with her sister ship *Vistafjord*) to Britain's Cunard Line—her classic name was maintained, however her registry was changed from Oslo to the Bahamas.

When Cunard Line joined the Carnival Corporation family in the early 1990s, the ship was again sold—this time to Saga Holidays of Great Britain.

Today, she sails from Southampton as MS *Saga Rose* on glorious itineraries worldwide.

Special Thanks and Acknowledgments . . .

The author would like to thank everyone in this story whose lives have so touched and influenced his—you know who you are. Your impact has been indelible.

The author would also like to thank authors Frank Browning and Russell Reich whose early readings of this manuscript—and whose cogent comments and many suggestions—have improved the telling of this story immensely.

Special thanks must also go to the Xlibris Corporation—especially to Dave Weinman and Beth Staples for their constant support and unwavering dedication.

And to Stephen Sondheim, Scott Heim, Maurizio Eliseo, Anthony Cooke, Donald Stoltenberg, PD James, Scott Heim, Diana Preston, Jeff Davis, Steven Ciabattoni, Anthony Paladino, Trevor Craft, William H. Miller, Paolo Piccione, Judy Carmichael, Brian Monahan, Trent Rhoton, and Greg De Felice—for your solid inspiration, continued encouragement, and enduring friendship.

And finally, to Rupert Sykes and Patrick Kirkpatrick...for making it all possible in the first place.

Steven Rivellino
January 2004

About The Author

Steven Rivellino is an accomplished writer, lecturer, and producer of theatrical entertainment—with credits spanning Broadway, Off-Broadway, television, and the corporate arena.

A member of the Circumnavigators Club, he has traveled the world extensively—far north of the Arctic Circle, south to Antarctica; from the Greenwich Meridian, east to the International Date Line.

He lives in New York City and Cedar Lake New Jersey; and is currently at work on a full-length history of America's first and only nuclear-powered passenger vessel NS *Savannah*.

Mysterious Places, Mysterious Dreams is his first book.

Notes on MPMD

Mysterious Places, Mysterious Dreams
was Art Directed by Steven Rivellino.

The interior text was set in 11.5-point Adobe Garamond—a
typeface based on the sixteenth-century type designs of
Claude Garamond, re-drawn by Robert Slimbach in 1989.

The original cover artwork entitled *Sagafjord By Night* was
painted by noted Maritime Artist Donald Stoltenberg.

§

www.mysteriousplacesmysteriousdreams.com